TWICE USED
SONGS

TWICE USED SONGS

PERFORMANCE CRITICISM
of the
SONGS *of* ANCIENT ISRAEL

Terry Giles *and* William J. Doan

HENDRICKSON PUBLISHERS

Twice-Used Songs: Performance Criticism of the Songs of Ancient Israel
© 2009 by Hendrickson Publishers, Inc.
P. O. Box 3473
Peabody, Massachusetts 01961-3473

ISBN 978-1-59856-272-9

Printed in the United States of America

First Printing — January 2009

An earlier version of chapter five appeared as William Doan and Terry Giles, "The Song of Asaph: A Performance Critical Analysis of 1 Chronicles 16:8–36," *Catholic Biblical Quarterly* 70 (2008): 29–43. Used with permission.

Library of Congress Cataloging-in-Publication Data

Giles, Terry.
    Twice used songs : performance criticism of the songs of ancient Israel / Terry Giles, William J. Doan.
        p. cm.
    Includes bibliographical references (p.   ) and indexes.
    ISBN 978-1-59856-272-9 (alk. paper)
    1. Hebrew poetry, Biblical—History and criticism. I. Doan, William, 1959–
II. Title.
    BS1405.52.G55 2008
    221′.0663—dc22
                                                    2008025907

For
Bonnie and Cheryl

Table of Contents

Publisher's Preface

Most of the English translations of the Bible found in this work are taken from the Revised Standard Version (RSV) and are not marked. Those translations that are taken from other English Bible translations or are the authors' own translations are marked accordingly.

Hebrew words found in this work have been transliterated using the General Purpose style of the *SBL Handbook of Style* with the exceptions of ʾ for *alef,* ʿ for *ayin,* and *kh* for *khet.*

Acknowledgments

W e would like to take this opportunity to express our gratitude to several groups of people. Terry was awarded a sabbatical semester during the spring of 2008 during which this book was brought to completion. We are grateful to the administration of Gannon University for this gift of time. Also we would like to express our sincere appreciation to Terry's faculty colleagues in the department of Theology at Gannon Univesity and Bill's colleagues in the School of Fine Arts of Miami University of Ohio. Their interest and support are constant encouragements. We also want to thank Adron Farris, graduate student in Miami's Department of Theatre, for his help with the bibliographies.

Sara Scott, Allan Emery, and the whole staff at Hendrickson have made this project enjoyable. Their editorial and administrative expertise is greatly appreciated.

Terry Giles
William J. Doan

Abbreviations

Books of the Bible

Gen	Genesis
Exod	Exodus
Num	Numbers
Deut	Deuteronomy
Josh	Joshua
Judg	Judges
Ruth	Ruth
1 Sam	1 Samuel
2 Sam	2 Samuel
1 Kgs	1 Kings
2 Kgs	2 Kings
1 Chr	1 Chronicles
2 Chr	2 Chronicles
Ezra	Ezra
Neh	Nehemiah
Ps(s)	Psalm(s)
Prov	Proverbs
Song	Song of Songs
Isa	Isaiah
Jer	Jeremiah
Ezek	Ezekiel
Dan	Daniel
Jon	Jonah
Mic	Micah
Hab	Habakkuk

Mark   Mark
Luke   Luke
1 Cor   1 Corinthians

General

AB   Anchor Bible
ABD   *Anchor Bible Dictionary*. Edited by David N. Freedman.
             6 vols. New York: Doubleday, 1992
B.C.E.   before the Common Era
BRev   *Bible Review*
BSac   *Bibliotheca sacra*
BZAW   Beiheft zur Zeitschrift für die alttestamentliche
             Wissenschaft
ca.   circa
CBC   Cambridge Bible Commentary
CBQ   *Catholic Biblical Quarterly*
C.E.   Common Era
ch(s).   chapter(s)
CTA   *Corpus des tablettes en cunéiformes alphabétiques décou-
             vertes à Ras Shamra–Ugarit de 1929 à 1939.* Edited by
             A. Herdner. 2 vols. Mission de Ras Shamra 10. Paris:
             Imprimerie Nationale, P. Guethner, 1963
ed(s).   editor(s), edited by, edition
e.g.   *exempli gratia*, for example
esp.   especially
et al.   *et alii*, and others
HTR   *Harvard Theological Review*
ICC   International Critical Commentary
JBL   *Journal of Biblical Literature*
JSOT   *Journal for the Study of the Old Testament*
JSOTSup   Journal for the Study of the Old Testament: Supplement
             Series
LXX   Septuagint
MT   Masoretic Text
NIV   New International Version
NJPS   *Tanakh: The Holy Scriptures: The New JPS Translation ac-
             cording to the Traditional Hebrew Text*
NRSV   New Revised Standard Version
OTL   Old Testament Library
p(p).   page(s)

PEQ	*Palestine Exploration Quarterly*
repr.	reprinted
RSV	Revised Standard Version
trans.	translated by
v(v).	verse(s)
vol(s).	volume(s)
VT	*Vetus Testamentum*
VTSup	Vetus Testamentum Supplements
WBC	Word Biblical Commentary
ZAW	*Zeitschrift für die alttestamentliche Wissenschaft*

Chapter 1: **Introduction**

This book is about "twice-used songs." Twice-used songs are those songs, scattered throughout the Hebrew Bible, that have become inserted into the midst of prose narratives. So placed, the songs have assumed a use in addition to that for which they were first composed. Their placement in a story makes the songs "twice-used."[1] But to the modern reader, the appearance of these songs is often awkward at best. At times they appear to interrupt the flow of the narrative or, in other important ways, to disrupt the story by supplying contradictory details or a quite distinct point of view compared with that of the surrounding narrative. And it is not a fluke. These twice-used songs appear throughout the Hebrew Bible, showing up in what most believe to be the very earliest parts as well as the very latest. The insertion of songs into a prose narrative was a technique that persistently popped up again and again. Yet modern readers of the Bible do not understand well the practice of inserting songs into a narrative—why and for what effect. This book is an effort to aid in that understanding.

Although scholarly articles have examined these twice-used songs individually (and often with widely varying conclusions),[2] only three book

---

[1] We will later examine the concept of "twice-used" in relationship to Richard Schechner's notion of performance as "restored," or "twice behaved behavior" (*Between Theater and Anthropology* [Philadelphia: University of Pennsylvania Press, 1985], 36–37).

[2] H. Gunkel, *The Psalms: A Form Critical Introduction* (trans. T. Horner; Philadelphia: Fortress, 1967); H. G. Reventlow, *Gebet im Alten Testament* (Stuttgart: Kohlhammer, 1986); S. Balentine, *Prayer in the Hebrew Bible* (Minneapolis: Augsburg Fortress, 1993); James Watts, "'This Song': Conspicuous Poetry in Hebrew Prose," in *Verse in Ancient Near Eastern Prose* (ed. J. C. de Moor and Wilfred G. Watson; Alter Orient und Altes Testament 42; Neukirchen-Vluyn: Neukirchener Verlag, 1993), 345–58; idem, "Psalmody in Prophecy: Habakkuk 3 in Context," in *Forming Prophetic Literature: Essays on Isaiah and the Twelve in Honor of John D. W. Watts* (ed. James Watts and Paul House; JSOTSup 235; Sheffield: Sheffield

length treatments consider the twice-used songs as a literary device in the
Hebrew Bible prose.[3] This volume takes the examination of the twice-used
songs in a new direction. Though mindful that, in many ways, we stand on
the shoulders of those who have gone before, we will apply techniques that
have not yet been brought to bear in the examination of these songs from
ancient Israel. We will use insights from performance criticism to help
understand why the ancient biblical storytellers included these twice-used
songs and what they hoped to accomplish by interrupting their stories
with songs.

Recycled Songs

In order to begin thinking together about these Hebrew songs, let us
consider how songs are twice-used in our own cultural experience. From
Gustav Mahler to Bob Dylan, the recycling of songs (or "twice-used") has
been an integral part of our cultural practice. Composers, musicians, and
lyricists recycle both their own work and the work of others. A simple
"Google Scholar" search of "recycled songs" produces more than three
thousand hits with articles and books ranging from classical to country,
to rock, pop, and folk. The topics of these books and articles represent a
broad continuum of inquiry, including the practice of recycling, cultural
identity, gender, technology, nationalism, subcultural identity, public memory, performance and the postmodern, and street consciousness. Recycling
is a given in the cultural transmission of songs. And we in the twentieth
century did not invent the practice. A good argument can be made that
the recycling of songs has been practiced as long as there have been songs
to recycle. The reasons for recycling are diverse, ranging from the preservation of style to the very pragmatic and financial need to sell CDs. And
there are reasons songs have economic potential—reasons they are so
appealing.

Songs are part of every oral tradition. They help make the unfamiliar
familiar, aid in memory, help create feelings of belonging, preserve and

---

Academic, 1996) 209–23; and idem, "Biblical Psalms outside the Psalter," in *The
Book of Psalms: Composition and Reception* (ed. Peter Flint and Patrick Miller; VTSup
99; Leiden: Brill, 2004), 288–309.

[3]James Watts, *Psalm and Story: Inset Hymns in Hebrew Narrative* (JSOTSup
139; Sheffield: JSOT Press, 1992); Hans-Peter Mathys, *Dichter und Beter: Theologen
aus spätalttestamentlichen Zeit* (Orbis biblicus et orientalis 132; Freiburg, Switz.:
Universitätsverlag, 1994); Steven Weitzman, *Song and Story in Biblical Narrative:
The History of a Literary Convention in Ancient Israel* (Indianapolis: Indiana University Press, 1997).

pass traditions from one generation to the next, and communicate on multiple levels through rhythm, melody, and harmony, all in addition to the lyrics. Our contemporary music scene is filled with remixes, remakes, covers, and recycled versions of preexisting songs. Remixes turn a tune into another style. For example, the group Project Q turned a ballad by Don McLean—"American Pie"—into a popular dance version. A cover version is usually an interpretation of a song by another band or group that tries to make the song its own. Dozens of artists have "covered" songs. As with "I Can't Get No Satisfaction" by The Rolling Stones, the more popular a song is, the more it is covered by others. Whatever the industry calls the practice, it is fundamentally a process of recalling the past into the present. But it is more than simply applying an old or familiar song or lyric to a new situation or context. Twice-used songs appear right on the border between innovation and preservation, displaying characteristics of both. Twice-used songs bring the past into the present in order to help create a future. They thus are powerful tools and, when wielded skillfully, can exert tremendous influence in the formation of a proposed action, attitude, or belief.

Powerful recent examples of recycling, or of twice-used songs, represent efforts to bind people together and unite them under a single belief. Following are the final lyrics to a recycled Marvin Gaye 1971 hit song, "What's Going On"—a song that, in its original rendition, begged for humanity and understanding following the Vietnam War. In September of 2001, a group of rock and pop superstars gathered to record a recycled version to raise money for an "AIDS in Africa" campaign. But just four days after completing the recording, the September 11 attacks sent the artists back into the studio to add another verse.[4] The complete lyrics can be found in various locations on the World Wide Web, but only the verse added in response to the September 11 attacks is provided here; this particular recycling is a kind of double-duty recycling or perhaps even a thrice-used example of the power of song.

"What's Going On?"

Somebody tell me what's going on
(What's going on)
We got human beings using humans for a bomb
But everyone wanna live
Don't nobody really want to die

---

[4]A. Weiskopf, "Artists Remake Classic Song to Benefit Sept. 11, AIDS Victims," *The Heights: The Independent Student Newspaper of Boston College* (January 15, 2002): 2.

You feeling me right
I can't be watching people die (die)
And watching people cry
Let me break it down for a minute
If there's enough room here for you and me
There's plenty of room for some humanity
Somebody tell me what's going on
(What's going on)
Somebody tell me what's going on
(What's going on)[5]

In 2005, Michael Stipe of the band REM covered "In the Sun" (originally written by singer-songwriter Joseph Arthur) to raise money for victims of Hurricane Katrina. Since the song was previously covered by Peter Gabriel for the 1997 tribute album *Diana Princess of Wales,* Stipe's version is at least the third recycling. Also in tribute to Princess Diana, Elton John recycled his own "Candle in the Wind" to honor the princess during her funeral. These are just a few examples of thousands of recycled songs that have made their way into the hearts and minds of countless listeners. The songs of Bob Dylan have generated hundreds of remakes, or recycled versions. Below is a list of a few Dylan remakes.

Bob Dylan: Top Ten Songs Covered

Blowin' in the Wind	375 versions
Don't Think Twice It's Alright	217 versions
I Shall Be Released	181 versions
Mr. Tambourine Man	176 versions
Like a Rolling Stone	172 versions
Knockin' On Heavens Door	150 versions
All Along the Watchtower	144 versions
It's All Over Now, Baby Blue	133 versions
I'll Be Your Baby Tonight	121 versions
The Mighty Quinn	118 versions

Source: "It Ain't Me, Babe: The Bob Dylan Cover Lists"
[cited January 28, 2008]. Online: www.bjorner.com/Covers.htm

In a series of scrapbooks and songbooks, Dylan has also published his handwritten lyrics and drawings, recycling his work as written poetry as well as recorded song. Who does not know at least some of the lyrics to

---

[5] "Christina Aguilera, What's Going On Lyrics," ST Lyrics [cited January 28, 2008]. Online: www.stlyrics.com/songs/c/christinaaguilera819/whatsgoin-gon233643.html

Blowin' in the Wind? Through YouTube entries, Wikipedia entries, and iTunes, this song is at our fingertips in a full range of musical styles.

Besides the ubiquitous recycling of songs intended to sell commercial products, recycling song material represents a rich history of cultural memory, of internalizing the words and rhythms of life. Recycling allows us to place something from the past into a present moment, to perform what *was* in the *here* and *now*. If we sing along with the recycled version of "What's Going On" or "Blowin' in the Wind," we participate in the creation of a new reality, a time and space that we share through the performance of the song. Impulses for innovation (the new setting of the here and now) and preservation (use of the old song) meet to create something unique. And the recycling process affords us the opportunity to make the song "sing" with the rhythms and flavors of who we are. The songs allow us to bind the past to some special moment of the present in order to help create a new sense of identity or belonging. As we will see in the pages that follow, constructed identity and the binding of a social unit with a belief or memory is a primary function of the twice-used songs of the Hebrew Bible as well.

Orality, the Written Word, and Performance

Songs live on the boundary between the oral and the written, between the performed and the literate. Describing the "oral-written interface," David Carr writes, "The focus was on inscribing a culture's most precious traditions on the insides of people."[6] Orality and writing are cultural partners in a grand design intent on mastery of a tradition. And so, contrary to the view of the influential theorist Albert Lord, who perceived orality and literacy on opposite ends of a continuum, Carr understands "an intricate interplay of orality and textuality, where written texts are intensely oral, while even exclusively oral texts are deeply affected by written culture."[7] Carr concludes, "Orality and writing technology are joint means for accomplishing a common goal: accurate recall of the treasured tradition."[8] Carr's statements are part of the platform upon which the following pages build. An examination of explicitly oral material (songs) now inserted by a prose author into his own written product provides a wonderful opportunity to

---

[6] David Carr, *Writing on the Tablet of the Heart: Origins of Scripture and Literature* (Oxford: Oxford University Press, 2005), 6.

[7] Ibid., 7. See also Jack Goody, *The Interface between the Written and the Oral* (Cambridge: Cambridge University Press, 1987); Alger N. Doane, "The Ethnography of Scribal Writing and Anglo-Saxon Poetry: Scribe as Performer," *Oral Tradition* 9 (1994): 420–39.

[8] Carr, *Writing on the Tablet of the Heart*, 7.

investigate how that "treasured tradition" was recalled and how the medium transferability (oral to written) of the song assisted the writer of the prose in accomplishing his or her own goal.[9] If our contention is correct, that the prose writers of the Hebrew Bible inserted the songs to assist the listener or reader in identifying with the prose narrative, then Carr's statement is instructive: "Indeed, that past is never 'past' in the way we might conceive it but stands in the ancient world as a potentially realizable 'present' to which each generation seeks to return."[10]

In addition, our premise, that there exist remnants of performance in both the biblical texts and in the likely recitation of these texts by the narrative authors, allows us to see how the performative quality of these songs played a central role in the recall of the past as a realizable present. The recitation, or public performance, of these texts presents us with a shared performer/spectator relationship. People came together to hear and to participate in moments of performance. Performance theorist and theatre practitioner Jill Dolan complements Carr's suggestion when he describes "inscribing a culture's most precious traditions on the insides of people." Although Dolan writes about contemporary performances, her concept of "utopian performatives" is very helpful for our purpose here:

> Utopian performatives describe small but profound moments in which a performance calls the attention of the audience in a way that lifts everyone slightly above the present, into a hopeful feeling of what the world might be like if every moment of our lives were as emotionally voluminous, generous, aesthetically striking, and intersubjectively intense. As a performative, performance itself becomes a "doing" in linguistic philosopher J. L. Austin's sense of the term, something that in its enunciation *acts*—that is, performs an action as tangible and effective as saying "I do" in a wedding ceremony. Utopian performatives, in their doings, make palpable an affective vision of how the world might be better.[11]

Songs have the potential to do just that: to "lift above the present." Consider the Song of Asaph, found in 1 Chronicles 16 (a song examined at length later in this study), which expresses precisely this vision of how the world *is* a better place because of what the Lord has done for the people of Israel:

---

[9]Jan Assmann, "Kulturelle und literarische Texte," in *Ancient Egyptian Literature: History and Forms* (ed. A Loprieno; Leiden: Brill, 1996), 76–77.

[10]Carr, *Writing on the Tablet of the Heart*, 11. See also Jan Assmann, *Das kulturelle Gedächtnis: Schrift, Erinnerung, und politische Identität in frühen Hochkulturen* (Munich: Beck, 1992).

[11]Jill Dolan, *Utopia in Performance: Finding Hope at the Theater* (Ann Arbor: University of Michigan Press, 2005), 5–6.

Song of Asaph

O give thanks to the LORD, call on his name,
Make known his deeds among the peoples.
Sing to him, sing praises to him,
Tell of all his wonderful works.
Glory in his holy name;
Let the hearts of those who seek the LORD rejoice.
Seek the LORD and his strength,
Seek his presence continually.
Remember the wonderful works he has done,
His miracles, and the judgments he uttered,
O offspring of his servant Israel,
Children of Jacob, his chosen ones. (1 Chr 16:8–13 NRSV)

This song transports the reader or listener to a new place by compressing marvelous and divine deeds, works, miracles, and judgments all into one present in which praise and song form the only sensible response.

One of the universals of performance, notes the influential theatre historian Marvin Carlson, is its sense of recall, "of the past reappearing unexpectedly and uncannily in the midst of the present."[12] This "reappearing" happens frequently in the twice-used songs of the Hebrew Bible. Each song, whether spoken or sung before its inclusion in the text of the Hebrew Bible, is a "reappearance" into the present, the here and now, of the scribe who places the song into the text. The reappearance of the past into the present is an event or occurrence, not just a quotation on a page (it is a song that comes alive in the singing, not just lyrics on a page).[13] It is something that happens, and this, too, is one of the universals of performance, particularly in relationship to theatre and drama. Performances happen. They occur. And in the occurrence, dynamics are unleashed that sweep up both presenters and spectators as active participants in the event. The twice-used nature of the songs that we will examine, in both their prose and their poetic versions, means that their presence in prose narratives is now "haunted" by the dynamics of their sung or performed past. It is not just the words of the song that are appropriated by the narrator but the past singing of the words, the performances of the song as well, that the narrator now uses. When the performative event (in our case the narrative

---

[12] Marvin Carlson, *The Haunted Stage: The Theatre as Memory Machine* (Ann Arbor: University of Michigan Press, 2001), 1.

[13] For a fuller discussion, see William Doan and Terry Giles, "Presentational versus Literary," in *Prophets, Performance, and Power: Performance Criticism of the Hebrew Bible* (New York: T&T Clark, 2005), 26–30.

itself), or at least part of the event, is structured around the recall of the past into the present (the inclusion of the twice-used song), something significant is shared as a result of the performance. And this significant performative event binds performers and spectators in a unique dance of making meaning by conjuring up the past into the present in order to create a shared experience of the here and now.

> All theatrical cultures have recognized, in some form or another, this ghostly quality, this sense of something coming back in the theatre, and so the relationships between theatre and cultural memory are deep and complex. . . . Theatre, as a simulacrum of the cultural and historical process itself, seeking to depict the full range of human actions within their physical context, has always provided society with the most tangible records of its attempts to understand its own operations. It is the repository of cultural memory, but, like the memory of each individual, it is also subject to continual adjustments and modifications as the memory is recalled in new circumstances and contexts. The present experience is always ghosted by previous experiences and associations while these ghosts are simultaneously shifted and modified by the processes of recycling and recollection.[14]

The twice-used songs of the Hebrew Bible certainly present us with both a tangible record of a culture's attempt to understand itself and a rich sample of the cultural memory of the people of ancient Israel. And just as Carlson suggests, the use of the songs in narratives constitutes an adjustment and modification of the artifacts of cultural memory to a new circumstance and context. Cultural memory, writes the Egyptologist and classicist Jan Assmann, is marked by its transcendence of the everyday, by its fixed point or horizon that "does not change with the passing of time."[15] "These fixed points are fateful events of the past, whose memory is maintained through cultural formation (texts, rites, monuments) and institutional communication (recitation, practice, observance). . . . In cultural formation, a collective experience crystallizes, whose meaning, when touched upon, may suddenly become accessible again across millennia."[16] The following five characteristics of cultural memory (concretion of identity, capacity to reconstruct, formation, organization, and obligation), established by Assmann are of central importance to the exploration of twice-used songs of the Hebrew Bible. These should be understood as follows:

1. *"The concretion of identity"* or the relation of the individual to the group. Cultural memory preserves the store of knowledge from

---

[14]Carlson, *The Haunted Stage*, 2.

[15]Jan Assmann, "Collective Memory and Cultural Identity" (trans. John Czaplicka), in "Cultural History/Cultural Studies," special issue, *New German Critique* 65 (spring–summer 1995): 125–33, here 129.

[16]Ibid.

which the members of a group derive an awareness of the group's unity and peculiarity. The objective manifestations of cultural memory are defined through a kind of identificatory determination in a positive ("We are this") or in a negative ("We are not that") sense. . . . The supply of knowledge in the cultural memory is characterized by sharp distinctions made between those who belong and those who do not, i.e., between what appertains to oneself and what is foreign (between *insiders* and *outsiders*).

2. Connected with this notion of group identity is cultural memory's *capacity to reconstruct*. No memory can preserve the past. . . . Cultural memory works by reconstructing, that is, it always relates its knowledge to an actual and contemporary situation. True, it is fixed in immovable figures of memory and stores of knowledge, but every contemporary context relates to these differently, sometimes by appropriation, sometimes by criticism, sometimes by preservation or by transformation. Cultural memory exists in two modes: first in the mode of potentiality of the archive whose accumulated texts, images, and rules of conduct act as a total horizon, and second in the mode of actuality, whereby each contemporary context puts the objectivized meaning into its own perspective, giving it its own relevance.

3. *Formation*. The objectivation or crystallization of communicated meaning and collectively shared knowledge is a prerequisite of its transmission in the *culturally institutionalized heritage of a society*. "Stable" formation is not dependent on a single medium such as writing. Pictorial images and rituals [and, we would add, performances] can also function in the same way. . . . As far as language is concerned, formation takes place long before the invention of writing.

4. *Organization*. With this we mean a) the institutional buttressing of communication, e.g., through formulization of the communicative situation in ceremony and b) the specialization of the bearers of cultural memory. The distribution and structure of participation in the communicative memory are diffuse. No specialists exist in this regard. Cultural memory, by contrast, always depends on a specialized practice. . . . In special cases of written cultures with canonized texts, such cultivation can expand enormously and become extremely differentiated.

5. *Obligation*. The relation to a normative self-image of the group engenders a clear system of values and differentiations in importance

which structure the cultural supply of knowledge and the symbols. There are important and unimportant, central and peripheral, local and interlocal symbols, depending on how they function in the production, representation, and reproduction of this self-image.[17]

Assmann's list of cultural-memory characteristics provides a valuable beginning by which to understand the function of the twice-used songs in the Hebrew Bible. In particular, we will be mindful of the way in which the songs are used to *reconstruct* the past in such a way as to assist in forming a *concrete social identity* among the reading and listening audience with the goal of creating a commitment or *obligation* to a specific ideal, value, or belief. But the way in which twice-used songs *perform* these cultural functions is quite different from the way prose narratives or other *literary* forms might be called upon to create cultural memory.[18] Songs are inherently performative, and so we will employ performative concepts in the investigation. Already there have been those who have begun looking at parts of the Hebrew Bible through a performative lens.

> Among literary approaches to the Old Testament, Meir Sternberg's *The Poetics of Biblical Narrative* is a major breakthrough in the field, as well as Robert Alter's insightful *The Art of Biblical Narrative* and Uriel Simon's *Reading Prophetic Narratives*. However, whereas the term "dramatic" is used in most literary-oriented works mainly to indicate particular structural elements, as well as the prevalence of conflict, dialogue, modes of characterization, and other drama-as-genre elements, this book [*The Bible as Theatre*] shifts the focus from a literary genre-oriented discussion to a medium-oriented one. It could, moreover, be argued that the entire traditional genre divisions of Epics, Lyrics, and Drama is a convenient late imposition on early

---

[17] Ibid., 130–32.

[18] In some ways, this is similar to the debate that has placed prose and poetry on opposite ends of a spectrum. See Johann G. von Herder, *The Spirit of Hebrew Poetry* (2 vols.; Burlington, Vt.: Edward Smith, 1833; repr., Naperville, Ill.: Aleph, 1971), 2:10, who was convinced of the emotional weight of poetry: a poetic image "exists only in its connection with the emotion that prompted it"; Robert Lowth, *Lectures on the Sacred Poetry of the Hebrews* (trans. G. Gregory; London: Chadwick, 1847), 153, who characterized poetry as emotive and prose as more cognitive, i.e., "the language of reason." See also James Kugel, *The Idea of Biblical Poetry: Parallelism and Its History* (New Haven: Yale University Press, 1981). Wilfred G. Watson, *Classical Hebrew Poetry: A Guide to Its Techniques* (JSOTSup 26; Sheffield: JSOT Press, 1984), 30–31, made a wonderful statement concerning the emotive function of poetry: "In spite of its brevity, this paragraph is one of the most important in the whole book. . . . In other words, *the main function* of the poetic features identified is to *express merismus* . . . (meaning that certain representative components of a larger object are mentioned instead of the whole)." Meir Sternberg, *The Poetics of Biblical Narrative: Ideological Literature and the Drama of Reading* (Bloomington: Indiana University Press, 1987), challenges the prose-poetry spectrum.

classical texts, the Old Testament included, which may—and do—comprise elements of all three literary genres in a much less neatly organized way. In analyzing biblical excerpts as theatrical, I contend that some of them can be performed verbatim, since the biblical "stage-instructions" pertaining to time, space, movement, costumes, props, lighting and other theatrical components, are often built-in.[19]

In this statement by Shimon Levy, one of the most important observations concerns the shift of focus from a genre-oriented discussion to a medium-oriented discussion. Levy is not alone in his observation about the convenience of traditional genre divisions. Michael Goldman, reflecting on the problem of "genre" when it comes to understanding the complexity of drama, notes that when it comes to discussion of drama and genre,

> most of these discussions, certainly the most influential, are deficient in a signal respect. They fail to engage drama fully as an experience, an ongoing moment-to-moment process for audiences or readers. They have in common a tendency to treat genre as a reflective category, a way of classifying and systematizing dramatic texts and performances after the fact. Everything changes, however, if we stop to think of genre as not entirely unlike rhyme, say, or ambiguity, as a feature, that is, whose primary interest for readers or audiences is as something that *happens* to us in a poem or play, *as* it happens [emphasis Goldman's].[20]

Both Levy's and Goldman's notions of drama and theatre, which center on a medium-oriented discussion of the nature of theatre and drama, one in which the experience of audience/readers is presented in terms of what happens to them, as it happens to them, requires an understanding of drama as a phenomenon, not only as a thing, such as a text or a place.

> Many problems not only in dramatic but literary theory would take on a sharply new perspective if, just to clear the air, let us say, we were to reverse the process and think instead of drama as the most general case of literature, with poetry, the novel, and so forth as specializations. We might do well in fact to imagine drama as the originary literary or artistic form, if only to offset the myth, nowadays unacknowledged because epistemologically incorrect, but nevertheless still dominant, of the literary origins of drama (from choral lyric, narrative, Solonic speeches in the agora, or whatever). Actually, the old habit of thinking about drama as a genre of "literature," a habit seemingly as old as criticism itself, has worked to obscure some important connections between drama and life—especially with some features of life we're likely to regard as intensely difficult, issues that bear on self and meaning, on persons and texts, on identity and community.[21]

---

[19]Shimon Levy, *The Bible as Theatre* (Portland, Oreg.: Sussex Academic, 2002), 5.

[20]Michael Goldman, *On Drama: Boundaries of Genre, Borders of Self* (Ann Arbor: University of Michigan Press, 2000), 3.

[21]Ibid., 6–7.

These important connections between drama and life are found in the twice-used songs of the Hebrew Bible, particularly as they relate to questions of identity and community and the ways in which the people of ancient Israel negotiated their relationship with God. The rest of this book will explore the dynamics of this negotiated relationship, particularly as articulated in twice-used songs.

What Do We Mean by Performance Criticism?

"Performance criticism" is a term frequently used by many people, with a resultant wide range of meanings. Under the umbrella of performance criticism, one will find those who write traditional performance history and who are more directly aligned with the study of theatre and drama; those who use records of performance to discuss literary issues; those who use performance for the anthropological and cultural study of identity, politics, and power; those who carry out semiotic analyses of performance; as well as those who discuss performance as an issue of dramaturgy—just to name a few. And so it seems appropriate to define the concept and set boundaries for the manner in which "performance criticism" will be used in this book.

In the discussion below, the following definitions, while found in the glossary, bear special emphasis at this point. *Theatre* occurs when one or more human beings, isolated in time and space, present themselves to another or others. *Drama* occurs when one or more human beings, isolated in time and space, present themselves in imagined acts to another or others.[22] *Dramaturgy* is the art and practice of dramatic composition and enactment. *Performance studies* is a field of academic study that focuses on the critical analysis of performance and performativity, incorporating theories of drama, dance, art, anthropology, philosophy, cultural studies, and more. Performance studies looks at how we ourselves perform in individual, social, political, religious, gendered, and other contexts. It is, moreover, a field with more than one origin story. One primary origin narrative focuses on the work of Richard Schechner and Victor Turner, thoroughly elaborated in Schechner's *Between Theater and Anthropology*. The other primary origin story focuses on the development of J. L. Austin's speech-act-theory with strong relationships to literary theory, feminism, and queer theory through the works of Judith Butler, Peggy Phelan, and many others. *Speech Act* involves doing and saying. In very simple terms, J. L. Austin taught us

---

[22]Bernard Beckerman, *Dynamics of Drama: Theory and Method of Analysis* (New York: Drama Book Specialists, 1979), 11, 21.

that when saying something, we *do* something; most famously exemplified by the "I do" pronouncements made at the time of marriage. *Performance criticism* examines the way in which these repeatable and socially recognizable events use specific techniques to powerfully express social values and themes. *Performance mode of thought* is a way of thinking that engages both the cognitive and the imaginative aspects of thought to conceive of reality not in propositions but in actions and being. Similar to the notion of "dramatic imagination," it is the shared imaginative space of performance where the performer/presenter and the spectator meet.

In establishing a definition for "performance criticism," it is useful to glance back at how the discipline developed. Just more than thirty years ago, performance studies formally emerged as a recognized discipline in the academy, a discipline that is both multi- and interdisciplinary by design. Under the wide and ideologically diverse umbrella of "performance studies," various approaches to performance criticism have emerged.[23]

The complexity of the use of the term "performance" or the phrase "performance criticism" is only intensified by the variety of disciplinary and interpretive uses that have developed over time. A leading historian of performance, Mary Thomas Crane, comments on this complexity in her effort to trace the highways and byways of performance theories, definitions, and critical practices:

> Judith Butler usefully distinguishes between theorists of "social drama," such as Victor Turner, who focus on what performance does in a culture to promote social cohesion and to resolve conflict, and theorists of "symbolic action," like Foucault, who "focus on the way in which political authority and questions of legitimation are thematized and settled within the terms of performed meaning." . . . Performance theorists like Turner and Richard Schechner argue that performance extends from the theatre to embrace play, games, sports, dance music, and ritual. For Schechner and Turner, social performances are reiterated behaviors that function in a culture to mediate liminal moments: periods of crisis or uncertainty that accompany individual or cultural transitions.[24]

Crane mentions three leading critics (Judith Butler, Victor Turner, Richard Schechner) who define performance not by "its representational

---

[23] Shannon Jackson, *Professing Performance: Theatre in the Academy from Philology to Performativity* (Cambridge: Cambridge University Press, 2004). Jackson's seminal study of the history and development of the complex nature of the word "perform" in the academy is the most thorough investigation of the problem of "performance" and the different disciplinary investigations that employ the term.

[24] Mary Thomas Crane, "What Was Performance?" *Criticism* 43.2 (2002): 16–87. The original Butler quote is from Judith Butler, "Performative Acts and Gender Constitution: An Essay in Phenomenology and Feminist Theory," *Theatre Journal* 40 (1988): 526n9.

or deceptive nature, but by repetition and liminality; they emphasize, in Turner's words, 'process and processual qualities: performance, move, staging, plot, redressive action, crisis, schism, reintegration, and the like.'"[25] In other words, "performance" is a cultural phenomena that can occur in a parade, a religious event, a school graduation, a sporting event, or in the theatre and on the stage.

The work of these critics in particular is central to the definition and practice of performance criticism employed here.[26] The work of Bernard Beckerman and Marco De Marinis, well-known theatre scholars whose conceptions of performance are more rooted in dramaturgical practice, is also central to our conception of a "performance mode of thought."[27]

Another perspective on "performance" and "performance criticism" that has taken hold and is opening up valuable new lines of inquiry is a cognitive and literary cultural theory about how embodied action shapes both thought and language. Crane provides a useful and succinct description of this line of thought.

> Francisco Varela, Evan Thompson, and Eleanor Rosch have argued that several converging strains of cognitive science seem closely akin to phenomenology in linking "human experience as culturally embodied with the study of human cognition in neuroscience, linguistics, and cognitive psychology." Rather than assuming, a priori, that discourse constructs the subject from outside, a cognitive approach sees cognition as "embodied action," emphasizing "that sensory and motor processes, perception and action, are fundamentally inseparable in lived cognition." Thus, "perception is not simply embedded within and constrained by the surrounding world; it also contributes to the enactment of this surrounding world."[28]

By contributing to the enactment of the surrounding world, cognition helps to create that world and give it meaning on both the page and in the body. Performance, whether *traditionally theatrical* or not, mirrors this process of "embodied action," or our ability to *re-present* what we perceive through some kind of embodied enactment: preaching, prophesying, oration, narration, singing, and so forth. The relationship between the

---

[25]Crane, "What Was Performance?"170. The original Turner quote is from Victor Turner, *The Anthropology of Performance* (New York: PAJ, 1986), 76.

[26]This is the case also in Doan and Giles, *Prophets, Performance, and Power: Performance Criticism of the Hebrew Bible* (New York: T&T Clark, 2005).

[27]See Text boxes. Doan and Giles, *Prophets, Performance, and Power,* 3.

[28]Crane, "What Was Performance?" 171. The original Varela, Thompson, and Rosch quotes are taken from Francisco Varela, Evan Thompson, and Eleanor Rosch, *The Embodied Mind: Cognitive Science and Human Experience* (Cambridge: MIT Press, 1993), 150, 173, 174.

performed and the real, even when the work of the imagination and our willing suspension of disbelief are involved, is complex and fascinating.

The questions about the nature of performance are clearly part of a complex and lively set of debates in academic circles, including the field of biblical studies. The following diagram charts out the complexities in the examination of performance.

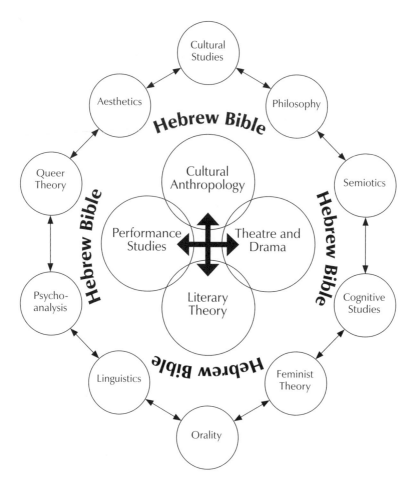

Source: The chart was first published in Terry Giles and William Doan, "Peformance Criticism of the Hebrew Bible," *Religion Compass* 6.3 (2008). Used with permission.

The diagram oversimplifies much of the context in order to set the stage, so to speak, for our investigation, which brings together biblical studies with both theatre and performance studies. *And the connection is just this: the way of thinking and the manner of communicating that are common in theatre and performance reside just beneath the surface of much of the Hebrew Bible text.*

In the diagram on p. 15, our investigation is at the center, where the four inner circles of cultural anthropology, performance studies, theatre and drama, and literary theory engage in a dance that is beautiful to watch. The outer ring represents academic disciplines, or fields of inquiry, all of which are concerned with performance and apply directly to the four inner circles representing aspects of human interaction.

As with politics and religion, when three people discuss theatre, performance studies, or biblical studies, there are at least four opinions! And so this chart will not satisfy everyone in the conversation. But together with this introduction it provides a useful context for understanding what is meant here by "performance."

Setting the Stage

As Bert States argues, "If something is to be remembered at all, it must be remembered not as what happened but as what has happened again in a different way and will surely happen again in the future in still another way."[29] In other words, significant events are conjured up time and again, invading the present and creating a future. Holidays, parades, and even songs are some of the mechanisms used to work this magic of cultural tradition. This study will examine the twice-used songs of the Hebrew Bible to better understand and appreciate the role these songs play in creating a cultural memory. The following chart provides a handy summary of the twice-used songs and their location in the Hebrew Bible.

Twice Used Songs

Common Title	Reference	Prose Introduction
Song of the Sea	Exodus 15:1–18	Then Moses and the people of Israel sang
Miriam's Song	Exodus 15:21	And Miriam sang to them
Song of Wells	Numbers 21:17–18	Then Israel sang this song
Victory Ballad	Numbers 21:27–30	Therefore the ballad singers say
Song of Moses	Deuteronomy 32:1–43	Then Moses spoke the words of this song until they were finished

---

[29] Bert O. States, *Dreaming and Storytelling* (Ithaca, N.Y.: Cornell University Press, 1993), 119.

Common Title	Reference	Prose Introduction
The Day the Sun Stood Still	Joshua 10:12–13	Then spoke Joshua to the LORD . . . and he said in the sight of Israel . . . . . . Is this not written in the Book of Jashar?
Deborah's Song	Judges 5:2–31	Then sang Deborah and Barak the son of Abinoam on that day
Song of David's Honor	1 Samuel 18:7 (21:12; 29:5)	And the women sang to one another as they made merry
Song of the Bow	2 Samuel 1:19–27	And David lamented with this lamentation over Saul and Jonathan his son, and he said it should be taught to the people of Judah; behold, it is written in the Book of Jashar. He said
David's Song	2 Samuel 22:2–51	And David spoke to the LORD the words of this song
Song of Asaph	1 Chronicles 16:8–36	Then on that day David first appointed that thanksgiving be sung to the LORD by Asaph and his brethren
Solomon's Temple Dedication	1 Kings 8:12–13 2 Chronicles 6:1–2	Then Solomon said . . . . . . Is it not written in the Book of Song? (3 Kgdms 8:53a [LXX])
Temple Dedication Chorus	2 Chronicles 5:13	And when the song was raised, with trumpets and cymbals and other musical instruments, in praise to the LORD
(Second) Temple Foundation Chorus	Ezra 3:11	They sang responsively, praising and giving thanks to the LORD

The prose narrators identify all these lyric insertions as songs, except "The Day the Sun Stood Still" in Joshua 10. But even the Joshua 10 poem can be included with the rest of the songs because of its association with the Book of Jashar, an association that seemed so important to the narrator of Joshua 10 that the source is mentioned just after the quotation of the song (10:13b). It should also be mentioned that the "Temple Dedication

Chorus" is not specifically identified as song in 1 Kings of the Hebrew Bible version but is so identified in the LXX version of the passage (3 Kgdms 8:53a) and therefore merits joining the other twice-used songs.

This study does not examine all the songs found in the Hebrew Bible; other "songs" contained in prose accounts are not included in our analysis (see the following chart). These songs, too, are twice-used, but they appear, in the majority of instances, as prayers and not as songs in their new prose contexts.

Songs Twice Used but Not as Songs

Common Title	Reference	Prose Introduction
Moses' announcement of the ark	Numbers 10:35–36	And whenever the ark set out, Moses said
Hannah's Prayer	1 Samuel 2:1–10	Hannah also prayed and said
Hezekiah's Prayer	Isaiah 38:10–20	A writing of Hezekiah . . . after he had been sick and had recovered from his sickness
Daniel's Prayer	Daniel 2:20–23	Then Daniel blessed the God of heaven. Daniel said
Jonah's Prayer	Jonah 2:3–10	Then Jonah prayed to the LORD his God

And besides these songs, used as prayers, other songs in the Hebrew Bible are not included in our examination. An argument could well be made that since the Hebrew Bible has assumed such a special place in Western culture, all the songs in the Bible are twice-used. And at some level, this is certainly the case. But this study limits its investigation only to those songs that have been appropriated by Hebrew scribes, inserted into prose narratives, and identified as songs. Thus the Psalms, the Song of Songs, and songs found in the poetry sections of prophetic materials (such as Isa 26:1–21; 27:2–5; 42:10–13) are not included although they, too, deserve fresh examination with tools from performance criticism.

Of the songs examined here, four categories present themselves. First is a set of three short songs that find a common association with the Book of Jashar. A close examination of the songs quoted from this book reveals that they share several characteristics that may provide insight into why prose writers use songs in the Hebrew Bible. In the second set, the respective prose writers quote the songs at length and introduced them as having been sung by the characters within the narrative. In these narratives, the singing of the song is part of the story. In the third set, the songs, though also recited at length by the prose narrators, are songs not sung. The prose writer introduces the reader to the song by claiming that the song was spoken or delivered in some other fashion—but not sung. These introductions should be taken seriously; it may well be that they serve as indicators that these "songs not sung" may have a slightly different rhetorical purpose or function than the songs that are sung by the characters of the narratives. The fourth and final grouping of songs is composed of short choruses, which range in size from just a few words to a sentence or two. One of the choruses makes several appearances, repeated by various prose narrators at different points along their respective stories. Although there are differences in the way that these twice-used songs are presented by the narrators borrowing them, all of the songs are tenacious. They are all important additions to the literary contexts in which they have been placed. And they all merit being twice-used.

The inclusion of twice-used songs in the narratives contained in the Hebrew Bible is a literary practice that has a long history, appearing in some of the earliest as well as some of the latest narratives. These twice-used songs

1. invariably predate the narratives to which they have been added;

2. often identify an author or performer, making that persona present to the reading or listening audience;

3. add little or nothing to the plot development of the narratives in which they now reside;

4. often conflict with the details of the narrative context and at times appear anachronistic in the narrative placement;

5. emphasize audience formation through the projection of a group identity;

6. contribute to the narrative an influence and persuasiveness that goes far beyond the mere recitation of the words of the song;

7. were, at least on one occasion, performed by an identifiable group known as the *moshelim,* or ballad singers.

These observations suggest that the twice-used songs in Hebrew narratives make an important contribution to the narratives by adding something other than further details to the plot or storyline. The songs were given life in the singing; they were meant to be performed. And the ghosts of these performances were powerfully present, acting upon the storywriters and influencing the decision to include the songs into the narratives. The twice-used songs operate according to a different kind of paradigm than do the narratives in which the songs are now embedded.

In describing the role of the twice-used songs in constructing a cultural memory, this study employs a number of concepts that focus on elements of performance and presentation within a theatrical, dramatic, and social-drama framework. Not all of these concepts apply equally to every song, but they do provide a matrix for analysis. Performance-critical concepts will be introduced as they are applied to one or more of the twice-used songs. A glossary of terms appears at the end of this volume to guide the reader through the use of terms and concepts. Readers unfamiliar with the terms may want to refer to the glossary repeatedly. But even readers well acquainted with the tools of drama, theatre, and performance may find the glossary helpful. Some of the terms admit to a wide variety of definition, and the glossary will give direction in our application of the terms and concepts. It is useful to begin here with a description of key relationships among terms and concepts.

Iconic and Dialectic Presentation

A performance, "gives us something and nothing to respond to."[30] The *something* a performance offers can be referred to as the iconic element of the performance: "the element offered to us for display."[31] Sound, color, movement—all of these are iconic elements heightened by the very fact that they are on display for spectators. *Iconic modes of presentation,* such as parades, political rallies, and other celebratory rituals, present and celebrate what is, the status quo, a moment frozen in time that celebrates identity. The twice-used songs are iconic presentations that were first embodied in the singer, and the movements, tonal qualities, and emotions of the singer all formed the something that were borrowed by the biblical storywriter.

The *nothing* offered by the performance is the dialectic element. This nothing is "the air that crackles from the interchange between one actor and another, between one moment and another."[32] It is the interplay between the place of presentation, the presenters, and the spectators. This give-and-take requires both the actor and the spectator as participants. It can well be characterized as a nothing, for this aspect of performance

---

[30] Bernard Beckerman, *Theatrical Presentation: Performer, Audience, and Act* (ed. Gloria Brim Beckerman and William Coco; New York: Routledge, 1990), 73.
[31] Ibid.
[32] Ibid., 74.

gives nothing but instead calls out from the spectator a powerful response essential for the creation of the imagined reality of the performance. The sensory response to the iconic, that which can be seen and heard, expands into the imaginative response to the dialectic, that which is created when the actor assumes the life of the character and the audience engages in the imaginative interplay along with the actor, particularly when characters engage in conflict and rising and falling tension, pulling the spectators into the emotional and psychological world of their action. *Dialectic modes of presentation*, the contextual narrative in which the twice-used songs are now placed, stress becoming and change.

The balance between iconic elements and dialectic elements determines the mode of presentation. Mixing the two, adding song to the narrative, or surrounding the song with the narrative will effectively make each stand in stark relief. But there is more. The something and nothing offered to us by these songs is part of the reason for the frustration expressed by commentators considering the text of the twice-used songs. The songs have *nothing* (or at most very little, and that in a problematic manner) to add to the story line of the narrative in which they are now placed. But the songs give to the narration *something* quite important. They are quite powerful "moments frozen in time," pausing the narrative, the dialectic, in order to pull the listener or reader into the story. The songs transform the audience and spectators from a group of individuals into a community—a "we" with a shared identity.

Actor-Character-Audience

An analysis of the twice-used songs will note the part played by actor, character, and audience. This interplay is quite prominent in some of the songs (the Song of David in 2 Sam 22, Song of Asaph in 1 Chr 16) but is present in all of the performed songs. The kind of actor-character-audience relationship encountered in the twice-used songs is primarily characterized by direct presentation, that is, presentation where the performer acknowledges the presence of the audience and makes that acknowledgment explicit.[33] In many of the songs, the actor-character-audience relationship goes beyond the recognition of the audience's presence and extends to audience participation. The songs involve the audience. This kind of direct presentation is an open form of exchange where the audience accepts the double nature of the presentation, knowing that the actor (scribe or reader) is not the character yet willfully and willingly suspending disbelief in order

---

[33] Ibid., 111.

to facilitate entrance into the relationship being offered to the audience through the actor's character. The audience and character are thereby given entrance into an imagined reality that can have a powerful impact on the nature of the audience even after the performance is complete.

The character and the character's actions are the site where actor and spectator meet, the imaginative space where they share beliefs, values, and feelings of belonging. In the twice-used songs, this imaginative space is a very important "location." It allows David to become a member of a postexilic audience (2 Sam 22), allows Yahweh to sing with a community celebrating release from Egypt (Deut 32), and makes applicable the security of the past to an uncertain and unsettled future (Num 21). This imagined space is where a cultural memory is celebrated and where a group identity is formed.

Audience Identity

It is important to remember that songs, including the twice-used songs of the Hebrew Bible, are used to *reconstruct* the past in such a way as to assist in forming a *concrete social identity* among the reading and listening audience with the goal of creating a commitment or *obligation* to a specific ideal, value, or belief. Just as, in the theatre and drama, a common ground (shared values) is established between presenter, presentation, and spectators in what is known as the communal audience, the songs examined here seek to promote an audience identity in which the values, language, and thoughts of all involved are as identical as possible, making multiple communication not only possible but effective as well. And this identity is not an accidental construct but an intentional project of the biblical storyteller. The storyteller wants to help shape the audience, to create values and priorities, to help spectators think of themselves in a specific fashion. The twice-used songs are not casually inserted into the narrative to simply entertain the reading or listening audience but are employed skillfully by the storyteller to do nothing less than help the audience reshape their own reality. The twice-used songs are powerful tools in accomplishing this goal.

Performative Mode of Thought

This investigation will, it is hoped, add to the insights furnished by literary-critical methodologies. The twice-used songs of the Hebrew Bible ask us to go beyond the fact of the written page, beyond a literary mode of thought, to the event of a performance, to a performative mode of thought in which the songs first were given life. The literary mode of thought, guiding the structure and shape of narratives, follows conventions and patterns readily discernible through literary-critical methodologies. The twice-used songs use different conventions and patterns. The songs are remnants of performances and so are usefully examined by methods commonly employed by performance critics. Because a mode of thought distinct from a literary mode was operative in employing the songs (and other performative material) in the Hebrew Bible, it is appropriate to seek a distinct set of tools by which to investigate the material. The nature of these tools is determined by the application to which the tools are put, by the performative mode of thought shaping performative communication.

The twice-used songs of the Hebrew Bible are first and foremost at the very nexus of conversations. These conversations take place between generations and between points of view. The conversations began long ago, before the Bible had any written components, and drew together, first, singer and song. And eventually those listening to songs became the singers, who, as narrators, sang in a new way songs drawn from the past and presented to a brand-new audience. Even today these twice-used songs draw people into conversation with the traditions they represent. We are simply part of this great stream. And although the tunes and melodies have long vanished, in the exploration of their enduring power and influence, the songs are still being sung.

A Few Key Texts for Understanding "Performance"

Austin, J. L. *How to Do Things with Words*. Cambridge: Harvard University Press, 1962.

Beckerman, Bernard. *Dynamics of Drama: Theory and Method of Analysis*. New York: Drama Book Specialists, 1979.

Butler, Judith. *Excitable Speech*. New York: Routledge, 1997.

Carlson, Marvin. *Performance: A Critical Introduction*. New York: Routledge, 1996.

Jackson, Shannon. *Professing Performance: Theatre in the Academy from Philology to Performativity*. Cambridge: Cambridge University Press, 2004.

Roach, Joseph, and Janelle Reinelt. *Critical Theory and Performance*. Ann Arbor: University of Michigan Press, 1992.

Schechner, Richard. *Between Theater and Anthropology*. Philadelphia: University of Pennsylvania Press, 1985.

———. *Performance Studies: An Introduction*. New York: Routledge, 2002.

Turner, Victor. *Dramas, Fields, and Metaphors*. Ithaca, N.Y.: Cornell University Press, 1974.

———. *From Ritual to Theatre*. New York: PAJ, 1982.

Chapter 2: **The Book of Jashar The Song Scroll**

A somewhat enigmatic and mysterious "book" quoted by several of the biblical authors provides the first signpost in our exploration of the ancient songs of Israel. Two or perhaps three lyrics quoted by prose authors of the Hebrew Bible are cited from the same source: *sefer ha-yashar*, or the "Book of Jashar" as it normally appears in English Bibles. This Book of Jashar deserves a closer look, for it may provide an important link between the oral performance of ancient songs and the twice-used appearance of those songs in the Hebrew Bible.

Sefer ha-yashar

Although seemingly straightforward, the name of the book calls for consideration. Certainly, to translate the Hebrew word *sefer* as "book" is a bit anachronistic, since codices, or bound books as we know them, were still hundreds of years in the future from the time when these texts were written. It would thus be best to understand "scroll" or "document" as the meaning intended. And although most English translations of the Bible treat Jashar[1] as a proper name, the use of the definite article before the noun (literally, "Book of the Jashar") normally indicates that the following word is a common noun, in this case "upright"[2] or a form of the verb "to

---

[1] Some scholars attempt to make the connection between "Jashar" and "Jeshurun," particularly as used in the Song of Moses (Deut 32:15); see, e.g., Edward Greenstein, "From Oral Epic to Written Verse and Some of the Stages in Between" (paper presented at the annual meeting of the Society of Biblical Literature, Washington, D.C., November 18, 2006).

[2] J. Alberto Soggin, *Joshua* (OTL; Philadelphia: Westminster, 1972), 122.

sing." In fact, of the several similar constructions used by biblical authors to refer to "books" or documents, this is the only one translated as a proper noun.[3] Consequently, some scholars have suggested that *sefer ha-yashar* be translated "Book of the Upright" or "Book of the Song." Both options are valid, and so we must look for contextual clues to determine which choice is best. It is at this point that the Old Greek translation of the Hebrew Bible may offer some help.[4] The LXX version of 1 Kgs 8:12–13 [3 Kgdms 8:53 LXX] includes a phrase not found in the Hebrew counterpart: it credits Solomon's lyric recitation to the "Book of the Song." Many scholars believe that the phrase accidentally dropped out of the MT and that the original phrase is exactly like that found in Josh 10:12 and 2 Sam 1:17. The argument goes on to suggest that the current LXX version of 1 Kings 8 arose from a simple transposition of two letters, resulting in the LXX "song," *shyr,* for the supposed original MT *yashar, yshr.* But perhaps it is the LXX that preserves the best reading. Indeed, whenever the book is mentioned, a lyric is present, and the word *yashar* does have definite similarities to the Hebrew verb for "sing." In any case, given that the scroll contained only lyrics as far as we know, it may be best to recognize this fact in the name of the scroll.

Whatever its name, the scroll, now lost, is known to us only by these few references coming from prose writers of the Hebrew Bible. In all cases, the prose writers quote lyric poetry from the scroll and insert these poems

---

[3] Parallel constructions are to be found in the "book of the covenant" (Exod 24:7; 2 Kgs 23:2, 21); "book of the generations of Adam" (Gen 5:1); "Book of the Wars of the LORD" (Num 21:14); "Book of the Chronicles of the Kings of Israel" (e.g., 1 Kgs 16:5); "Book of the Chronicles of the Kings of Judah" (e.g., 1 Kgs 15:7); "Commentary on the Book of the Kings" (2 Chr 24:27); "book of the law of Moses" (Josh 23:6; 2 Kgs 14:6); "book of the acts of Solomon" (1 Kgs 11:41); "book of the law of the LORD" (e.g., 2 Chr 17:9); "book of the law of God" (Josh 24:26). Other writings are also known: the "Book of the Kings of Israel" (1 Chr 9:1; 2 Chr 20:34); "Book of the Kings of Judah and Israel" (2 Chr 16:11); "Book of the Kings of Israel and Judah" (2 Chr 27:7); "Chronicles of the Kings of Israel" (2 Chr 33:18); "Chronicles of Samuel the seer" (1 Chr 29:29); "Chronicles of Gad the seer" (1 Chr 29:29); "Chronicles of Nathan the prophet" (1 Chr 29:29); "history of Nathan the prophet" (2 Chr 9:29); "prophecy of Ahijah the Shilonite" (2 Chr 9:29); "visions of Iddo the seer" (2 Chr 9:29); "chronicles of Shemaiah the prophet and of Iddo the seer" (2 Chr 12:15); "chronicles of Jehu the son of Hanani" (2 Chr 20:34); "Chronicles of the Seers" (2 Chr 33:19); "story of the prophet Iddo" (2 Chr 13:22); a book written by the prophet Isaiah son of Amoz containing the history of Uzziah (2 Chr 26:22); "chronicles of King David" (1 Chr 27:24); "book of the records of your fathers" (Ezra 4:15); "Book of the Chronicles" (Neh 12:23); "vision of Isaiah the prophet the son of Amoz" in the "Book of the Kings of Judah and Israel" (2 Chr 32:32; Isa 1:1).

[4] H. Thackeray, "New Light on the Book of Jashar (a Study of 3 Regn.VIII 53b LXX)," *Journal of Theological Studies* 11 (1910): 518–32.

(songs) into their own narrative accounts. These prose narrators all take for granted that the readers are familiar with the scroll, for never is there offered an explanation of the scroll's identity or function. Could it be that the scroll (and although it is not a precise translation of the Hebrew, we shall call it the *Song Scroll*) was a collection of songs used in performances for special religious and state functions?[5] It is quite likely that the scroll contained more than just the three songs identified by Hebrew prose writers. Perhaps the Song of the Sea, the Song of Deborah, and others were also borrowed from the *Song Scroll*.[6] Regardless, the *Song Scroll* served an important function in ancient Israel. At the very least, the scroll was widely recognized by a number of the biblical writers and by their reading and listening audiences. Whatever its early history, the legacy of the *Song Scroll* is now firmly embedded in the text of the Hebrew Bible.

Choral Response Performance

Before we look at the individual songs contained in the *Scroll*, it is helpful to make a few observations about the collection as a whole. If we are correct in assigning Solomon's Temple Dedication Song (1 Kgs 8:12–13; and 2 Chr 6:1–2) to the *Song Scroll* (following the lead of the LXX), then all three attested examples of lyrics taken from the *Scroll* share several fascinating features. The first general characteristic of all three songs is that they display a change of person within the song that is characteristic of a choral response performance. The Day the Sun Stood Still of Josh 10:12–13 and Solomon's Temple Dedication Song of 1 Kgs 8:12–13 and 2 Chr 6:1–2 are, in this aspect, exactly the same. Both are composed of two sentences (following the MT version of 1 Kgs 8:12). In Joshua 10 (The Day the Sun Stood Still), the song opens in a first-person address to Sun and Moon followed by a third-person description of resultant activity. First Kings 8 (Solomon's Temple Dedication Song) opens in a third-person description, moving on to a first-person address to the implicit attending audience. Both songs can easily be performed as choral responses. Likewise the third song from the *Song Scroll*, the longer song of 2 Sam 1:19–27 (the Song of the

[5] William Schniedewind, *How the Bible Became a Book* (Cambridge: Cambridge University Press, 2004), 54. P. Kyle McCarter, speaking of the 3 Kgdms 8:53 LXX reference to the "Book of the Song," calls it "an entirely appropriate title" (*II Samuel* [AB 9; Garden City, N.Y.: Doubleday, 1984], 74). The NJPS identifies the scroll as a collection of war songs. S. Mowinckel provides argumentation to this end ("Hat es ein israelitisches Nationalepos gegeben?" *ZAW* 53 [1935]: 130–52).

[6] C. F. Kraft, "Jashar, Book of," in *The Interpreter's Dictionary of the Bible* (ed. George A. Buttrick et al.; 4 vols.; New York: Abingdon, 1984), 2:803.

Bow), shifts back and forth from direct address in verses 19a, 20, 21a, 24, and 26 to a third-person description in 21b–23 and 25b. Interspersed is a repeating refrain found in verses 19b, 25a, and 27.[7] The song moves in the following fashion:

19a	Direct address
19b	Refrain
20	Direct address
21a	Direct address
21b–23	Third-person description
24	Direct address
25a	Refrain
25b	Third-person description
26	Direct address
27	Refrain

So, although somewhat more complex, the Song of the Bow can easily be imagined as a response performance by two groups, with all joining in on the repeating refrain.[8] All three songs are constructed to allow a choral response performance.

Besides the movement, resident in all three songs, allowing a response performance, a second common characteristic becomes evident. The way in which persons are addressed in all three songs is quite similar. First, each song directly addresses listeners not visibly present (Sun, Moon, Israel, citizens of Gath, mountains of Gilboa, daughters of Israel, the deceased Jonathan,[9] Yahweh). Each uses immediate forms of discourse to address a person or personification not immediately present. Although this distant person or personification is addressed, the words seem to have a more immediate impact on the audience that is present. That is, the prayer or eulogy, though addressed to a deity, or deceased, or far-off mountain, is mouthed more to

---

[7] See also the syllable-and-meter-based model provided by David N. Freedman, "The Refrain in David's Lament over Saul and Jonathan," in *Ex orbe religionum: Studia Geo Widengren oblata* (ed. C. J. Bleeker et al.; Leiden: Brill, 1972), 1:125–26.

[8] Wilfred G. Watson, *Classical Hebrew Poetry: A Guide to Its Techniques* (JSOT-Sup 26; Sheffield: JSOT Press, 1984), 296–97; Freedman, "The Refrain in David's Lament," 115–26.

[9] This kind of second-person address is said to be common in a funerary lament. See A. A. Anderson, *2 Samuel* (WBC 11; Dallas: Word, 1989), 13.

communicate with those gathered round the speaker. This is quite consistent with performed addresses—spoken *to* another character in the performance but spoken *for* the hearing of the attending audience. Second, in all three songs, the third-person description makes most sense when intended for a present audience. The descriptions are not needed for the speaker or for the character whose actions are being described. Instead the descriptions inform the presumed audience of something that they did not witness and knowledge of which can be to their benefit. This leads to a third common characteristic of the three songs.

In all three songs, an identity is projected out from the song and is enjoined upon the reading or listening audience by means of the third-person description. In Joshua 10 the audience becomes identified with the conquering nation, in 2 Samuel the audience assumes the role of mourner, and in 1 Kings 8 (2 Chr 6) the audience owns and celebrates the temple and the temple-dwelling Yahweh, who has chosen this people for a special possession. Each song changes the singer and the listener by providing to them a new identity, and it is this new identity that reinforces the strength of the surrounding prose. This identity-creating function constitutes the special contribution that each song makes to its present narrative setting. Indeed, it is the song that allows for the identity to be performed inside the narrative.

Act-Scheme

The characteristics found in all three songs—direct address, implicit audience, projected identity—are concepts commonly investigated in performance criticism. The manner in which address, audience, and identity are all woven together constitute what is called, in performance-critical studies, a "performative-scheme" or "act-scheme." The act-scheme is the presentational form, the event or set of dynamics that plays before us. Act-schemes fall into recognizable patterns (in some ways analogous to literary syntax) that facilitate communication between the performer(s) and spectators.[10] These act-schemes or patterns are "instruments of expression and action"[11] determined by social and cultural conventions familiar to both the presenter and the spectator. For example, consider the pantomime artist. What most likely comes to mind is the act-scheme of being trapped inside a box, the mime artist using her or his hands to create the boundaries of

---

[10]Bernard Beckerman, *Theatrical Presentation: Performer, Audience, and Act* (ed. Gloria Brim Beckerman and William Coco; New York: Routledge, 1990). In ch. 7 (pp. 101–9) Beckerman describes the relationship between the act-scheme and the act-image.

[11]Ibid., 104.

the box while simultaneously working the shoulders and knees to represent the box getting small and smaller. Another instance is the pantomime routine of climbing a rope, expertly creating the illusion of the body going up in space while, in fact, it remains stage bound. Similar examples abound in magic performances as well. Classic card tricks, disappearing objects, objects pulled from a hat—all are examples of act-schemes upon which an entire presentation can be built by adding, subtracting, adapting, and revising according to the dynamics of the performer-audience relationship, the skill of the performer, and the social context in which the performance takes place. Like words to sentences, act-schemes are the building blocks of performance.

The act-schemes of any theatrical period emerge from a very complex social context.[12] "In other words, the governing conditions of performance go a long way toward determining the kinds of act-schemes a society will generate."[13] These governing conditions may range from political to religious authority, to cultural and subcultural practice, or to individual or familial practice. Understanding the governing conditions of performance lets us know when we are watching a ballet rather than a jazz dance performance or an opera rather than a musical. Through repetition we come to know the fundamental elements of these schemes. We recognize their performative structures. The toe shoes, the tutu, the pirouette are separate and distinct for us from the flat jazz shoe and the slides, glides, and musical phrases that fit together for us in one mode but not in another.

Act-schemes are modes of presentation, autonomous yet essential to the kinds of presentational forms a culture generates. As those familiar with contemporary biblical scholarship will recognize, talk of "act-schemes" and "culturally determined conditions of performance" is, in important ways, similar to the types of discussion that take place in both form-critical and rhetorical-critical investigations. And there is some degree of overlap. The major difference, however, is that form criticism and rhetorical criticism, as usually conducted, are literary criticisms of structures, types, or literary genres (the formal structures of the literature) and the social settings in which they were used, whereas performance criticism focuses on the event or the dynamic complex of action of a performance. Performance criticism does, however, offer its own unique contribution. Whereas form criticism may identify legends, epics, ascension hymns, and the like and rhetorical criticism focuses on the stylistic features of prose

---

[12]The use of the term "theatrical" in this study is parallel to Beckerman's use of the term: a structured act of presentation between performer(s) and spectators. It is not referring to any particular theatre or dramatic genre.

[13]Beckerman, *Theatrical Presentation,* 105.

and poetry (again literary types) that help make the composition persuasive and influential, performance criticism considers movement, voice, costume, dialogue, activity, and the way events play out in performative episodes built upon particular schemes. In trying to sift out the proper domain of each of these types of criticism, notice the characteristics of act-schemes cited by Bernard Beckerman, a leading authority on the history of theatre and drama:

> Whatever fanciful notions of the origin of drama we may have, by the time the verifiable examples of Greek drama emerge, we encounter highly sophisticated act-schemes. Their characteristics are widely known: alternating sequences of individuals and groups (odes and episodes), costumes that distort and monumentalize the performers, groups moving and speaking in formal patterns, individuals speaking in set meters and following strictly defined paths. . . . In ancient Greece that act-scheme arises from the social balance between individual and community, with the individual endowed with an appearance that heightens his superhuman qualities. Whatever passions or circumstances these schemes signify, the schemes themselves embody forces other than the fictive or mimetic.[14]

Act-schemes operate within a "code," that is, a pattern or system of conventions that are culturally determined. This code, or system of conventions, or peculiar and recognizable structure, functions as the bridge allowing the performer and the spectator to communicate through specific kinds of performance. Street theatre, opera, musical theatre, political speech or rally, sermon, and football half-time shows (the list could go on and on) are examples of codes common to our society that provide the recognizable context by which performers and spectators connect with each other along the continuum of the social drama to the formal artistic performance. In attempting to describe the codes used by other and distant societies, we need to consider these questions: What are or were the kinds of presentation needed? What are or were the contexts for these acts of presentation? What are or were the political, social, and religious forces shaping these acts of presentation? Beckerman employs the fifth-century Greek theatre as a primary example of the complexity of this code, but this is also very useful to our examination of the use and placement of the three songs from the *Song Scroll* in the Hebrew Bible.

Beckerman points out that the code of the fifth-century theatre of ancient Greece was built on structuring performances for large numbers of people and creating a formal program of events that would unite diverse features, such as tragedy, comedy, and the choral ode. The key feature of these formal programs was the use of performance to resolve conflict,

---

[14]Ibid., 104.

echoing the code of the dithyrambic contest that most scholars believe preceded Greek tragedy. "Although we may not be able to show a direct correspondence between dramatic form and the inclusion of the dithyrambic contest in the Dionysian festival, still we can see the act-scheme as a formulation of an echoing agon that reverberates throughout the festival. . . . The same reverberation between presentational contexts and act-schemes occurs in other societies."[15]

The inclusion of selections from the *Song Scroll* in the prose of the Hebrew Bible suggests that a code was present, surrounding the inserted songs. It is not enough for the narrators to quote lyrics (or make up a lyric) they believe helpful to their stories; it is important that they identify these lyrics from a recognizable collection—the *Song Scroll*—and it is the mention of the collection that points us to the existence of the code (brought to mind by the identification of the *Song Scroll*) and its embodiment in a particular act-scheme (each particular song contained within the *Song Scroll*). Mention of the *Song Scroll* would have immediately brought to mind specific expectations in the mind of the reader or the listener, even before the words of the specific song were read or heard. This act-scheme is just as much a part of the communication effected by the biblical narrator as are the words of the songs the narrator quotes. Recall the mention of Bob Dylan's "Blowin' in the Wind" in the first chapter, above. Simply seeing the title on the page is likely to have triggered the melody flowing through your head, or at least the choral response: "The answer, my friend, is blowin' in the wind."

Remember what we discovered about the three songs taken from the *Song Scroll*. All three are structured to project an identity onto the listening or reading audience. They engage the spectator by directly addressing the audience and inviting the audience to actively participate. As Beckerman and others have pointed out, theatre historians agree that the early stages of theatre and drama made use of word, dance, music, and song. Combining these in various ways made the appearance of highly defined act-schemes possible, including act-schemes that provided for direct audience participation. "That appearance, it is often claimed, *has the purpose both of striking awe into the audience and arousing belief*" (italics added).[16]

It is worth considering that the songs borrowed from the *Song Scroll* by the biblical narrators drew part of their social influence and so their appeal to the biblical writers from the particularly powerful way they articulated an influential, culturally expressed act-scheme code. If this is the case, then everything we can learn about this potentially present act-

---

[15] Ibid., 105
[16] Ibid., 107.

scheme code would be a valuable aid in our understanding and appreciation of the presence of these songs within their new narrative settings.

Our working hypothesis is this:

> An act-scheme, or system of conventions, that includes the scribe/compiler
> (both as writer and reader/performer), an implicit group of spectators, and
> the use of song within a compressed narrative affected a new identity for the
> hearing or reading audience through their both hearing and participating in
> the embedded song from the *Song Scroll* and its surrounding narrative.

Although no claim is made that a specific dramatic tradition in the Hebrew
Bible is identifiable, such as that seen in the evolution of tragedy in the
Greek theatre, it will be argued here that elements of a dramatic tradition
do appear in the *Song Scroll* selections. Some additional explanation of the
process of theatre history may shed light on the way act-schemes influence
both literary and performance traditions.

"Myth and history are the first sources of dramatic performance. The
distinction between the two, however, is not entirely clear. In utilizing
the resurrection of Christ as the initial situation for their trope, the *Quem
quaeritis*, the Winchester monks thought of the event as both symbolic and
historical; indeed, it was symbolic because it was historical."[17] The monks,
functioning as a "surrogate for the congregational witness," used performance to bring the essence of the moment into being. That is to say, they
used performance to make the resurrection present for the congregation
in the here and now. The Greeks also used myth, history, ritual, and oral
tradition for the building blocks of performance. "For much of drama,
performance combines a system of presentation with derived narrative
materials leavened by the sensibility of the artists concerned."[18] This is
precisely the process that occurs when the biblical narrator places existing
song material into a new narrative structure.

Essentially, performance traditions, particularly in the case of dramatic presentation, are made up of some interaction between narrative
materials and act-schemes. There is a story to be told, and one needs
a way to tell it. What we see in these songs, and in their insertion into
the narrative text, is a combination of the ways of telling the story. And
what is fascinating and suggests the value of performance criticism is that
the emerging literary tradition occurred within a primarily oral culture
that included performative elements. The "scribe-reader" and "performer-
spectator" dynamics are interwoven, playing off and impacting each other.
Their boundaries are permeable.

---

[17] Ibid., 107–8.
[18] Ibid.

At the level of the act-scheme, dramatic presentation "offers a theatrically effective pattern that has inherent interest for the audience."[19] These act-schemes also present certain dynamics of the particular social structures they come from; they represent meaningful exchanges for members of that group. For example, in our time, slam poetry nights have become an increasingly popular event in recent years. These communal events provide an organized outlet for individuals to express themselves in creative, edgy ways: singing, chanting, rapping, and rhyming their feelings and ideas on race, class, global politics, and gender. The event provides a performative framework of an open microphone, tables, and chairs aimed toward the microphone, a signup sheet in order to go from spectator to performer, and a live audience anticipating both performance and participation. In this contemporary context for meaningful exchange, those who are not likely to embrace the "slams" are not likely to be there. The act-scheme's heightened form—"the fact that it is sufficiently intense to sustain audience interest—further embodies a trace of the extraordinary; that is, no matter how much it utilizes *actual* features of the audience's life, it transforms these features into a pure state."[20]

It will be argued here that selections from the *Song Scroll* were included by the biblical narrator because these selections had already proven their ability to hold interest, to transform the listener in some fashion. The analysis of the songs will identify and discuss the patterns of activity (act-schemes) that structure these songs along with what the act-schemes represent or signify, with an eye toward better understanding the important role and presence of the *Song Scroll* in ancient Israel.

The Day the Sun Stood Still (Joshua 10:12–13)

The Day the Sun Stood Still

Sun, hold position at Gibeon
And Moon, in the valley of Aijalon.

And the sun held position
The moon stood still
Until [the] people rose against their enemies
    (authors' translation).

---

[19] Ibid., 109.
[20] Ibid.

The narrator of Joshua 10 readily admits that the song existed before his composition.[21] Moreover, the narrator's rhetorical question, "Is this not written in the Song Scroll?" (10:13b, authors' translation) implicitly acknowledges that the readers of the narrative would have recognized the song from its original presentation in the *Song Scroll*. The narrator inserted the song into a battle account[22] that is marked by repeated divine interventions, including the stilling of the sun. It was a remarkable day—like no other—when Yahweh listened to the voice of a man (10:14). In its Joshua 10 setting, the song now provides a lyric comment and highlight to a portion of the battle account in the surrounding prose. But this was not the only use to which the song was applied.

The twice-used nature of the song—and so by implication an earlier use of the song—is noticeable through some of its connective ties to the narration. For several reasons, the song of verses 12 and 13 has been considered by scholars to be awkwardly placed in Joshua 10. Indeed, the prose, too, shows signs of conflating two independent sources.[23] First, the prose beginning of verse 12, confirmed in verse 14, indicates that Joshua spoke to Yahweh. Yet the song itself implies that Joshua addressed Sun and Moon. It is most unusual to find Joshua, leader of the Israelites, addressing Sun and Moon in prayer. This fact was not lost on the narrator, and a corrective was created in verse 12, presenting the prayer petitioned before Yahweh. Second, the prose account mentions only the staying of the sun (v. 14) whereas the song includes the moon in its lyrics. And further, the very verb used to describe the sun's activity in the prose conclusion of verse 13b is, in the song (v. 13a), applied to the moon and not the sun. These observations lead one to wonder about the function of the song and why the Joshua compiler thought it valuable to interrupt his narrative by this short verse. Would not the account flow much better had the song been left out? One commentator on this passage thinks that the poem, along with its prose frame, is a fitting climax to the episode of the battle of

---

[21] Trent Butler assigns an exilic date to the composition of Joshua and refers to the poem as "an even more ancient source" (*Joshua* [WBC; Waco: Word, 1983], 117). Richard Nelson favors recognition of a Deuteronomistic authorship for Joshua that occurred in stages from the later preexilic into the exilic times (*Joshua* [OTL; Louisville: Westminster John Knox, 1997], 5–9). Likewise Carol Newsom, "Joshua, Book of," *ABD* 3:1002–15.

[22] The poem has been dated to the tenth century, hundreds of years before the composition of the prose narrative. See John Holladay, "The Day(s) the *Moon* Stood Still," *JBL* 88 (1968): 166–78. Soggin, *Joshua,* 122, comments, "No doubt the quotation originally goes back to another event, and was later attached to the present narrative."

[23] Baruch Margalit, "The Day the Sun Did Not Stand Still: A New Look at Joshua X 8–15," *VT* 42 (1992): 466–91.

Gibeon but that "in the more extended context, however, the poem plays no role and even interrupts the natural plot sequence from the battle to the pursuit of the kings."[24]

In the face of this awkward placement, naturalistic theories have been put forth attempting to explain that the unusual phenomenon standing behind the poem is reason for the poem's appearance. Perhaps the most fanciful of these theories concerns the planet Venus and a very drastic but quite abrupt bump in its normally predictable orbit.[25] Some scholars have attempted to reconstruct a meteoric incident from the words of the song.[26] Others, not convinced by the attempts of a naturalistic explanation but still looking for an actual description, seem quite content to ignore the song, apparently convinced that it adds nothing to the tale being told in Joshua 10.[27]

If, indeed, the Joshua compiler was reinterpreting his received tradition (at least as far as the song goes), we must assume that he had in mind a reason for his actions. And this reason was not plot or narrative development, for if such were the case, the poem is misplaced and should find its more proper spot just before verse 10, there functioning as a comment on the panic inflicted by Yahweh on Israel's enemies.[28] Something else is at work. According to James Watts, the Joshua compiler simply bungled it by breaking out into this catchy but irrelevant song.[29] But need this be our conclusion? It seems likely that The Day the Sun Stood Still was composed before its insertion into its present context. And it also seems most likely that the Joshua compiler thought that the composition improved with insertion of the poem. Yet the poem does not, in any readily evident fashion, improve the narrative qualities of the literary section, and so we must look elsewhere, other than in the plot of the story, if we are going to appreciate the role of the song in the Joshua narrative. One commentator refers to the song only as an "archaic poem" and considers "the name and contents of the book [Song Scroll] not the most important issue," choosing to focus on the point that "the Hebrew tradition understood its scripture as based upon even more ancient sources."[30] But beyond these attempts—or the despair of attempts—to find an event corresponding to the poetry of the song, another interpretive path can be found. If the compiler felt

---

[24]James Watts, *Psalm and Story: Inset Hymns in Hebrew Narrative* (JSOTSup 139; Sheffield: JSOT Press, 1992), 172.

[25]Immanuel Velikovsky, *Worlds in Collision* (New York: Macmillan, 1950).

[26]W. J. Phythian-Adams, "A Meteorite of the Fourteenth Century," *PEQ* 78 (1946): 116–24.

[27]Soggin, *Joshua*, 123–25.

[28]Margalit, "The Day the Sun Did Not Stand Still," 482, 487.

[29]Watts, *Psalm and Story*, 172.

[30]Butler, *Joshua*, 117.

compelled to change the thrust of the poem and if the poem makes no significant contribution to the narrative of Joshua 10, why is it there? Why did the compiler choose to enter the poem into the account?

We need to begin our search by asking a question suggested by Bernard Beckerman's comments above. Is there a way in which the song transports the audience from the *actual* to a *pure* state and in this transformation captures a sustained audience interest?[31] This focus on audience response points in a very different direction from that allowed by a concern for plot development.

Richard Nelson constructs four categories by which to group the various interpretive approaches generally taken to the song. First are the approaches that, like the examples just mentioned, seek to identify a naturalistic phenomenon residing behind the poetic description. Second are those that seek to reconstruct an omen from the poem.[32] Third are those that see in the poem an invective against the astral protective deities of Gibeon, Beth-horon, and Aijalon. The fourth approach, adopted by Nelson, understands the mythopoetic qualities of the poem and views the poem as a call for the sun and moon to "stand frozen or fixed, or perhaps silent, in stunned reaction to an awe-inspiring victory."[33] In effect, we have an Israelite description of "shock and awe" in which even the sun and moon are impressed with Israel's military prowess and the victory won by Yahweh. And indeed, the prose conclusion seems to reinforce the remarkable nature of the experience: "There has never been a day like it before or since, when Yahweh listened to the voice of a man" (v. 14).

This description of "shock and awe," if it was intended, seems to be a secondary use of the song, for, as Baruch Margalit argues, originally the poem followed a darkened-sun motif known in other day-of-Yahweh constructions.[34] A comparison of Joshua 10 with the battle narrative in Exodus 14 reveals remarkable similarities that may indeed support the darkened-sun intent of Josh 10:12–13, especially when also read with the very similar construction of Hab 3:11 in mind. If this was, in fact, the original thrust of the poem, the Joshua compiler must have reinterpreted (or misinterpreted) the poem, changing the poem from a darkened-sun motif to a depiction of a brilliant, shining sun. But the prose context, both the introduction and conclusion, changes the tenor of the poem in other and not-so-subtle fashions. First, the poem is quite clear in indicating that

---

[31] Beckerman, *Theatrical Presentation*, 113.

[32] Holladay, "The Day(s) the *Moon* Stood Still," 172–78, is a good example of this approach.

[33] Nelson, *Joshua*, 145.

[34] Margalit, "The Day the Sun Did Not Stand Still," 490–91.

Joshua directly addresses Sun and Moon. Twice the Joshua compiler tones down this questionable practice of addressing celestial bodies in prayer, by offering that Joshua, in fact, addressed Yahweh with his request. Second, if indeed the thrust of the poem is that Sun and Moon were silenced in awe at the Israelite victory, the Joshua compiler was compelled to change this also. In the conclusion offered by verse 13b, the sun and moon clearly become simply markers of time and not impressed bystanders. The day was lengthened, and this was as a result of Yahweh's influence, not because of an awestruck Sun and Moon.

As an example of a battle song, the song of Joshua 10 presents some very interesting claims to a reading or listening audience. The song offers Joshua's request for Sun to station itself at Gibeon while Moon is to stay at the Valley of Aijalon.[35] This position of the sun to the east and the moon to the west implies a request for early-morning daylight conditions—a definite advantage for the Israelite warriors. The Israelites are said to have marched from Gilgal all night (about eighteen miles), arriving at Gibeon (west of Gilgal) in the early morning. The battle, described in the prose of Joshua 10, began at Gibeon, continued in a westerly direction to Beth-horon, and from there progressed in a southwesterly direction toward Azekah (about thirty-one miles from Gibeon) and Makkedah (of unknown location but thought to be in the vicinity of Lachish), whose nearby caves offered un-reliable refuge to the five kings of the Amorites introduced in verse 5 and where Joshua established his base camp following the remarkable battle. A request for Sun to hold position at Gibeon (to the east) and Moon over the valley (to the west) would mean that the sun was suspended in its early-morning position[36] and Israel's enemies were forced to look directly into the rays of the "morning sun" while, at the same time, the sun was at Israel's back for the duration of the battle and not positioned at midday as suggested by verse 13b. Had the sun and the moon followed their normal courses, this Israelite advantage would have turned to a disadvantage in the afternoon, as then the Israelite warriors would be forced to look di-rectly into the sun's rays while pursuing the enemy westward. And tired those warriors must have been, for not only did they engage the enemy for the duration of the prolonged day; they marched at least 50 miles as well. Surely, this remarkable feat lifts us from (using Beckerman's terms) the realm of an *actual* to a *pure* experience, one well capable of sustaining audience interest. And could it be that this heightened and sustained level of audience involvement is exactly what our narrative writer wished to ac-complish by the insertion of the song?

---

[35] Nelson, *Joshua*, 142.

[36] Margalit, "The Day the Sun Did Not Stand Still," 479.

Already anticipating this direction of enquiry, John Holladay's advice seems quite sound when he suggests that interpreters seek to "interpret it [the song] in terms of its own thought world."[37] What Holladay identifies as "thought world" is, in performance criticism, the social context that governs the kinds of performance people engage in and the context that makes these performances understandable. Integral to the thought world of the song is recognition that it is a performative piece of communication that has now become twice-used in its Joshua setting.

A hint of this thought world may be evidenced in a small, easily overlooked grammatical detail found in verse 13. The Hebrew word translated as either "people" or "nation" (*goy*) lacks the definite article, making the noun less specific. Definite articles are used elsewhere in the song (contrary to what has been characterized as "suitable" early Hebrew poetics),[38] and its absence before "people" is part of the rationale leading some commentators to render the phrase "until he defeated his enemies' force!"[39] Could it be that the mention of "people" or "nation" in verse 13 without the definite article is intentionally open-ended? Does the lack of specificity allow greater ownership of the song? Without a specifically identified enemy, the term can be applied and reapplied to a variety of perceived foes. Certainly, the song is here twice-used with an antecedent earlier than the Israelite encounter and this earlier antecedent has in Joshua become appropriated to apply to the Israelite victory over the Canaanites. And if the Joshua compiler was an exilic writer, the nonspecificity by which he referred to the villains of the song would have lent the song to easier application by, and greater identification with, the listening or reading exilic and postexilic audience.

This application to a listening or reading audience takes us back to an observation made earlier in this study, about the collection of three songs taken from the *Song Scroll*. The change of persons embedded in the structure of the songs raises the possibility that the *Song Scroll* was a collection of choral responses. And since all of the prose writers seem to expect that their reading or listening audiences will recognize the songs as excerpts from the *Song Scroll*, could it be that the inclusion of those songs into the prose accounts was designed to help create an identity with the reading or listening audiences in which they could literally sing along and so enter into the story being told through the narration?

---

[37] Holladay, "The Day(s) the *Moon* Stood Still," 167.

[38] Ibid., 168.

[39] Robert Boling and G. Ernest Wright, *Joshua* (AB 6; New York: Doubleday, 1982), 274.

If this is the case and the change of persons is a marker signifying a choral response that allows entry into the story, then this song contains a striking parallel to one of the oldest performative structures generally recognized by theatre historians of Western theatre and drama: the *dithyrambic contest*, a choral storytelling form. Eli Rozik argues that it is the dithyramb and other ancient choral forms, and not ritual per se, that ultimately led to Greek tragedy.[40] According to Rozik, these were structures that led to the generation of theatre, structures with certain qualities that, on the level of medium, made the transition to tragedy possible.[41]

> My contention is that tragedy could have originated in choral storytelling, by developing its potential theatricality, and, probably, in already existing theatrical forms. . . . Since storytelling is a verbal art, it naturally includes the verbal components of dialogue. If storytelling is printed, the concomitant nonverbal aspects of dialogue are described by means of words; but if storytelling is performed orally, these aspects can be, and usually are, conveyed by the storytellers themselves, who enact each character in turn, whenever the narrative features dialogue, by means of imprinting images of the speaking characters on their own bodies. This probably is the ground for transition from one medium to the other.[42]

Rozik's clear understanding of the medium of choral storytelling, the performative nature of this act, and its theatrical and dramatic potential is useful to this study. As he points out, on the level of medium, certain qualities of the dithyramb and other ancient choral forms highlight various performative structures, including choral presentation, possible enacted direct speech, verbal components of dialogue, dance, and song.[43]

Each of these aspects of choral storytelling is a way of engaging actively in the making of social meaning and of exchanging those social experiences. Each is a medium for communal participation, where the voices and bodies, the tools of everyday, ordinary communication, can be transformed into something extraordinary. Suddenly a collection of individuals, gathered to hear the scribe, can be transformed into a choral community with a shared identity that is deeply rooted in the communal memory of the song. It is this shared identity that gets to the heart of the song's function in Joshua 10.

---

[40] Eli Rozik, *The Roots of Theatre: Rethinking Ritual and Other Theories of Origin* (Iowa City: University of Iowa Press, 2002), 145–53. Investigating the evolution of Greek tragedy, Rozik examines the relationship between dithyrambs, ritual, and tragedy and argues that the alleged connections between these elements do not necessarily lead to the conclusion that tragedy derives directly from ritual.

[41] Ibid., 150.

[42] Ibid., 151.

[43] Ibid., 150–52.

The Song of the Bow (2 Samuel 1:19–27)

Communal memory or cultural memory and shared identity are also at the heart of the Song of the Bow in 2 Sam 1:19–27.[44] The song's repeating pattern of direct address, third-person description, and refrain establishes a rhythm of engagement in which the spectators are both witnesses and participants, confirming their shared values as inheritors of both the song and the slain glory the song laments. Direct presentation creates dramatic identification with the symbols and figures of the song, identification that carries intense psychological impact for the spectators. The implicit crowd assembled in the song "Your glory, O Israel" provides the background, or common ground of understanding. What is implicit (the glory sung about in the song) is made explicit when embodied by the spectators gathered around the scribal performer, folding the past into the present and crystallizing audience belief.[45] The dislocation between past and present is overcome by the insertion of this song into the narrative.

The character of David, lost in grief, filled with passion for Saul and Jonathan, emanates from the song as a force that can be felt by the spectators. "Implicit in the discussion of dramatic modes is the recognition that drama primarily treats the human beings who generate the action as forms of energy. They communicate force and response first. Only secondarily do they emerge as entities, independent of the action they undergo."[46] The force or energy of character(s) is what charges the air with electricity during performance, creating an interplay of energies between the act, the performer, and the spectator. The energy of David's character bursts forth from the first line of the Song of the Bow:

Song of the Bow

Thy glory [beauty], O Israel, is slain upon thy high places!

How are the mighty fallen!

---

[44]The idea of "cultural memory" applies to all the songs found in the *Song Scroll*, and as with many of the concepts considered in this study, it is applied here to the Song of the Bow in an illustrative manner. Indeed, cultural memory is an important concept relevant to all the twice-used songs. The treatment of the Song of the Sea in ch. 3, below, will return to this idea.

[45]The Song of the Bow has many features of the iconic modes of presentation. Chapter 3, below, will discuss this concept more thoroughly.

[46]Bernard Beckerman, *Dynamics of Drama: Theory and Method of Analysis* (New York: Drama Book Specialists, 1979), 210.

Tell it not in Gath,
publish it not in the streets of Ashkelon;
lest the daughters of the Philistines rejoice,
lest the daughters of the uncircumcised exult.

Ye mountains of Gilboa
let there be no dew or rain upon you,
nor upsurging of the deep!

For there the shield of the mighty was defiled,
the shield of Saul, not anointed with oil.
From the blood of the slain,
from the fat of the mighty,
the bow of Jonathan turned not back,
and the sword of Saul returned not empty.
Saul and Jonathan, beloved and lovely!
In life and in death they were not divided;
they were swifter than eagles,
they were stronger than lions.

Ye daughters of Israel,
weep over Saul,
who clothed you daintily in scarlet,
who put ornaments of gold upon your apparel.

How are the mighty fallen in the midst of the battle!

Jonathan lies slain upon thy high places.

I am distressed for you, my brother Jonathan;
very pleasant have you been to me;
your love to me was wonderful,
passing the love of women.

How are the mighty fallen,
and the weapons of war perished![47]

The description of the poem as song is made explicit in the translations of both the NJPS and the NRSV, the latter of which renders 2 Sam 1:18 as "and he [David] said it [the Song of the Bow] should be taught to the people of Judah." And in terms of the story being told by the compiler of Samuel, some scholars consider that the song is misplaced, since it appears to serve as a more fitting completion to the public mourning described in 2 Sam 1:11–12,[48] or that the chapter as a whole fits better if it concludes

---

[47]The division of the stanzas are the authors', not that of the RSV. The authors' preference for "beauty" in the place of "glory" in the first line is noted in brackets.

[48]Anderson, 2 Samuel, 14.

1 Samuel and so brings to an end the episode of Saul.[49] Common to these observations is the presumption that the narrative originally did not include the song and that the song was added at a later date. These assessments carry weight especially if it is assumed the function of the song is to carry on or complement the narrative plot. If, however, this song, like the others considered in this study, had a function other than moving along the plot of the story, then perhaps its placement is strategic and intentional.[50] And a clue to the function of the song as pointing to something other than plot may be found in the literary structure of the song. Holladay makes a strong case for his conclusion that "word-play is the key to the structure of the poem."[51] And wordplay is not what we would expect if plot were the focus of attention.

That the song predates the composition of the narrative, as indicated by the compiler of Samuel, seems most assured.[52] McCarter is of the opinion that it is reasonable to think that the song was composed as a eulogy for Saul and Jonathan, as claimed by the Samuel compiler.[53] Indeed, McCarter goes so far as to offer that it seems a "sound" conclusion that David himself composed the song and consequently the very personal expressions of grief over a friend lost.[54] Should this in fact be the origin of the song (or at least a very early legend associated with the song), we must also then consider that it was popularized among the people of Judah and made its way into the well-known and presumably respected scroll—the *Song Scroll*—only to be finally quoted at length by the Samuel compiler and that the compiler had a goal in mind. Overall, the Samuel compiler does

[49] H. W. Hertzberg, *I and II Samuel* (trans. J. Bowden; OTL; Philadelphia: Westminster, 1964), 236.

[50] James Watts, *Psalm and Story: Inset Hymns in Hebrew Narrative* (JSOTSup 139; Sheffield: JSOT Press, 1992), 171. Anderson, *2 Samuel*, 15, referencing Otto Eissfeldt, *The Old Testament: An Introduction* (Oxford: Blackwell, 1965), 115, mentions that the song may have had "power to arouse courage and boldness in young men." Although Anderson indicates that there may have been other reasons for the inclusion of the song, he does not expand on what those reasons may have been.

[51] William Holladay, "Form and Word-Play in David's Lament over Saul and Jonathan," *VT* 20 (1970): 156.

[52] Ibid., 154.

[53] McCarter, *II Samuel*, 78–79. See also Masao Sekine, "Lyric Literature in the Davidic-Solomonic Period in the Light of the History of Israelite Literature," in *Studies in the Period of David and Solomon and Other Essays* (ed. Tomoo Ishida; Winona Lake, Ind.: Eisenbrauns, 1982), 2. David N. Freedman dates this composition to the monarchic period of the tenth century or later ("Divine Names and Titles in Early Hebrew Poetry," in *Magnalia Dei, the Mighty Acts of God: Essays on the Bible and Archaeology in Memory of G. Ernest Wright* [ed. Frank Moore Cross, Werner Lembke, and Patrick Miller; Garden City, N.Y.: Doubleday, 1976], 55–107).

[54] McCarter, *II Samuel*, 79. See also Holladay, "Form and Word-Play," 154.

indeed seem intent on offering a "continuing hope for social unity grounded in belief" to an audience that represents a "wide spectrum of attitudes and beliefs."[55]

It is likely, then, that this continuing hope is grounded in cultural memory, that is, a shared set of experiences the significance of which is evident in the creation and circulation of the *Song Scroll*. The *Song Scroll* is just that, a collection of lyrics giving voice to this cultural memory. Cultural memory is not a small matter. "The concept of cultural memory comprises that body of re-usable texts, images and rituals specific to each society in each epoch, whose 'cultivation' serves to stabilize and convey that society's self-image. . . . Through its cultural heritage a society becomes visible to itself and others."[56] In the Song of the Bow (as with the other songs in the *Song Scroll*), the Samuel audience is reasserting its identity and presence. That audience is probably Jerusalemite and of a Jerusalem late in the monarchy. The scholarly consensus is that the books of 1 and 2 Samuel, mainly in their present form, originated before the destruction of Jerusalem in the sixth century B.C.E., although how much before is still an open question.[57] By all estimates, the Song of the Bow was well established in the repertoire of Judah before its insertion into the tale spun by the Samuel compiler.

The Song of the Bow is more than a lament expressing grief over the loss of a fallen hero. It is a reaffirmation of group identity. The song became part of a cultural memory that helped form a continued hope for social unity that could be embodied repeatedly through the performance of the song. This is what makes the role of the Samuel narrator so interesting in this instance. To achieve and sustain social unity requires some sort of leadership—a vision or a conviction about what to think and how to feel or even how to remember the past. The character of David provides the narrator with the opportunity to embody and give voice to this leadership. Who is this David? What do his voice and body communicate to his spectators? What uses might the Samuel narrator make of David's grief and passion?

---

[55]James Flanagan, "Samuel, Book of 1–2," *ABD* 5:961.

[56]Jan Assmann, "Collective Memory and Cultural Identity" (trans. John Czaplicka), in "Cultural History/Cultural Studies," special issue, *New German Critique* 65 (spring–summer 1995): 125–33, here 132–33. Chapter 3, below, will explore in more depth specific characteristics of cultural memory as defined by Assmann.

[57]Walter Brueggemann, "Samuel, Book of 1–2," *ABD* 5:966. McCarter, *II Samuel*, 13, seems to be of the opinion that the narrative surrounding the Song of the Bow, 1 Sam 16:14 to 2 Sam 5:10, represents material from the reign of David.

Solomon's Temple Dedication (1 Kings 8:12–13; 2 Chronicles 6:1–2)

Solomon's Temple Dedication

YHWH . . . said that he dwells in thick darkness,
but I myself have built a mighty house for You,
a place for You to dwell forever (authors' translation).

The LXX version of the 1 Kings passage follows the song with a postscript: "Is it not written in the Book of Song?"[58] The song is also included in the Chronicles version of the same story (borrowed extensively from Kings). The presence of the song and the LXX's reference to the Book of Song have often bewildered commentators. One writer, despairing of understanding the history of the song, comments, "The original purport and circumstances of this ode, of which only the first lines are quoted, are wholly obscure."[59] How the song was used before its inclusion in Kings and later Chronicles is obscure, yet it must have had such an influential social presence that the writer of Kings inserted the song into the narrative and later the inheritor of the Kings tradition, the writer of Chronicles, retained it.

The Chronicles version of the song appears in the midst of a single literary unit extending from 2 Chr 5:2 to 7:22, which parallels 1 Kgs 8:1–9:8. Whereas the Kings account shows roughly equal interest in the construction and the dedication of the temple, the Chronicler shows a much greater interest in the dedication of the temple and much less interest in the preparation and building of the temple. We might infer that, for the Chronicler, the emphasis was on what the temple represented—the presence of Yahweh—and not on the temple itself. The Chronicler is intent on establishing a sense of identity that could be assumed by a people long after the Solomonic temple was gone.[60] The writer of Kings, on the other hand, is more interested in the glories of the physical structure. Writing in a time when the temple was still standing ("they are there to this day" [1 Kgs 8:8]), the author seems intent on persuading the reading or listening audience

---

[58] J. Wellhausen, *Die Composition des Hexateuchs und der historischen Bücher des Alten Testaments* (3d ed.; Berlin: Georg Reimer, 1899; repr., Berlin: de Gruyter, 1963).

[59] James Montgomery, *The Book of Kings* (ICC; Edinburgh: T&T Clark, 1951), 190.

[60] A fourth-century date for the compilation of Chronicles seems accurate. See Sara Japhet, *I and II Chronicles* (OTL; Louisville: Westminster John Knox, 1993), 24–26.

of the preference they should give to Jerusalem over other contemporary and even foreign competitors for allegiance.[61]

The 2 Chronicles narrative leading up to the song in 6:1–2 relies heavily upon 1 Kings 8 except for the text of 2 Chr 5:11–13a, which is not found in 1 Kings 8. These verses added by the Chronicler emphasize the role of the Levites, a group that the Chronicler also brings to the attention of the reader by exchanging "priests" in the source document of 1 Kgs 8:3 with "Levites" in 2 Chr 5:4. The Chronicler also removes the stone description of the Mosaic tablets (2 Chr 5:10), which is quite clear in the Kings source document (1 Kgs 8:9: *lukhot ha'ebanim*). If indeed the Chronicler's audience has available a replica of the ark (the original having been destroyed by the fiery conflagration associated with the Babylonian destruction), they would have no expectation of finding the original tablets, especially if not inscribed on stone plaques but on a more perishable material.

For the readers or listeners of Chronicles, the temple and its glories are long past. Yahweh's presence cannot be verified by a thick cloud or even by the glories of a state structure. Yahweh is present in the continuing acting out of a postexilic people who own the Solomonic past as its own. And the Chronicler's rendition of the "to this day" phrase may provide an intriguing hint on how this identity is to be encouraged. In Kings, the "they are there to this day" phrase refers to the poles of the ark. Second Chronicles 5:10 preserves the "to this day" notation as well but reads, "it is there to this day," referring not to the poles as in 1 Kings but to the ark itself. It is not unusual for commentators to consider the change of verbal form in Chronicles an insignificant corruption or editorial change predating the work of the Chronicler,[62] but consider the result of this one small change. The presence of the ark—or, better, its replicate—in the postexilic temple would have provided a very meaningful rallying point. Even after the trauma of Babylonian conquest, destruction, and resultant exile, this religious symbol remains "to this day" perhaps as a model of the staying power that the Chronicler wishes to impart to the community itself. Just as "to this day" the ark has survived—so, too, have you survived, the people who will sing, "I have built thee an exalted house—a place for thee to dwell forever" (2 Chr 6:2). Although, granted, the primary referent of "house" is the temple (preexilic in Kings, postexilic in Chronicles), it is not long before the secondary referent of "house" as people will assert itself within the worldview of the Chronicler.

---

[61]A preexilic compilation of Kings is probable, with appropriate additions (particularly at the end of 2 Kings) made by an exilic "Deuteronomic" redactor. See John Gray, *I and II Kings* (OTL; Philadelphia: Westminster, 1970), 36.

[62]Japhet, *I and II Chronicles*, 578. The RSV seems to agree with Japhet's assessment, presenting the Kings version in Chronicles.

And so, even though both Kings and Chronicles present the Song of Solomon's Temple Dedication (and very similar renditions of the song, following the MT rather than the LXX,[63] of both 1 Kings and 2 Chronicles),[64] the narratives in which these songs appear have different purposes and so, too, do the presentations of the songs. The Kings account binds the readers to the temple—the physical structure—and the social institutions, both political and religious, that the temple represents. The Chronicles account binds the reader to a memory, a heritage, now to be reembodied by the reading or listening audience and used to imagine a communal identity projecting into the future.[65] This double purpose to which the song is applied is quite consistent with the nature of performative material, as demonstrated throughout this chapter.

Conclusion

If, as already suggested, the inclusion of these songs in their respective narrative was designed to help create an identity, these performative features of choral responses and storytelling provide the medium for doing exactly that. The content of the songs, with the change of persons, lack of specific enemy, dislocation and compression of time, and expectation of audience recognition, makes it possible for the song to be twice-used and to bind the past and the present together in the person of the reading or listening audience. At the very least, the mechanism for moving that audience to a pure state or, in Jill Dolan's terms, to utopian performatives[66]— profound moments that lift everyone above the present—is established by inserting these songs into the narratives.

---

[63]The LXX version of 1 Kings (i.e., 3 Kgdms) adds "The LORD has set the sun in the heavens" before the first phrase of the MT. Othmar Keel, "Der salomonische Tempelweihspruch: Beobachtungen zum religionsgeschichtlichen Kontext des ersten Jerusalemer Tempels," in *Gottesstadt und Gottesgarten: Zur Geschichte und Theologie des Jerusalemer Tempels* (ed. Othmar Keel and Erich Zenger; Quaestiones disputatae 191; Freiburg im Breisgau: Herder, 2002), 9–24, argues that the song in both 1 Kings and Joshua gives evidence of sun worship in Jerusalem in an open-air sanctuary later encompassed and darkened within the confines of a building.

[64]First Kings reads *banoh baniti* at the beginning of v. 13 whereas 2 Chronicles reads *weʾani baniti* to begin the same phrase. Both renditions serve to emphasize the subject of the verb *baniti*.

[65]In some ways, the Kings account and the Chronicler's account illustrate the distinction made by Beckerman between actual and ideal presentation. See Beckerman, *Theatrical Presentation*, 113.

[66]Jill Dolan, *Utopia in Performance: Finding Hope at the Theater* (Ann Arbor: University of Michigan Press, 2005), 5–6.

Chapter 3: **The Song of the Sea**
(Exodus 15:1–18)

Introduction

The last chapter considered three relatively short songs bound together by their common association with the *Song Scroll*. Performative concepts such as "act-scheme," "implicit audience," and "projected identity" were applied in order to understand the placement and function of the songs within their respective narratives. This chapter moves to a lengthier song that now finds a home in the central narrative of biblical Israelite identity—the exodus story. The Song of the Sea is part of a story that has been told and retold for generations and gives us a wonderful opportunity to visit a recycling process applied to an ancient song that has now become part of the biblical communal memory. The Song of the Sea allows us to expand the use of performance-critical analysis by more broadly considering the nature of performance and of presentation with particular emphasis, discussion, and application of the iconic mode of presentation.

> The retelling of stories already told, the reenactment of events already enacted, the re-experience of emotions already experienced, these are and have always been central concerns of the theatre in all times and places, but closely allied to these concerns are the particular production dynamics of the theatre: the stories it chooses to tell, the bodies and other physical materials it utilizes to tell them, and the places in which they are told. Each of these production elements are also, to a striking degree, composed of material "that we have seen before," and memory of that recycled material as it moves through new and different productions contributes in no small measure to the richness and density of the operations of theatre in general as a site of memory, both personal and cultural.[1]

---

[1]Marvin Carlson, *The Haunted Stage: The Theatre as Memory Machine* (Ann Arbor: University of Michigan Press, 2001), 4–5.

Retelling and recycling "what we have seen before" are characteristic of the several songs from ancient Israel that have made their way into prose sections of the Hebrew Bible.[2] This chapter will examine the Song of the Sea from Exod 15:1–18 with tools gleaned from performance-critical analysis. And through performance criticism, it will investigate the manner in which the Song of the Sea presents a retelling and recycling of one of the most significant epic memories given witness in the Hebrew Bible.

Modern scholarship has clearly demonstrated that the poem of 15:1–18, though now a literary whole, has a structure that is the composite of either two (vv. 1b–12 and 13–18) or three (vv. 1b–12; 13a and 14–16; 13b and 17–18) constituent segments. It is readily accepted that the poem existed earlier than, and independently from, its present context within the prose of the book of Exodus. Frank Cross suggests a twelfth- or eleventh-century B.C.E. date for the oral composition of the poem, followed by a written form of the poem in the tenth century.[3] David Freedman supports a twelfth-century composition date for the poem.[4] Here it is accepted that although the poem had a long oral history, the composition of its written form was no earlier than the eighth century.[5]

Although the form of the poem has received ample attention from scholars,[6] there has been no clear agreement on the genre to which the song may belong.[7] The narrative, or story line, of the poem, on the other

---

[2] Songs inserted into poetic contexts necessitate a separate analysis.

[3] Frank Moore Cross, "The Song of the Sea and Canaanite Myth," in *Canaanite Myth and Hebrew Epic* (Cambridge: Harvard University Press, 1973), 121–25.

[4] David N. Freedman, "Early Israelite Poetry," in *Pottery, Poetry, and Prophecy: Studies in Early Hebrew Poetry* (Winona Lake, Ind.: Eisenbrauns, 1980), 177–78. A postexilic date for the poem found scholarly support at the beginning of the twentieth century but has since lost its consensus as understanding of Hebrew philology has become more refined. See A. Bender, "Das Lied Exodus 15," *ZAW* 23 (1903): 1–48. A recent proponent of the postexilic date for the poem is Martin Brenner, *The Song of the Sea: Ex 15:1–21* (BZAW 195; Berlin and New York: de Gruyter, 1991), 177.

[5] Arguments for the dating need not detain us here. The decision here in favor of an eighth-century written composition is determined, in part, by the work of Avi Hurvitz on the P source (see his "Dating the Priestly Source in Light of the Historical Study of Biblical Hebrew a Century after Wellhausen," *ZAW* 100 supplement (1988): 88–99 as well as by what seems to be a reasonable historical context for the whole of the poem as it now appears in Exod 15.

[6] "Exodus 15 has become a standard example of early Israelite poetry" (John Durham, *Exodus* [WBC; Waco: Word, 1987], 204). See esp. David N. Freedman, "The Song of the Sea," in *Pottery, Poetry, and Prophecy*, 179–86; idem, "Strophe and Meter in Exodus 15," ibid., 187–227; James Muilenburg, "A Liturgy on the Triumphs of Yahweh," in *Studia biblica et semitica* (Wageningen, Neth.: H. Veenman, 1966), 233–51.

[7] Brevard S. Childs, *The Book of Exodus* (OTL; Philadelphia: Westminster, 1974), 243.

hand, has received too little attention.[8] This story line shows ample evidence of layering or growth. Even a quick reading of the poem uncovers some of the awkwardness that the poem presents. In Exodus 15 the song is placed in the exodus story line at the occasion of the miraculous defeat of Pharaoh's army at the Red Sea. Yet it is quite probable that verse 17 (and 13b) of the song was written from Jerusalem,[9] perhaps even with the temple in mind, and so disrupts quite handily the story line of Exodus 15. Similarly, verses 13–16 (excepting 13b) more naturally provide commentary on the Israelite journey through Transjordan after the stay at Sinai and the abortive attempt to enter the promised land through Kadesh-barnea (narrated at the end of Numbers, from ch. 14 on).

Performance criticism may help answer several questions that thus arise. First, what can performance criticism tell us about the dynamics of the song that gave it a life of its own prior to its adoption by the Exodus 15 editor? And second, what performance-critical observations about the appropriation of the song into its present prose context might help explain the inclusion of even the seemingly anachronistic elements of the song in its present narrative context?

Performance Criticism and the Structure of the Poem

Literary criticism has taught us that pieces of literature have their own structural logic and, according to that logic, can be grouped and categorized into specific literary genres. Similarly, performance criticism shows that performances also, according to their respective types, have a structural logic. Scholarship has subjected Exodus 15, as a piece of literature, to analysis in order to make plain its literary structure but has yet to submit it to performance criticism in order to make plain its performative structure. Exposing this performative structural logic is our first task.

As indicated above, the poem of Exod 15:1–18 has at least two versions: the one prior to its inclusion into Exodus 15 and the one that made its way into Exodus 15. In other words, the work has a "performed song" version and a "literary poem" version. On the basis of a variety of considerations (content, genre, motifs, and diction), Thomas Dozeman considers verses 1–12 and 18 to be the performed-song version of the work.[10] This song, he suggests, can be divided into three parts:[11]

---

[8] Ibid., 244.

[9] Other sites, including Gilgal, have also been suggested.

[10] Thomas Dozeman, "The Song of the Sea and Salvation History," in *On the Way to Nineveh* (ed. Stephen Cook and S. C. Winter; Atlanta: Scholars Press, 1999), 96–113, 103.

[11] Ibid., 100.

Introduction	vv. 1–3
Body	vv. 4–11
Conclusion	vv. 12, 18

This pre-Exodus 15 version of the song is closer to recognizable extrabiblical genres and can be identified as a victory hymn that is preexilic and possibly premonarchical in origin.[12]

Dozeman argues persuasively that the pre-Exodus version has the same thematic structure as that present in Ugaritic texts: conflict, victory, and proclamation of divine kingship.[13] As Dozeman understands it, the thematic pattern is built around an *inclusio* with the refrain of verse 6 serving as the core of the pattern.

Victory	vv. 1–3
Conflict	vv. 4–5
Victory	v. 6
Conflict	vv. 7–10
Victory	vv. 11–12
Proclamation of divine kingship	v. 18

This pre-Exodus version of the performed song displays a mythic pattern that allows us to ask questions about the performative aspects of the symbolic presentation.

Songs, by their very nature, connote presentation and performance. "Presentation" and "performance" are overlapping terms, but each "stresses a different aspect of a mutual act."[14] Songs are meant to be given life by the human voice, making the human being both the producer and the product of the song. In other words, there is a mutually dependent relationship between the song that is to be presented and the performance required to achieve the presentation. In the overlap of presentation and performance, we become engaged with both the thing being presented and the how of presentation, or the performance of the thing itself. "Presentation suggests a multiplicity of meanings. It is rooted in the idea of offering a gift, in particular offering a gift by making it present, of the moment. Presentation thus not only incorporates the act of giving, but also the act of being—of the donor being in touch with the receiver of the gift."[15] Beckerman identifies the very core of what distinguishes performance-critical analysis from other methods: both the temporal and the spatial qualities that connect

---

[12] Ibid., 100–101.

[13] Ibid., 102, referring to *CTA* 2.

[14] Bernard Beckerman, *Theatrical Presentation: Performer, Audience, and Act* (ed. Gloria Brim Beckerman and William Coco; New York: Routledge, 1990), 1.

[15] Ibid.

the presenter and spectator in a here-now relationship where each consciously shares in the presence of the other.

A pyramid image emerges that is central to understanding the song in both its presentational and its performative context. At the apex of this pyramid we place the receiver(s), for whom both the gift (song) and its performance are intended.

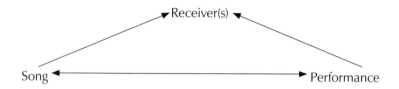

In the case of a song, we need to first investigate *what* is being given before examining *how* it is given. From a presentation-as-gift perspective, the Song of the Sea is best understood for its symbolic or iconic value. It is a celebratory act of glorification, the kind of show that can be described as "an apt instrument for a man or a city to celebrate a special event. . . . They are overflowings of our spirit."[16] Iconic modes of presentation and performance, suggests Beckerman, are presentations-as-gifts by their very nature. We have innumerable examples of these throughout history: holiday celebrations, parades, fireworks, pageants, and so on.[17] These celebratory acts focus on demonstration and glorification, not factual re-creation of an event. Fireworks may bring to mind the noise and fury of battle but have changed that battle into a beautiful spectacle of light and sound. Beckerman uses the simple example of a small-town Memorial Day parade to demonstrate the essence of iconic presentation: "It [the Memorial Day parade] celebrates the past and the present, the past glory, suffering, and achievements of the people, together with their present unity and idealism. In that sense the show confirms established values, and it does so by mere demonstration."[18] Iconic modes of presentation are distinguished by the following three major features:

1. The performer(s) stresses *being* rather than *becoming*. Demonstration and embodiment of what is are more important than moving dialectically toward what could be.

---

[16] Ibid., 2–3.

[17] Beckerman, ibid., ch. 3, presents an extensive examination of iconic presentation. The key elements of iconic presentation applied here are drawn primarily from that chapter.

[18] Ibid., 43.

2. "The action that is performed involves less the overcoming of temporal resistance and more the ritual enactment of prescribed movements."[19] Spectators are more aware of an "unfolding display" than the "relief of suspense" associated with dialectic modes of performance. In other words, speech and gesture are precise, controlled, and patterned. As in the case of the Song of the Sea, the rhythmic and repetitive pattern of the language provides the framework for the precise enactment of the song.

3. "The effect produced by the demonstrative event is illumination more than catharsis. We have a sense of an act falling into place (a puzzle solved, a miracle wrought)."[20]

Beckerman's contention appears correct that iconic modes of performance move spectators "toward awe, wonder, and ultimately insight into mystery."[21] Using the three main principles of iconic presentation and performance described above, we will now examine the pre-Exodus version of the performed song (vv. 1–12, 18) in order to try to understand the attraction it presented to the Exodus narrator, thereby persuading him to include it in the story of Exodus.

Embodiment (Being Rather Than Becoming)

From a performative perspective, the singers of the Song of the Sea embody several ideas. Primary among these are (a) an explicit relationship with Yahweh (b) knowledge of who Yahweh is and what is required of the relationship with him, and (c) a claiming of a past, a communal history, in which Yahweh earns the admiration embodied in the song.

In verses 1–2, the phrases "My strength," "my salvation," "my God," "my father's God," "whom I will praise," and "whom I exalt" immediately allow the song's performers to own and personify an intimate and personal relationship with Yahweh. There is no hint of conflict between the performers and their God, no suggestion that we are about to experience a forward-moving action that results in a newly defined relationship to Yahweh. The performers embody what is, a relationship established on admiration and exaltation. One can imagine the sounds and gestures of such a performance, communicating a sense of pride, security, and deep

---

[19] Ibid., 55.
[20] Ibid.
[21] Ibid.

satisfaction to the spectators. What is in the song is beautiful, complete, and worthy of celebration.

The Song of the Sea firmly establishes who Yahweh is by celebrating him as savior, God, and warrior. As the song progresses, the past is recalled not to reenact the events of the past but to allow the presenters to embody the admiration and exaltation of the first two verses. The refrain of verse 6 reinforces this for both performers and spectators: "Your right hand, O LORD, is majestic in power. Your right hand, O LORD, shatters the enemy." The situation presented in the song is consistently restated so that the role of admirers and exalters of Yahweh is sustained by the performers and the past and future are embodied in the present:

Song of the Sea (portion)

Who is like thee, O LORD,
    among the gods?

Who is like thee,
    majestic in holiness,

terrible in glorious deeds,
    doing wonders? . . .

The LORD will reign
    for ever and ever. (vv. 11, 18)

The song compresses time. Past and future are woven into the present, and this temporal compression is important to note if we are to understand the appropriate placement of the song in Exodus 15.

Unfolding Display

Unlike dialectic modes of presentation, where conflict is enacted in order to move toward resolution (a "process of becoming" evident in plot line or series of performed actions), iconic modes of presentation tend to display or describe the results of action as part of the process of embodying what is.[22] In this sense, the past is invaluable to the iconic mode of

---

[22] For a complete discussion of dialectic modes of presentation see ibid., ch. 4, 56–72. Ronald Hendel, "A Book of Memories," *BRev* 18 (2002): 38–45, 52–53, describes these differences in Exod 15 as "real history" and "existential actuality" and comes close to a description of what is referred to here as dialectic and iconic modes of presentation.

presentation. By displaying past events as the foundation for what *is*, performers and spectators are united in terms of identity. The annual Christmas pageant in its many forms is an example, from the simplest outdoor manger scene with its mixture of people, farm animals, and props to the largest, most theatrically extravagant spectacular with music, camels, and flying angels backed by a forty-foot, digital blue screen in the background. No matter how simple or complex, a nativity pageant, like a parade, unfolds before us frame by frame. There are no surprises. We know what the final scene will be. We trust and rely on the fact that there will be no surprises, that the story will be presented to us with all the component parts we need and expect. Our communal relationship to the others present with us is rooted in the unfolding display of this pageant, which will end with the Christ child in a manger. If there are any surprises, they are purely theatrical, brought about by the technology available in many of today's megachurches, where these pageants can take on an extreme magnitude in terms of the spectacle.

In what unfolds before us in the pre-Exodus version of this song, verses 3–10 function like these pageants. Yahweh's victories are rhythmically displayed so that both performers and spectators can exalt in them. They pass by in grand procession and, with each display, the spectator becomes more and more identified with the communal parade. Pharaoh's military chariots and his officers, Yahweh's foes and his enemies are paraded past the spectators as memories that display the power and majesty of God. Verses 3–5 and 7–10 focus specifically on display, relying on the spectators' knowledge of the past to connect them to the images:

Song of the Sea (portion)

The floods cover them;
    they went down into the depths like a stone. . . .

At the blast of thy nostrils
    the waters piled up,

the floods stood up in a heap;

the deeps congealed
    in the heart of the sea. . . .

Thou didst blow with thy wind,
    the sea covered them;

they sank as lead
    in the mighty waters. (vv. 5, 8, 10)

Twice-Used Songs: Performances Usurped

In its pre-Exodus incarnation, the Song of the Sea provided an iconic means of communal solidarity in which both performer and spectator celebrated a social memory. Like other songs now appearing in prose contexts within the Hebrew Bible,[23] the song of Exodus 15 has been harnessed into a prose literary context. The song changes and becomes twice-used when set into prose. "Far from being a description totally independent of the prose account, the poetic tradition of Exodus 15 shares its basic features."[24] Clear evidence of this intentional transformation is found in 15:19, a prose summary of the song that repeats verbatim a phrase found in 14:29. In other words, the song has been transformed by its insertion into Exodus 15. Another example of this twice-used function of songs appears in 2 Sam 22, in which is inserted a song that we have simply in song form as Psalm 18. When performances become appropriated into a secondary usage, dynamics are present that change how the performance now functions. "Often the poem is earlier in date than its framework and originally served a different purpose in its independent state."[25] We are fortunate also with Exodus 15 in that with good probability two stages of composition, one a performative stage and the other a literary stage, have been identified. Now that we have analyzed performative aspects of the performed song, it is our task to consider the structural logic of the literary poem (vv. 1–18) and ask how this literary structure may have transformed the performed song into a literary poem.

Dozeman completes his comparison of the Song of the Sea with Canaanite myth by pointing out that the addition of Exod 15:13–17 adds thematic structures that are also seen in Ugaritic texts:[26]

Temple construction vv. 13b, 17b

Conquest   vv. 14–16

Establishment of kingdom   vv. 13a, 17a

In contrast to the relatively simple structure suggested by Dozeman for the performed song of the pre-Exodus 15 version, the literary logic of the Exodus 15 literary poem is quite detailed as suggested by Freedman:[27]

---

[23] Particularly Deut 31:30–32:43; Judg 5:1–31; 2 Sam 22:2–51.

[24] Childs, *The Book of Exodus*, 245.

[25] Ibid., 248.

[26] Dozeman, "The Song of the Sea and Salvation History," 102, referring to *CTA* 3 and 4.

[27] See Freedman, "The Song of the Sea," 180–86. Not Freedman's excellent translation but rather the more familiar RSV is used here. The structure of the song as he has provided it, however, is given.

Song of the Sea

Preface (vv. 1–2)

> The LORD is my strength and my song,
>> and he has become my salvation;
>
> this is my God,
>> and I will praise him,
>
> my father's God,
>> and I will exalt him.

Inclusio: Introduction (vv. 3–5) frames the poem along with verses 17–18

> The LORD is a man of war;
>> the LORD is his name.
>
> Pharaoh's chariots and his host
>> he cast into the sea;
>
> and his picked officers
>> are sunk in the Red Sea.
>
> The floods cover them;
>> they went down into the depths like a stone.

Refrain 1 (v. 6)

> Thy right hand, O LORD,
>> glorious in power,
>
> thy right hand, O LORD,
>> shatters the enemy.

Stanza 1 (vv. 7–10)

> In the greatness of thy majesty
>> thou overthrowest thy adversaries;
>
> thou sendest forth thy fury,
>> it consumes them like stubble.
>
> At the blast of thy nostrils
>> the waters piled up,
>
> the floods stood up in a heap;
>
> the deeps congealed in the
>> heart of the sea.

The enemy said,
    'I will pursue, I will overtake,

I will divide the spoil,
    my desire shall have its fill of them.

I will draw my sword,
    my hand shall destroy them.'

Thou didst blow with thy wind,
    the sea covered them;

They sank as lead
    in the mighty waters.

Refrain 2 (v. 11)

Who is like thee, O LORD,
    among the gods?

Who is like thee,
    majestic in holiness,

terrible in glorious deeds,
    doing wonders?

Stanza 2 (vv. 12–16a)

Thou didst stretch out thy right hand,
    the earth swallowed them.

Thou hast led in thy steadfast love
    the people whom thou hast redeemed,

thou hast guided them by thy strength,
    to thy holy abode.

The peoples have heard, they tremble;

pangs have seized on the inhabitants of Philistia.

Now are the chiefs of Edom dismayed;[28]

the leaders of Moab,
    trembling seizes them;

all the inhabitants of Canaan have melted away.[29]

Terror and dread fall upon them;[30]

---

[28] Or perhaps more in tune with the Hebrew poetry, "Then they were dismayed—the chieftains of Edom" (Freedman).

[29] Again more along the lines of the Hebrew poetry, "They completely collapsed—the kings of Canaan" (Freedman).

[30] Freedman maintains the poetic rhythm, translating, "You brought down upon them—a numinous dread."

because of the greatness of thy arm,
    they are as still as a stone,

Refrain 3 (v. 16b)

till thy people, O Lord,
    pass by,

till the people pass by
    whom thou hast purchased.

Inclusio: Conclusion (vv. 17–18)

Thou wilt bring them
    in,

and plant them
    on thy own mountain,

the place, O Lord,
    which thou hast made for thy abode,

the sanctuary, Lord,
    which thy hands have established.

The Lord will reign
    for ever and ever.

The structure suggested by Freedman makes clear the refrain created by the repeating phrases found in verses 6, 11, and 16b. The refrains "provide the skeletal structure on which the poem is built."[31] These refrains separate the stanzas of 7–10 and 12–16a as well as the stanza that functions as an *inclusio*, "book-ending" the poem in verses 3–5 and 17–18. Freedman suggests that we conceptualize the poem in the shape of a pyramid, with the refrain of verse 11 forming the apex, or top, of the pyramid.[32]

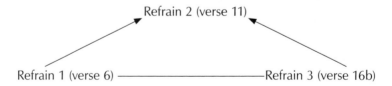

Built around the three refrains are three stanzas. The *inclusio* stanzas function much like an introduction (vv. 3–5) and a conclusion (vv. 17–18)

---

[31] Freedman, "The Song of the Sea," 189.
[32] Ibid.

to the song. The first stanza (vv. 7–10) celebrates Yahweh's victory at the sea. The second stanza (vv. 12–15) forms a similar celebration of Yahweh's guidance and protection while the Israelites wandered through hostile territory to arrive safely at Yahweh's chosen abode.

Verses 1 and 2 appear as a preface to the poem. Verse 1, repeated in Exod 15:21, where it is cast as the Song of Miriam, repeats and functions much like the refrains of verses 6, 11 and 16b. Verse 2 may have served as an introduction to the liturgical use of the song, suggesting a liturgical setting for public use of the song in worship.[33]

The Prose Context of the Performance

The inclusion of the Song of the Sea in the prose of Exodus is not accomplished as smoothly as one might expect or hope. The difficulties that arise when the poem of Exodus 15 is compared with its prose context from Exodus 14 are well known, and these difficulties are not limited to the discrepancies between the Song of the Sea and its prose context. Similar difficulties can be found when other twice-used songs are compared with the prose contexts in which they are now embedded. For example, it has been said that the song of Deuteronomy 32 "does not sit easily in its context."[34] Judges 4 has been cited as "a prime example of an Israelite historian interpreting a source, and having a bad day of it."[35] And the difficulties associated with the Song of the Sea in Exodus 15 have been characterized as a "misguided hermeneutic" employed by the prose writer.[36] But other voices have weighed in on the assessment as well. One commentator has sought to explain the differences between the prose of Exodus 14 and the poetry of Exodus 15 as the result of a "strong theological or traditional motive operating to shape a different understanding of the event than that which may have shaped the poetry and this in its turn has generated a quasi-midrashic understanding of the poem."[37]

This "motive" at work in the song is only in part a result of the traditional or theological forces at work in the construction of the prose context. Just as important are performative and nonperformative patterns

[33] Ibid., 182.

[34] David Peterson and Kent Richards, *Interpreting Hebrew Poetry* (Minneapolis: Fortress, 1992), 68.

[35] Baruch Halpern, "The Resourceful Israelite Historian: The Song of Deborah and Israelite Historiography," *HTR* 76 (1983): 396.

[36] Ibid., 397.

[37] Walter Houston, "Misunderstanding or Midrash? The Prose Appropriation of Poetic Material in the Hebrew Bible," *ZAW* 109 (1997): 354.

that reside in the song turned poem and the prose context in which the poem now finds itself. The poems are "ghosts" of the songs that went before, and the performative mode of thought embodied in the song still haunts the literary context now giving a home to the poem.

Ghosting in the Song of the Sea

The retelling, reenactment, and reexperiencing of events have conditioned, as Marvin Carlson and others note,[38] the very processes by which theatre and performance are composed, given form, and altered over time by various theatrical cultures around the world. This recycling process, which Carlson calls "ghosting," is central to how performance is received by spectators and, in turn, how the spectators' reception influences the performance traditions, ultimately influencing the composition of the text. Applying this logic, we see a hermeneutic circle or, better, a cycling of sorts, constructed for the twice-used songs.

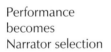 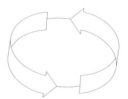

Performance
becomes
Narrator selection

Spectator reception
becomes
Reader reception

In its simplest terms, this recycling points to the cultural practice of returning to stories, myths, songs, and other narrative materials that are not only well known but likely to generate a certain and predictable response. As Carlson points out, we find this practice not only in traditional Western cultures but Asian, Indian, and Arabic cultures as well.[39] What are the stories we want to hear over and over? What are the songs we want to sing over and over? The songs that confirm who we are, that tell us it all means something. For the Exodus narrator, the selection of material within the narrative was very much concerned with the problem of reception, or with what the readers/listeners needed and wanted. The narrator's choice of material, from the range of historical material available to him, largely determined his effect on his spectators.

---

[38] Carlson, *The Haunted Stage*, 7. See also Richard Schechner, *Between Theater and Anthropology* (Philadelphia: University of Pennsylvania Press, 1985); Bert O. States, *Dreaming and Storytelling* (Ithaca, N.Y.: Cornell University Press, 1993); Roland Barthes, *Image, Music, Text* (trans. Stephen Heath; New York: Hill & Wang, 1977).

[39] Carlson, *The Haunted Stage*, 34–35.

"All reception is deeply involved with memory, because it is memory that supplies the codes and strategies that shape reception, and, as cultural and social memories change, so do the parameters within which reception operates."[40] What is particularly applicable to the Exodus 15 poem is Carlson's suggestion that "the reception process itself might be characterized as the selective application of memory to experience."[41] The movement from the performed tradition of the Song of the Sea into the literary tradition of the poem found in Exodus 15 is a selective process of establishing memory *as* experience that can be captured in a performable text. In this way, myth, history, reality, and the fragmented experience of various groups can be structured into a unified cultural memory that is accessible through both text and performance. So, although a literary analysis of Exodus 15 is useful, this literary analysis alone does not recognize the prior performative dimension of the song.

A further examination of the iconic nature of the literary version of the Song of the Sea deepens our understanding of the symbolic and celebratory power of the song, particularly as it retells, recalls, and reestablishes memory and the experience of memory as the site of cultural experience for the people of Israel. The three distinctive features of iconic modes of presentation—embodiment, unfolding display, and illumination—are not only retained in the literary version of the Song of the Sea but are, in fact, enhanced through the refrain structure identified by Freedman.

After establishing the personal relationship with Yahweh, embodying a specific notion of being (Yahweh's admirers, his people), the first refrain restates the awesome power of Yahweh the warrior: he who cast Pharaoh's chariots into the sea. The stanzas present a continuous unfolding display of memory after memory in the formal emerging history of Yahweh's relationship to the people of Israel. The explicit images of Pharaoh's army drowning in the Red Sea becomes the rhythmic source of the stanzas, which surely washed over listeners like the waves heaped up at the blast of Yahweh's nostrils.

The rhythmic rowing of the enemy is present in the repetitive phrasing of their futile efforts: "I will pursue, I will overtake, I will divide the spoil. . . . I will draw my sword." But Yahweh blew his breath and the waves of the sea covered the enemy.

The second stanza changes in both its imagery and its rhythm, although it continues to celebrate the power of Yahweh to guide his people

---

[40]Ibid., 5. Here Carlson refers to the parameters of reception that Hans Robert Jauss has called "the horizon of expectation." See Hans Robert Jauss, *Toward an Aesthetic of Reception* (trans. Timothy Bahti; Minneapolis: University of Minnesota Press, 1982).

[41]Carlson, *The Haunted Stage*, 5.

across both time and space. In an unfolding display of Yahweh's power, we are led systematically across Philistia, Edom, and Moab, but now the imagery is dominated by shuddering, trembling, and collapsing, being swallowed by the underworld and struck dumb like a stone—images and tones associated with more earthbound phenomena such as quakes, storms, and other "natural" events.

Illumination

As each series of images is embodied by the performers, displayed to the spectators, and now usurped by the narrator, we sense an act falling into place. There are no surprises, no concerns that the ending will change from what we know it to be (like the expected movie conclusion where the hero will win out in the end). Each piece of the puzzle fits. Yahweh indeed is a mighty fortress, a savior, and a warrior whose power is majestic. There is no one like him, and he is a worker of wonders. The proclamation of divine kingship, identified by Dozeman in verse 18, stands as the performative final mark of punctuation to the song. Even time is shattered and consumed by Yahweh:

Song of the Sea (Divine Kingship)

The LORD will reign
for ever and ever.

Across the sea and across the land, the literary version of the Song of the Sea clearly establishes a singular sense of direction: the sanctuary of Yahweh's hands. This is the point of illumination. The time and space of human existence, filled as it is with trials, tribulation, enemies, and battles for power, are nothing compared with the divine power of Yahweh. In essence, the literary version of the song uses the iconic mode of presentation inherent in the preliterary version to effectively deepen the performative structure. The song provides the ghosted memory of the parade floats now passing by the reader in quick succession, each giving an ever-deepening reaffirmation, on the part of the reader, that Yahweh will reign forever and ever.

Conclusion: Cultural Memory

One final concept merits discussion to draw together, as it were, all aspects of the performative function (e.g., ghosting, illumination, etc.) of the Song of the Sea. The ghosted memory of the parade floats that pass before the reader or listener of the song constitutes an important expression of cultural memory. And it is this idea of cultural memory that highlights the function of the Song of the Sea. Consider the Song of the Sea in light of Assmann's statements, quoted in the last chapter, that "the concept of cultural memory comprises that body of re-usable texts, images, and rituals specific to each society in each epoch, whose 'cultivation' serves to stabilize and convey that society's self-image."[42] Upon this memory "the group bases its awareness of unity and particularity."[43]

The construction of a sense of group unity and particularity (a sense of "we") includes, as Assmann suggests, the following five characteristics of cultural memory:[44]

1. *The concretion of identity:* a particular set of information or store of knowledge from which the group derives its unity and distinctiveness. In the Song of the Sea, it is the recitation of the mighty acts of Yahweh during the exodus from Egypt.

2. *Ability to reconstruct:* the ability to understand the present in terms of the particularized view of the past common to the group. This is remarkably present in the Song of the Sea through the inclusion of events transpiring much later than the story line allows (vv. 12–18).

3. *Formation:* the crystallization of communicated (informal) meaning. In the Song of the Sea, it is fidelity to Yahweh.

4. *Organization:* the techniques, used or specialized, by which the ideas are communicated. The very popularity of the Song itself embodies the shared cultural memory.

5. *Obligation:* the values and obligations that are assumed by the group to maintain its normative self-image. In the Song of the Sea, the fidelity to Yahweh and the implied loyalty to Jerusalem (vv. 17–18) would constitute the norms and values.

Cultural memory is important in defining the group, in warding off a relativism that considers one perspective or identity as good as another.

---

[42]Jan Assmann, "Collective Memory and Cultural Identity" (trans. John Czaplicka), in "Cultural History/Cultural Studies," special issue, *New German Critique* 65 (spring–summer 1995): 125–33, here 132.
[43]Ibid.
[44]Ibid., 130–31.

Cultural memory is formative in education and normative in that it provides a structure by which to understand rules of conduct.[45] "Through its cultural heritage a society becomes visible to itself and to others."[46] The Song of the Sea provides a wonderful example of the encapsulation of Israel's cultural memory.

The poem of Exod 15:1–18 is the literary retelling of a song that had a long history in ancient Israel. Elements of plot and detailed consistency with the prose material preceding Exod 15:1–18 are matters of little consequence. The function of the song is not to further the narrative story of the exodus but to draw the reader (or listener) into the drama of the story by presenting a device whereby the reader (or listener) can "sing along" and so be part of the telling of the story. The song offers the chance for embodiment: physical and vocal participation. Like a parade welcoming home the troops or celebrating an important victory or like a holiday pageant celebrating the historical, mythological, or ritualized moments central to our cultural identity, the iconic nature of the song reminds us how important it is to be part of a past that defines our present and sets the stage for our future.

---

[45]The discussion of the Song of Moses (Deut 32) in ch. 6, below, will highlight the educational value of these iconic expressions of cultural memory.

[46]Assmann, "Collective Memory and Cultural Identity," 133.

Chapter 4: **The Song of Deborah** *(Judges 5:2–31)*

The Song of Deborah in Judg 5:2–31, like the Song of the Sea, is a very old performance composition. And like the Song of the Sea, the Song of Deborah has attracted the attention of literary critics who have subjected the song to analysis according to literary form (poetry)[1] or examined the contribution of the song to historical understanding.[2] This chapter, which builds upon the conclusions already provided by literary-critical studies, also considers the contribution of this twice-used song to an iconic presentation within the context of the Judges narrative account.

The Song of Deborah, as it appears in Judges, is one of the oldest intact pieces of literature in the Hebrew Bible; it can be dated to the late tenth or early ninth century B.C.E.[3] Its juxtaposition to a prose narrative (Judg 4)

---

[1] A good example is Richard Paterson, "Victory at Sea: Prose and Poetry in Exodus 14–15," *BSac* 161 (2004): 42–54. James Watts, *Psalm and Story: Inset Hymns in Hebrew Narrative* (JSOTSup 139; Sheffield: JSOT Press, 1992) has produced a fine examination of the poetic literature in prose contexts but gives little attention to the manner in which the prose narrator labels the poetic insertions. Watts writes, "The psalms in narrative contexts which are the subject of this essay all share a formal characteristic involving praise to God" (p. 15). Nevertheless, he includes in his study material identified by biblical narrators as prayers (Jonah and Hannah), a writing (Hezekiah), and words that were spoken (Moses, Daniel, and David).

[2] Baruch Halpern, "The Resourceful Israelite Historian: The Song of Deborah and Israelite Historiography," *HTR* 76 (1983): 379–401, examines the Song of Deborah as poem and searches for historical reliability.

[3] A. Globe, "The Literary Structure and Unity of the Song of Deborah," *JBL* 93 (1974): 493–512; M. Coogan, "A Structural and Literary Analysis of the Song of Deborah," *CBQ* 40 (1978): 143–66; David N. Freedman, *Pottery, Poetry, and Prophecy: Studies in Early Hebrew Poetry* (Winona Lake, Ind.: Eisenbrauns, 1980), 152n63; Halpern, "The Resourceful Israelite Historian," 379; J. Alberto Soggin,

describing the same event as that celebrated in the song has provided a
rare opportunity for literary critics to compare and contrast and to investigate the manner in which the prose writer dealt with his poetic source.
The presence of the song in a prose narrative also gives the performance
critic an opportunity to investigate the manner in which the prose writer
assimilated a performative event.

In his influential book on Hebrew poetry, Wilfred Watson wrote, "The
poet was in the first instance, *a performer* who sang in front of an audience"
(italics added).[4] Watson goes on to explain that the performer was bound
to his audience by identifiable conventions and a "special technique"[5] that,
in part at least, can be analyzed within the present literary version of the
song. Watson has articulated, perhaps unknowingly, the very essence of
performance from a theatrical perspective: "Theatre is man presenting
himself through the medium of activity."[6] The poet (performer) singing his
song (activity) before an audience is perhaps the oldest model we have for
understanding this complex relationship. Not only is the performer bound to
the audience by identifiable conventions; vice versa the audience is bound
to the performer by either accepting or rejecting those conventions and
by exerting their own influence on the conventions, changing them over
the course of time. In this reciprocal relationship, we witness the timeless
dynamic of a performer (formal or informal) making direct contact with
spectators in recognizable patterns.[7] The examination here of the Song of
Deborah will focus on this song[8] as a performed activity within the context
of *iconic* and *direct* modes of presentation, putting flesh onto the bones of
Watson's observation.

Judges (trans. John Bowden; OTL; Philadelphia: Westminster, 1981), 80–81, points
out that the song knows and uses the definite article and the use of expected forms
of plural constructs both point to a date slightly later than the Gezer calendar.

[4] Wilfred G. Watson, *Classical Hebrew Poetry: A Guide to Its Techniques* (JSOT-
Sup 26; Sheffield: JSOT Press, 1984), 68.

[5] Ibid., 68. It is unfortunate that although Watson makes this observation,
he fails to consider it seriously either in the choice of material for analysis or in
the method of analysis conducted.

[6] Bernard Beckerman, *Dynamics of Drama: Theory and Method of Analysis*
(New York: Drama Book Specialists, 1979), 211.

[7] Bernard Beckerman, *Theatrical Presentation: Performer, Audience, and Act*
(ed. Gloria Brim Beckerman and William Coco; New York: Routledge, 1990),
126.

[8] A song, as a medium of activity, relies heavily on its lyrics, or words set to
rhythm and music, as the means for connecting to an audience. And Lyric Poetry,
a historic genre, considered poetry to be sung. In the case of the Song of Deborah
in its prose context, "lyrics," "song," and "poem" are used here interchangeably.

The Song of Deborah in Its Prose Context

There are quite clear discrepancies between the prose account of Judges 4 and the song of Judges 5. The prose account plainly states that only two tribes (Naphtali and Zebulun) took part in the military engagement (Judg 4:6, 10), whereas the song lists Ephraim, Benjamin, Machir, and Issachar in addition to Naphtali and Zebulun as participants in the conflict (5:14–18).[9] Barak's location from which he was summoned to the fight is also in dispute (Kedesh in 4:6, Issachar in 5:15).

Working his way through these and other less obvious discrepancies, Halpern concludes that the prose account depends on the song. The differences between the prose and the song need not be considered evidence that the prose writer showed little regard for his source text (Judg 5). Rather, the discrepancies arise because the prose author of Judges 4 exercised high regard for the song and assumed a very literal method of interpretation of the song. The prose writer interpreted the poetic parallelism and poetic metaphor quite literally. When it was added to material taken from other traditional sources, the result was the discrepancies mentioned above. The ancient Israelite historian "applied close, narrow reading, not a little creative association, and a good deal of synthetic ingenuity to recover an epoch long gone."[10] Our task here is to investigate whether an understanding of the song as performed text can help us flesh out the nature of that narrow reading, creative association, and synthetic ingenuity.

We do well to begin our application of performance criticism to Judges 5 by remembering the purpose of the prose context in which the song now finds itself. Of that larger context, Walter Houston wrote what must surely come close to hitting the mark when he described the intent of the ancient prose writer: These writers "are not researching ancient texts to make what they can of them for a reconstruction of the past. They are

---

[9]Halpern, "The Resourceful Israelite Historian," 382, argues that actually ten tribes make up the fighting force found in the song, widening the gap between the two tribes (Zebulun and Naphtali) who alone fought in Judg 4.

[10]Ibid., 401. Elsewhere Halpern writes of the prose author, "He was almost exclusively dependant upon Judges 5 for particulars of the Deborah story. And his intentions were nothing but the best. But his tendency here and there was to seize on a given problem, on a certain question that cropped up, and to solve it by the most agonizingly literal attention to his source-text. He did not invent; he merely reified the text, treated it as though it were some legal deposit intended to be read as it was written down" (Baruch Halpern, "Doctrine by Misadventure: Between the Israelite Source and the Biblical Historian," in *The Poet and the Historian: Essays in Literary and Historical Biblical Criticism* [ed. Richard Elliott Friedman; Harvard Semitic Series 26; Chico, Calif.: Scholars Press, 1983], 49).

writing the story of their nation to confirm to them the faithfulness of
their God; it is a message which reflects upon the present (and indeed the
future) as much as upon the past. . . ."[11] Though not sufficient to explain
the differences between the song and its prose context, this idea of writing
in order to confirm the group's identity in relation to their God gives us a
point of entrance into understanding the function of the Song of Deborah
in Judges 5.

The prose writer of Judges 4 certainly must have concluded that
the inclusion of the Song of Deborah enhanced and lent authority to his
own prose narrative. In some fashion, the song was authoritative both
for the writer and for those whom he imagined as his readers. The Song
of Deborah carried with it a degree of social authority and influence
that the writer of Judges 4 deemed valuable to use for his own purpose.
The inclusion of the song of Judges 5 into the prose narrative makes
that prose more palatable and invests the prose with a greater degree of
authority. The appropriation of an authoritative text (the song) by the
writer of the prose submitted the authority of the song to the designs of
the prose writer.[12]

Halpern identifies as literary reification part of the appropriation
process that occurred with the song in Judges 5 as well as with the Song
of Moses in Exodus 15. Of these older texts—the songs as well as other
source material used by prose narrators—Halpern writes,

> Now, the words—even the letters—are a sacred truth. They generate ad hoc
> meanings, new, fresh truths, that are taken to be as valid as the ideas their
> authors meant to express. . . . Certain texts are routinely deprived of their
> metaphoric interstices, converted into hollow verbal shells to be filled at the
> interpreter's pleasure. They are depleted semantically, of internal relation-
> ships, nor indeed on contextual bearings; but on the reader's whimsy.[13]

What Halpern calls semantic depletion—the movement away from the
metaphorical and iconic—is also characteristic of the movement from a
performative mode of discourse to a literary mode of discourse. Indeed,
Watson, citing the earlier work of Albert Lord and Milman Parry, observes that the effect of writing on oral poetry is that it "tends to destroy

---

[11] Walter Houston, "Misunderstanding or Midrash? The Prose Appropriation
of Poetic Material in the Hebrew Bible," *ZAW* 109 (1997): 345. Houston prefers to
liken the interpretive strategies used by the prose writers to midrash, similar to
that employed by medieval rabbis.

[12] "When literature is suddenly authoritative, it becomes a matter of manipulation to read one's own agenda into it" (Halpern, "Doctrine by Misadventure," 57).

[13] Ibid., 61.

spontaneity."[14] What Halpern calls reification Watson refers to as a loss of spontaneity, and this is not simply or only a result of the religious appropriation of source texts but a function of movement from a performative mode of thought to a literary mode of discourse. And this movement from one to the other represents a fundamental conflict between the literary and the presentational mind. "We must remember that material meant to be presented is not necessarily connected by style or theme, 'but by the idea of common presentation.'"[15] Halpern's description of semantic depletion is significant to our understanding of the performative mode of thought. A performance, notes Beckerman, "gives us something and nothing to respond to. The 'something' is in the form of people doing extraordinary things with their voices, bodies, with the world around them. . . . The nothing we respond to is no less important. . . . It is a nothing that serves as a screen onto which we project our expectations and emotions."[16] The "something" we respond to is the iconic element in a performance or presentation. In the case of a song, it is the singer(s), their gestures, movements, facial expressions, and so on. And when the song incorporates or involves spectators, the line is blurred and the spectators become part of the iconic display. Depleting the iconic is indeed a movement away from the performative. The idea of the iconic will return later in our analysis of the Song of Deborah.

The recognition of different modes of discourse can provide another lens through which the contradictions between the prose and the lyric texts of Judges 4 and 5 can be viewed. Although it does seem altogether reasonable to conclude, with Halpern and others, that the prose writer knew and presupposed the lyric account, it is also likely that the "song assumes the reader's familiarity with the events which have just been narrated."[17] In other words, the purpose of both accounts needs to be considered when one evaluates the differences or similarities that they display. The narrative is designed to inform a readership and preserve a body of knowledge. The lyric text is designed to do something quite different. The song takes elements of the story and gives them "a dramatic force they lack in the body of the narrative."[18] The result "is not so much contradiction as thematic

---

[14] Watson, *Classical Hebrew Poetry*, 71.

[15] William Doan and Terry Giles, *Prophets, Power, and Performance: Performance Criticism of the Hebrew Bible* (New York: T&T Clark, 2005), 26. The internal quotation is from Beckerman, *Theatrical Presentation*, 91.

[16] Beckerman, *Theatrical Presentation*, 73.

[17] B. G. Webb, *The Book of Judges: An Integrated Reading* (JSOTSup 46; Sheffield: JSOT Press, 1972), 139.

[18] Ibid.

enhancement."[19] The enhancement in the lyric is particularly evident in the manner in which sexuality[20] and "a woman's point of view gives the psalm [the Song of Deborah] its distinctive feel."[21] Likewise the lyric depiction of Yahweh "adds considerable detail and color to the restrained depiction of divine actions in the narrative."[22] The "psalm does not repeat so much as supplement the prose account with added details, emotions, scenes and characterizations."[23]

The observations made by Watts and others above are important in analyzing the compositional relationship between the lyric and the prose. First Wellhausen[24] and now Halpern[25] and many others[26] argue that the prose is dependent upon the "poetic" versions of the Deborah story. Watts offers a two-stage compositional history, with the prose account mainly dependent upon the poetic version. Yet the prose and the poetic have different "thematic interests," and so an additional explanation must be offered for the inclusion of both prose and poetic in the Judges account.

> It is possible that the details derive from a common tradition behind the prose and poem, but the amount of borrowing makes the hypothesis of direct dependence [of the prose on the poetry] more likely. However, the strong sense of difference which still prevails between narrative and psalm makes it extremely unlikely that the narrative was composed as an explanation and companion-piece to the poem. Judges 4 is rather a reworking of the psalm's tradition for different thematic and narrative purposes. The reunion of the poetic and prose traditions was therefore probably secondary to the composition of the prose account. . . .

> The psalm's narrative role is best explained by presuming that the Song of Deborah was composed first, served as a basis for a prose account with different thematic interests, was later combined together with that narrative, and still later came to be incorporated as a single unit into the redactional framework of the book of Judges.[27]

---

[19] Watts, *Psalm and Story*, 89.

[20] M. Bal, *Murder and Difference: Gender, Genre, and Scholarship on Sisera's Death* (trans. M. Gumpert; Bloomington: Indiana University Press, 1988), 134.

[21] Watts, *Psalm and Story*, 88.

[22] Ibid., 91.

[23] Ibid., 92.

[24] F. Bleek, *Einleitung in das Alte Testament* (Berlin: Reimer, 1878), 187–89.

[25] Baruch Halpern, *The First Historians: The Hebrew Bible and History* (San Francisco: Harper & Row, 1988), 78–82; idem, "The Resourceful Israelite Historian."

[26] E.g., Peter Ackroyd, "The Composition of the Song of Deborah," *VT* 2 (1952): 160–62.

[27] Watts, *Psalm and Story*, 94–95.

Identifying and analyzing the "different thematic interests" found in lyric texts is the contribution made by performance criticism. Watts anticipates some of this analysis when he comments, "The use of the Song of Deborah in the context of the Deborah narrative enriches the latter with more explicit praise, celebration and ridicule than Hebrew prose narrative style usually contains."[28] In other words, the lyric enhances the whole by contributing a performative mode of thought to the Hebrew narrative. The lyric adds a sense of emotive awareness to the cognitive emphasis from the preceding narrative.[29] This emotional awareness revolves around the euphoric celebration of a military victory won against an imposing enemy only through the agency of a divine help whose presence is evident in the victory itself. But certainly, would not the same have been accomplished by a Song of Sampson or a Hymn of Gideon? Why a song here and why Deborah? Perhaps these questions are answered not by focusing attention on the singer but on the song and, more, on the listener. What about this song allowed an emotional connection to a receptive audience who presumably were tempted to sing along and join the chorus, adding their own voice to that of the narrator in Judges 4? These questions direct the next part of our investigation.

Song in Prose

The inclusion of poetry (including songs) within the context of a prose account is a technique that is attested throughout the ancient Near East.[30] Poetic prologues introduce the epics of Anzu and Erra and the Old Babylonian version of Gilgamesh. A poetic epilogue is to be found at the end of *Enlil and Ninlil*. For literature that mixes poetic pieces within the prose account, Watts suggests that we are best directed to ancient Egyptian literature if we are to find any close parallels to the same technique as that used in the biblical texts.[31] In particular, it is the Piye Stela that provides the nearest parallel to the Hebrew use of song in a prose account[32] because, as in both Judges 4 and Exodus 14, poetry in the Piye Stela is twice introduced as a song:

---

[28] Ibid., 96.

[29] Watts notes that "the psalm is used to conclude the episode on a note of high emotion in Judges 5" (ibid., 97).

[30] James Watts, "Song and the Ancient Reader," *Perspectives in Religious Studies* 22 (1995): 135–47.

[31] Ibid., 137.

[32] Miriam Lichtheim, *Ancient Egyptian Literature: A Book of Readings* (3 vols.; Los Angeles: University of California Press, 1973–1980), 3:66–80.

Piye Stela

And the troops of the Hare nome shouted and sang, saying:

> "How good is Horus at peace in his town,
> The Son of Re, Piye!
> You make for us a jubilee,
> As you protect the Hare nome!"[33]

Then at the end of the stela the song concludes:

This was their song of jubilation:

> "O mighty ruler, O mighty ruler,
> Piye, mighty ruler!
> You return having taken Lower Egypt,
> You made bulls into women!
> Joyful is the mother who bore you!
> The man who begot you!
> The valley dwellers worship her,
> The cow that bore the bull!
> You are eternal,
> Your might abides,
> O ruler of Thebes!"[34]

These examples from the Piye Stela are important, as our interest in the Song of Deborah is not simply the presence of poetry in prose but poetry identified by the prose writer as song. We want to know how song is used in prose contexts.[35] Watts senses the importance of this distinction:[36] "What do psalms achieve as narrative conclusions which prose alone can

---

[33] Ibid., 72–73.

[34] Ibid., 80.

[35] The presence of song and not just poetry in the prose is an important distinction to bear in mind, as most commentators merge the categories in their discussion of biblical texts. For performance critics, the distinction between poetry and song is vital, since the techniques used in the delivery of each are different and the social place of each is not the same.

[36] Watts is not, however, careful in the application of the distinction. He identifies Exod 15, Judg 5, and Jud 16 as well as 1 Sam 2 as "psalms used in narratives as victory songs" even though 1 Sam 2 is identified by the prose author as a prayer and so should be viewed as such and not as a song by the performance critic (Watts, "Song and the Ancient Reader," 139). He later includes Jon 2 and Dan 2 in the examination, falling prey to the same error, since both the Jon 2:3–20 and the Dan 2:20–23 texts are labeled by the prose writer as prayers and not songs (p. 140).

not?"[37] The answer, he suggests, is that "hymnic poetry in this position invites readers to join in the celebration, an effect which is especially strong in the victory songs of Exodus 15, Judges 5, and Judith 16."[38]

This intended purpose, an invitation for the reader to join in the celebration, is an open door for the application of performance criticism to better understand how the reader (or, better, listener) actualized the invitation to join the song.

The Power of Song

It is not uncommon for the Song of Deborah to be described as a "victory song."[39] This designation is useful, as it allows the reader to understand the literature within a genre of similar pieces that spans the ancient Near East. Perhaps, however, we can take the description a bit further and seek a more nuanced description, taking into account not only the content of the song but the intended function as well. In taking this next step, the work of folklorist R. Serge Denisoff may give us valuable direction. Denisoff, working with folksongs of protest, outlines a taxonomy and provides typological features of a larger group of songs—"songs of persuasion."[40] "Persuasion," writes Denisoff, "refers to the purposes of opinion and behavior formation that the songs were put to rather than to the intent of the composer."[41] This requires a functional analysis of the role of the song in the "group, movement, community and society in which it is enacted."[42] By definition, this functional analysis places emphasis on

---

[37] Ibid., 139.

[38] Ibid. It can be argued, however, that the same effect was not intended by the writer of 1 Samuel and therefore the poetry found in 1 Sam 2 was more aptly labeled a prayer and not a song by the prose writer.

[39] Ibid.; Mark Smith, "The Poetics of Exodus 15 and Its Position in the Book," in *Imagery and Imagination in Biblical Literature: Essays in Honor of Aloysius Fitzgerald, F.S.C.* (ed. Lawrence Boadt and Mark Smith; Catholic Biblical Quarterly Monograph Series 32; Washington, D.C.: Catholic Biblical Association of America, 2001), 24; Peter Craigie, "The Song of Deborah and the Epic of Tukulti-Ninurta," *JBL* 88 (1969): 253–65; Alan Hauser, "Two Songs of Victory: A Comparison of Exodus 15 and Judges 5," in *Directions in Biblical Hebrew Poetry* (ed. Elaine Follis; Sheffield: JSOT Press, 1987), 265–84; Richard Patterson, "Victory at Sea: Prose and Poetry in Exodus 14–15," *BSac* 161 (2004): 42–54.

[40] R. Serge Denisoff, "Songs of Persuasion: A Sociological Analysis of Urban Propaganda Songs," *Journal of American Folklore* 79, no. 314 (October–December 1966): 581–89.

[41] Ibid., 581.

[42] Ibid.

the content and usage of the material or its function in its historical and social setting. "Songs of persuasion can only be perceived functionally when they are performing the requirements of invoking some form of reaction or interaction."[43] Denisoff's suggestion as to the function of the songs is explored here concerning the Song of Deborah, for it is quite evident that the prose narrator has assumed, for the song that he has appropriated, a purpose and function different from the purpose and function envisioned by the composer of the song. And that purpose or function is probably not a narrative function.[44]

According to Denisoff, songs of persuasion regularly display one or more of the following six goals:[45]

1. The song attempts to solicit and arouse support and sympathy for a social or political movement.

2. The song reinforces the value structure of individuals who are active supporters of the social movement or ideology.

3. The song creates and promotes cohesion, solidarity, and high morale in an organization or movement supporting its worldview.

4. The song is an attempt to recruit individuals into joining a specific social movement.

5. The song invokes solutions to real or imagined social phenomena in terms of action to achieve a desired goal.

6. The song points to some problem or discontent in the society, usually in emotional terms.

In formulating these perceived goals for songs of persuasion, Denisoff notes that often the songs of protest assume a structure that is readily identifiable.[46] These structural prerequisites include features that speak specifically to the performability of the song: the song points to a perceived

---

[43] Ibid., 582.

[44] Contra Watts, *Psalm and Story*, 19, who consistently analyzes the poetic pieces for their narrative value or contribution to the plot: "Thus at least part of the psalm's narrative role is to repeat and supplement the prose account of chapter 4" (p. 85).

[45] Denisoff, 582.

[46] See John Greenway, *American Folksongs of Protest* (Philadelphia: University of Philadelphia Press; London: Oxford University Press, 1953); Edith Fowke and Joe Glazer, *Songs of Work and Freedom* (Chicago: Labor Education Division,

problem-situation in the social system, uses simplistic musical structure to facilitate attention and participation, and is familiar to audience in order to facilitate ease of communication.

"One of the major functions of the song of persuasion is to create solidarity or a 'we' feeling in a group or movement to which the song is verbally directed."[47] Songs of persuasion stress unity in the conditions of the moment and a projected unity for the future as the result of struggle. Strength comes from this unity, a strength that is often expressed explicitly in the lyrics of the song. "The need for solidarity is essential, especially for an organization espousing views deemed by other sectors of the society to be subversive or radical, if that organization is to survive."[48] In victory songs, like those so identified in the Hebrew Bible, this "we" emphasis, or sense of solidarity, is celebrated as the result of winning the struggle. But the need for persuasion continues in order to solidify and institutionalize the group feeling. This persuasion that solidifies can also be applied to the process of attracting new members or new believers who wish to experience the exultation of participation in either the struggle or the victory. In other words, the song extends participation in the event to a new group or a new generation by creating solidarity with the original actors in the drama. The simple choruses currently popular among evangelical Christian churches illustrate this idea well. And they easily fit Denisoff's description. They are simple, become quickly familiar, and articulate the perceived remedy of some personal or social problem.

Denisoff argues that "the manner by which a song of persuasion fulfills the functions based on the prerequisites cited provides a guideline by which to identify and categorize songs of persuasion."[49] The functions, he suggests, are achieved by either magnetic songs or rhetorical songs. The magnetic song is meant to persuade individuals to support or join a particular movement. It draws people in and binds them together. An example outside the folk song tradition but applicable to our context might be "Onward Christian Soldiers." In the folk tradition, a good example would be "Give Peace a Chance." Both are songs that make explicit reference to certain goals and values, establishing a sense of a group mind-set. Magnetic songs are also constructed "to create social cohesion or a feeling of solidarity among membership of a social movement or specific world view."[50]

Roosevelt University, 1960); and Archie Green, "A Discography (LP) of American Labor Union Songs," *New York Folklore Quarterly* 17 (1961): 187–93.

[47] Denisoff, "Songs of Persuasion," 583.
[48] Ibid.
[49] Ibid., 584.
[50] Ibid.

The rhetorical song is "written to identify or describe some social condition, but one which offers no explicit ideological or organizational solutions, such as affiliation with an action or movement."[51] Such songs pose questions or suggest resistance to certain social institutions. They may be songs about war, destruction, or social and political organizations without referring to specific wars or organizations. Like the 1960s war song "Eve of Destruction," the time and place of performance become the specific context for the song's meaning.

As Denisoff points out about modern protest and propaganda songs (two types of songs of persuasion), rhetorical songs can be further subdivided into the universal and the specific. Universal rhetorical songs can transcend the specific moment of composition, whereas specific songs of persuasion deal with singular events, usually bound to them through explicit references in the lyrics.

"Magnetic songs of persuasion follow several structural patterns with numerous deviations, frequently contingent on the needs and the type of movement employing the songs." Useful to our analysis of the Song of Deborah is one of the structures found in propaganda songs from the folk tradition, the *situation-remedy* structure. This structure is a classic form stating or describing a situation in negative terms. "Stating a situation in negative terms, the performer customarily states the solution to the social condition in the final verses: organize a union, join a movement, sit-down, or sit-in."[52]

A basic pattern of the situation-remedy structure includes the following significant features:

1. stating a situation in negative terms (problem);

2. "transfer," or referring to an authoritative source (religion, tradition, government) in order to validate the problem;

3. provide the remedy.[53]

Denisoff provides a different focus to the analysis of songs such as the Song of Deborah than that focus often guiding the analysis conducted by biblical scholars. This function of promoting group identity is quite different from the proposed function of plot contribution or narrative development, which provides the foundation to the type of analysis conducted

---

[51] Ibid.
[52] Ibid., 585.
[53] Ibid., 585–86.

by Watts, who analyzes the Song of Deborah "in terms of the psalm's contribution to the plot, its verbal and thematic links to the prose, and its effect on characterization."[54] Watts's analysis is thorough and helpful. His investigation seems quite appropriate for scrutinizing poetic insertions into prose contexts and provides a platform from which to extend the investigation into the insertion of lyrics into prose contexts. But we now need to go further. We need to investigate dimensions of reader identity, reader affect, mode of presentation, and the performer/spectator relationship. These analytical concepts, common in theatre studies, will be brought to bear on the investigation of these lyric remnants of oral performances now embedded in prose literature.[55]

Accepting the premise by Denisoff, that this kind of song if persuasion is intended to involve the listeners in the reality of the song, we are now poised to ask, How does this reality participation occur? Carlson's suggestions may be helpful. He has made an in-depth and compelling argument for the ways in which traditional theatre histories employ the recycling of material to "encourage particular structures of reception in its potential audiences."[56] Text, the actors' bodies, the production of plays, and the theatre spaces all participate in this recycling, or ghosting, in which spectators encounter the identical thing they have encountered before, but in a different context.[57]

> Theatre as a simulacrum of the cultural and historical process itself, seeking to depict the full range of human actions within their physical context, has always provided society with the most tangible records of its attempts to understand its own operations. It is the repository of cultural memory, but, like the memory of each individual, it is also subject to continual adjustment and modification as the memory is recalled in new circumstances and contexts. The present experience is always ghosted by previous experiences and associations while these ghosts are simultaneously shifted and modified by the processes of recycling and recollection.[58]

In the case of the Song of Deborah, even though we are not investigating a traditional theatrical event or an event that would fall under the normative experience of traditional theatre, we are investigating an event that moved from an oral, performative tradition to the literary tradition of the Hebrew Bible, a literary tradition that was itself dependent on oral performance in

---

[54] Watts, *Psalm and Story*, 82.

[55] Working definitions of these terms are provided in the glossary of Doan and Giles, *Prophets, Performance, and Power*.

[56] Marvin Carlson, *The Haunted Stage: The Theatre as Memory Machine* (Ann Arbor: University of Michigan Press, 2001), 16.

[57] Ibid., 7.

[58] Ibid., 2.

what was essentially an illiterate culture. Memory is a key component of the communicative process, especially in a preliterate society.

As Carlson notes, many scholars have recognized the centrality of memory to the development of texts, particularly the dramatic text.

> Derrida and others have argued that all texts are in fact haunted by other texts and can be best understood as weavings together of preexisting textual material—indeed, that all reception is based upon this intertextual dynamic. . . . I think it still may be argued that the dramatic text is distinguished in part by the extent and specificity of its relationship to previous texts, literary and nonliterary. Among all literary forms it is the drama preeminently that has always been centrally concerned not simply with the telling of stories but with the retelling of stories already known to its public.[59]

Carlson argues that this specific kind of intertextuality found in the drama goes beyond the "usual patterns that intertextuality considers." "It involves the dramatist in the presentation of a narrative that is haunted in almost every aspect—its names, its character relationships, the structure of its action, even small physical or linguistic details—by a specific previous narrative."[60]

Inclusion of the song, it can be argued, makes earlier performance of the song part of the sacred truth,[61] identified by Halpern, since its inclusion in the text is haunted, in Carlson's terms, by the earlier performances or singing of the song that the text invokes. The prose and the lyric versions do not stand in opposition to each other; rather, they represent the two traditions simultaneously: the performance tradition and the emerging literary tradition. The past and the present are reified by the literary process of inclusion, and thereby the ghost of the past's performance is made available to the readers and the listeners of the present as well as the future.

Iconic Presentation and the Song of Deborah

Many pre-Renaissance forms of drama placed an emphasis on drama as demonstration (iconic presentation), particularly in Western forms of drama from the Greeks through the Middle Ages. These dramas of demonstration were primarily centered on holidays and days of celebration, organized gatherings of the citizenry around ideas of social identity or, in the case of medieval liturgical drama, an idea of God and the church. The result was a variety of shows of glorification: parades, contests, pageants, cycles, and even sports contests.

---

[59] Ibid., 17.
[60] Ibid.
[61] Halpern, "Doctrine by Misadventure," 61. See quote above in note 10.

Whether David dances his triumph in the streets or the Romans bring home their spoils of victory, whether Renaissance princes assert their authority in magnificent entries or modern states vaunt their patriotism on revolutionary anniversaries, parades and processions are communal demonstrations of universal appeal. As shows, they are also a key to an entire aspect of performance that is insufficiently recognized.[62]

As established in the previous chapter, performances that emphasize display, demonstration, exemplification, and celebration are examples of an iconic mode of presentation. These kinds of shows celebrate "past and present, the past glory, suffering, and achievements of the people, together with their present unity and idealism. In that sense the show confirms established values, and it does so by mere demonstration."[63]

Iconic modes of performance have a number of features that are found in Denisoff's taxonomy of the features of songs of persuasion. Songs of persuasion, victory songs, and songs of celebration all constitute some kind of "showing," or performative structure. By their nature they produce a kind of "widespread sharing" that is derived, as in the case of the original singers of these songs, from that original poet/performer and the audience who witnessed and participated in the song.[64] Iconic modes of presentation, particularly those emphasizing demonstration and celebration, present a kind of "glorified stasis" or display of being whose focus is to "endow [the show] with all the glorification that a community is capable of bestowing."[65] As already mentioned earlier, Beckerman asserts that there are three distinguishing features of iconic presentation. First, the performer stresses being rather than becoming. Second, the action that is performed involves less the overcoming of temporal resistance and more the ritual enactment of prescribed movements. Finally, the effect produced by the demonstrative event is illumination more than catharsis—a sense of an act falling into place.[66]

Outlined below are the ways in which the Song of Deborah displays the three primary features of iconic presentation and how the song also incorporates the features of songs of persuasion. The powerful poetic and metaphoric images of the song merge historical event with enacted celebration and provide the focal action centered on willingly offering oneself to the Lord.

---

[62] Beckerman, *Theatrical Presentation*, 43.
[63] Ibid.
[64] Ibid., 45.
[65] Ibid.
[66] Ibid., 55.

1. *Stresses Being Over Becoming:* The work reinforces the value structure of individuals who support the movement or ideology; it creates and promotes cohesion and solidarity; and it points to some
problem or discontent, usually in emotional terms.

In the Song of Deborah: We find multiple references to the Lord, God of
Israel; multiple references to the people of Israel; references to those "who
offer themselves willingly" (NRSV) to the Lord; praise for the tribes who
participated; praise for the leadership of those who participated; as well as
reference to those who were cursed for not participating.

2. *Ritual Enactment:* The work has a simplistic structure to facilitate
attention and participation and a familiar construction in order to
facilitate ease of communication. It extends participation by creating solidarity with the original actors in the drama and repeats the
motif of strength in cohesion.

In the Song of Deborah: We find a rhythmic structure enhanced by
repetition of chosen words and phrases; the naming of clans and individuals familiar to the spectators; the use of a first-person singer to engage the
spectators with commands such as, "tell of it you who ride . . . , you who
sit . . . Awake, awake Deborah! . . . Arise Barak" (NRSV); and a narrative
progression of events already known to the spectators.

3. *Illumination Over Catharsis:* The work institutes the creation of a
solidarity, or "we" feeling through the promotion of group identity.
It projects a sense of unity for the future as well as a celebration as
a result of winning the struggle. Such a text states the situation,
transfers an authoritative source, and provides the remedy.

In the Song of Deborah: As a counterpart to Judg 4:1–24 (and to what
is already a familiar series of events) the song does not move readers or
hearers to a new conclusion. Rather it projects unity for the future as in the
notice, "So perish all your enemies, O LORD! But may your friends be like
the sun as it rises in its might" (NRSV). And it provides reinforcement of
how the Lord triumphs over oppressors.

In addition to these three distinguishing features, other aspects of
iconic modes of presentation have specific application to our analysis of
the Song of Deborah. As Beckerman notes, iconic modes of presentation
represent that aspect of all types of show processes "that seeks to con-
cretize itself, to resist change, to make itself into a permanent emblem."

Indeed, Beckerman argues, this tendency to seek concretization is most fully expressed in shows of celebration, which would include victory songs and other songs of persuasion. "One way in which the concretizing impulse works is by stressing the act as illustration or example . . . by framing the focal action within a celebratory structure."[67] The opening declaration of the Song of Deborah is a good example of such a structure: "Then Deborah and Barak son of Abinoam sang on that day, saying: When locks are long in Israel, when the people offer themselves willingly—bless the LORD!" (Judg 5:1–2 NRSV). We are prepared with these opening words for the illustration and celebration of victory to follow. A contemporary example of this is when a master of ceremonies or narrator addresses the spectators with "Ladies and gentlemen," similar to what we commonly encounter in the biblical prophetic oracles, "Thus says the LORD." Simply put, we are prepared for the presentation to prove and confirm what we already believe.

Direct Presentation

Chapter 2, on the Book of Jashar, introduced the significance of direct presentation as a tool of performance criticism. As the chart illustrates, the Song of Deborah provides direct presentation to the reading or listening audience; in essence, by the inclusion of the song, we (readers/spectators) are prepared to participate in what can be called direct presentation, which "is an open exchange between performer and spectator."[68] In iconic modes of presentation, direct forms of presentation by actors can display a broad range of styles. Historically, this range includes nondramatic prologues and epilogues, narrators, single and mass choral ensembles, and even "characters" who suddenly appear to speak the apology of the author directly to those gathered. "What is normally called dramatic presentation is actually a form of direct presentation. The performer acknowledges the presence of the audience and presents the show making that acknowledgment explicit."[69] Direct contact, argues Beckerman, can involve groups as well as individuals. "Large groups may be subdivided into smaller units that bear a hierarchical link to the whole. This is especially true in shows of glorification."[70]

---

[67] Ibid., 46.
[68] Beckerman, *Theatrical Presentation,* 111.
[69] Ibid.
[70] Ibid., 113.

Conclusion

"Then sang Deborah and Barak." With these words we are attuned to the singer in a performed "now," or present, that transports us through the past by means of direct presentation. The song itself, functioning as a parade or pageant, unfolds for spectators, making them (us) participants in a shared enactment of identity. The first-person "I" used throughout the song creates and sustains the immediacy of performance, granting the singer authority over time by establishing a spatial presence for the unfolding celebration: "to the LORD I will sing, I will make melody to the LORD, the God of Israel" (NRSV). The singer, by gathering the spectators-participants together, creates a space in which a demonstration of the Lord God of Israel's might and power can be celebrated and shared. The song is the performance structure for creating the show of celebration and involving the spectators as both spectators and participants in a complex exchange of direct contact.

In the case of the Song of Deborah, we have both rhythmic and, implicitly, kinetic precision where all (kings, travelers, peasantry, kin, and chiefs) are in service to the glorious image. "So on that day God subdued King Jabin of Canaan before the Israelites. Then the hand of the Israelites bore harder and harder on King Jabin of Canaan, until they destroyed King Jabin of Canaan" (4:23–24 NRSV).

Chapter 5: **The Song of Asaph** *(1 Chronicles 16:8–36)*

In many important ways, the songs of the Hebrew Bible exist at the boundary, or on the edge (at least according to categories common today).[1] In that they bring into the narrative text a memory and an event from the past, the songs exist on the boundary of past and present and the boundary of oral and literate. These boundaries and their permeation are important in the formation of the biblical text, at least as we know it today, and are receiving renewed attention from biblical scholars. As seen in the preceding chapters, new questions are being asked about the thought processes that went into the composition of the performed songs of ancient Israel and the placement of these songs into a narrative context. Performance criticism is an emerging methodology that can help shape questions guiding our investigation of these boundary texts. And just like the texts being considered, performance criticism is a boundary methodology. It is the examination of the conventions, content, structure, and style of generally oral presentation, which may be transferred to a written medium and leave characteristic marks on resultant literature. Performance criticism readily borrows insights derived from, for example, form criticism and rhetorical criticism as well as from performance and theatre studies. Central to a performance-critical investigation is concern with a *performance mode of thought,* that is, a particular type of orality in which "oral performances were conveyed and compositional characteristics of which still reside embedded in the written literature."[2] The examina-

---

[1] An earlier version of this chapter appeared as William Doan and Terry Giles, "The Song of Asaph: A Performance Critical Analysis of 1 Chronicles 16:8–36," *CBQ* 70 (2008): 29–43. A translation of the Song of Asaph is found at the end of this chapter.

[2] William Doan and Terry Giles, *Prophets, Performance, and Power: Performance Criticism of the Hebrew Bible* (New York: T&T Clark, 2005), 5.

tion of the Song of Asaph in 1 Chr 16:8–36 begins by considering further what is meant by this performance mode of thought.

Performance Mode of Thought

Before we proceed to 1 Chronicles, a word must be said as a reminder about the nature of performance criticism in the world of drama and literature studies. As pointed out in chapter 1, above, theatre and performance studies scholars have acknowledged the historical tendency to use terms such as "drama" and "dramatic" in primarily literary-oriented ways, referring to traditional structural elements that have become associated with various dramatic-literary traditions from the Greeks to the present. These structural elements, such as conflict, dialogue, and character, tend to point primarily toward an Aristotelian understanding of the drama, which, indeed, is a literary perspective. It is important to remind ourselves, however, these terms are being used here as part of a medium-oriented discussion, one where "drama" and "theatre" are understood in terms of performed or performative concepts. "It could, moreover, be argued that the entire traditional genre divisions of Epics, Lyrics, and Drama is a convenient late imposition on early classical texts, the Old Testament included, which may—and do—comprise elements of all three literary genres in a much less neatly organized way."[3]

Shimon Levy encourages us to see dramatic structures in all sorts of literary genres. Indeed, "drama" is best understood as an event and not a particular literary form or text. These dramatic structures that Levy refers to are the stuff of a performance mode of thought. The notion that "drama" is best understood as an event is fundamental to a performance-critical methodology. When we identify and analyze elements of "drama" from this perspective, different questions are asked, new thoughts are entertained. "Everything changes, however, if we stop to think of genre as not entirely unlike rhyme, say, or ambiguity, as a feature, that is, whose primary interest for readers or audiences is as something that *happens* to us in a poem or play, *as* it happens."[4]

In both Levy's and Goldman's notions of drama and theatre, moving to a "medium-oriented discussion" or to a focus on the experience of audience/readers in terms of what happens to them, as it happens to them, we find an understanding of "drama" as a nexus of social and inter-

---

[3]Shimon Levy, *The Bible as Theatre* (Portland, Oreg.: Sussex Academic, 2002), 5.

[4]Michael Goldman, *On Drama: Boundaries of Genre, Borders of Self* (Ann Arbor: University of Michigan Press, 2000), 3.

personal interactions, not just a thing such as a text or a place. Eli Rozik posits a similar definition of theatre-as-medium: "Being a medium (i.e., a system of signification and communication) *theatre is an instrument of thinking, articulating, and communicating thoughts to others*, similar to and no less efficient than natural language. The theatrical experience should thus be conceived in terms of communal thinking"[5] (italics added). In understanding "drama" as a medium, we are not free of the problems of genre and literary form, but we simply do not start there. As Goldman urges, we need to think of "drama" in terms of its connections to life, "especially with some features of life we're likely to regard as intensely difficult, issues that bear on self and meaning, on persons and texts, on identity and community."[6]

And so performance criticism is concerned with the investigation of a "system of signification and communication," that is, a performance mode of thought. There are places in the Hebrew Bible where this kind of orality is most evident. One such example, found scattered throughout the Hebrew Bible, is the set of twice-used songs. These songs, composed earlier, sung and performed as pieces in their own right, have been appropriated by narrative writers and inserted in strategic places within narrative compositions.[7] When a narrator so employs a song, more than the lyrics are appropriated. The narrator also appropriates the social place and influence—that is, the performative power—of the song to enhance the power of his own composition. Narrators borrow these songs in order to add persuasive power to their own narrative compositions. The nature of these songs makes them prime candidates for performance criticism examination. The Song of Asaph is one such song.

The Composite Song of Asaph: 1 Chronicles 16:8–36

The Chronicler skillfully uses the Song of Asaph to achieve a desired effect. It adds to the surrounding narrative a powerful element of audience formation. This chapter will examine the manner in which the Chronicler used the Song of Asaph to augment his narrative. It will survey some of the Chronicler's editorial changes and the effect of these changes in audience formation. And it will consider the special iconic role played by the song in the Chronicler's audience development.

---

[5] Eli Rozik, *The Roots of Theatre: Rethinking Ritual and Other Theories of Origin* (Iowa City: University of Iowa Press, 2002), 22.

[6] Goldman, *On Drama*, 7.

[7] Ralph W. Klein, "Psalms in Chronicles," *Currents in Theology and Mission* 32 (2005): 264–75, here 264.

The Song of Asaph derives its name from the account of its commissioning. The song, commissioned by David and performed by Asaph and his brothers (1 Chr 16:7), is a composite drawn from Ps 105:1–15 (for 1 Chr 16:8–22), Ps 96:1b–13a (for 1 Chr 16:23–33), and Ps 106:1, 47–48 (for 1 Chr 16:34–36).[8] Since we possess not only the song as presented by the Chronicler but the sources of the song as well, we have an opportunity to examine how the Chronicler's use of selected material changed the lyrics by inserting them into a prose context.[9] Further, since the Chronicler borrowed the narrative from 1 Samuel 5–6, we can also observe how the narrative material was changed when the lyrics were inserted.[10]

This analysis employs two working assumptions about the Chronicler. The first is that the Chronicler composed most likely in the fourth century

---

[8]See J. M. Meyers, *1 Chronicles* (AB 12; New York: Doubleday, 1965), 121; J. A. Loader, "Redaction and Function of the Chronistic 'Psalm of David,'" in *Studies in the Chronicler* (ed. W. C. van Wyk; Johannesburg: Weeshuipers, 1976), 69–75; H. G. M. Williamson, *1 and 2 Chronicles* (New Century Bible; Grand Rapids: Eerdmans, 1982), 32; Sara Japhet, *I and II Chronicles* (OTL; Louisville: Westminster John Knox, 1993), 316; R. Mark Shipp, "'Remember His Covenant Forever': A Study of the Chronicler's Use of the Psalms," *Restoration Quarterly* 35 (1993): 31–39.

[9]James Watts, *Psalm and Story: Inset Hymns in Hebrew Narrative* (JSOTSup 139; Sheffield: JSOT Press, 1992), 164, presents a clear case for the Chronicler as author of the song. The unity of the song in Chronicles is rarely challenged. Martin Noth, *The Chronicler's History* (trans. H. G. M. Williamson; JSOTSup 50; Sheffield: Sheffield Academic, 1987), 35, however, considers vv. 5–38 and 41–42 secondary, and Peter Ackroyd, *I and II Chronicles, Ezra, Nehemiah* (London: SCM, 1973), 64–65, does not think that the Chronicler arranged or composed the song.

[10]The Chronicler is not at all shy about borrowing from other writers. In addition to the extensive borrowing from Samuel and Kings, the genealogical material in 1 Chr 1 comes from Genesis; 1 Chr 4:28–33 from Josh 15 and 19; 6:54–81 from Josh 21; and 2 Chr 36:22–23 from Ezra 1:1–3. In addition, it is widely recognized that the Chronicler used extrabiblical sources. John Kleinig states that "the Chronicler uses extra biblical sources much more freely and creatively than is the case with the biblical sources, which may indicate that he distinguishes them in their status and authority" ("Recent Research in Chronicles," *Currents in Research: Biblical Studies* 2 [1994]: 43–76, here 48). Graeme Auld, however, contends that the Chronicler's use of Samuel, though possible, is not very likely ("What If the Chronicler Did Use the Deuteronomistic History?" *Biblical Interpretation* 8 [2000]: 137–50, here 149). See H. G. M. Williamson, "History," in *It Is Written—Scripture Citing Scripture: Essays in Honour of Barnabas Lindars, SSF* (ed. D. A. Carson and H. G. M. Williamson; Cambridge: Cambridge University Press, 1988), 25–38; Kai Peltonen, "Function, Explanation, and Literary Phenomena: Aspects of Source Criticism as Theory and Method in the History of Chronicles Research," in *The Chronicler as Author: Studies in Text and Texture* (ed. M. Patrick Graham and Steven McKenzie; JSOTSup 263; Sheffield: Sheffield Academic, 1999), 18–69.

B.C.E.,[11] although the arguments made here hold equally well for a date from the sixth through the fourth century. The second is that the psalms used by the Chronicler were in the public domain; that is, they were songs that people knew and recognized. The Song of Asaph is a composite, formed by a skillful combination of three separate source psalms. The psalms, including those used by the Chronicler, were not intended primarily for private consumption but were, by nature, public in design. Consequently, although it can never be proven one way or another, it does seem most plausible that if the Chronicler knew these psalms, others did too and that his audience would have recognized any changes made by the Chronicler to the psalms. The Chronicler is acting as a member of a community and, through selection and editing of material, is, in many ways, creating a new Davidic drama composed of existing genres, forms, and material—a drama whose boundaries are fluid and that requires communal participation and acknowledgment. Goldman, when talking about the nature of drama, acknowledges this same fluidity: "While genre is clearly about boundaries, the sensing of boundaries, it seems also to be the case that it's about the permeation of boundaries."[12] Indeed, as Tamara Eskenazi observes, "Chronicles replicates the song and makes the reader a participant in the celebration. What we have is surely not summary, perhaps not even a depiction of a scene, but a reenactment."[13] In the case of 1 Chronicles 16,

---

[11] Most scholars date the Chronicler's work to between 350 and 300 B.C.E. See Kleinig, "Recent Research in Chronicles," 46; Trent Butler, "A Forgotten Passage from a Forgotten Era 1 (Chr. XVI 8–36)," *VT* 28 (1978): 142–50, here 146; Japhet, *I and II Chronicles*, 27–28; Simon De Vries, *1 and 2 Chronicles* (Forms of Old Testament Literature 11; Grand Rapids: Eerdmans, 1989), 16–17. The same point could be made, perhaps even more forcefully, if 1 Chr 10 to 2 Chr 36 was composed earlier in stages, beginning at the end of the sixth century B.C.E., as suggested by William Schniedewind, "The Chronicler as an Interpreter of Scripture," in *The Chronicler as Author: Studies in Text and Texture* (ed. M. Patrick Graham and Steven McKenzie; JSOTSup 263; Sheffield: Sheffield Academic, 1999), 158–80, here 159; James Newsome, "Toward a New Understanding of the Chronicler and His Purposes," *JBL* 94 (1975): 4–18; and Frank Moore Cross, "A Reconstruction of the Judean Restoration," *JBL* 94 (1975): 4–18, repr. in *From Epic to Canon: History and Literature in Ancient Israel* (Baltimore: Johns Hopkins University Press, 1998), 167–69. See David N. Freedman, "The Chronicler's Purpose," *CBQ* 23 (1961): 436–42. William Rudolph posits a date of composition ca. 400 B.C.E. with additions, including some in 1 Chr 15–16 to the Maccabean period ("Problems of the Book of Chronicles," *VT* 4 [1954]: 401–9, here 402).

[12] Goldman, *On Drama*, 27.

[13] Tamara Eskenazi, "A Literary Approach to Chronicles' Ark Narrative in 1 Chronicles 13–16," in *Fortunate the Eyes That See: Essays in Honor of David Noel Freedman in Celebration of His Seventieth Birthday* (ed. A. Beck et al.; Grand Rapids: Eerdmans, 1995), 258–74, here 269.

the Chronicler's edits and narrative inventions, by drawing on psalmic material, narrative material, and historical material to create a new experience for hearers and readers, facilitate a permeation of the emerging boundaries of literary forms. This permeation of boundaries creates the kind of fluidity associated with the imaginative power of performance, particularly of drama, where past, present, and future are free to create the here and now of a shared experience.

Several outlines of the composite song appearing in 1 Chronicles 16 have been proposed.[14] That adopted here is presented by Mark Throntveit:[15]

> I. Thanksgiving hymn (vv. 8–34)
>   A Introductory calls to thanksgiving (vs. 8–13)
>   B For past judgments (vs. 14–22)
>   C For present sovereignty (vs. 23–29)
>   B′ For future rule (vs. 30–33)
>   A′ Concluding call to thanksgiving (vs. 34)
>
> II. Concluding liturgy (vs. 35–36a)
>   A Liturgical summons (vs. 35a)
>   B Petition (vs. 35b)
>   B′ Benediction (vs. 36a)
>   A′ Congregational response (v. 36b)

This outline recognizes the use of key words and phrases found within the song as well as the concentric structure that is also characteristic of 1 Chronicles 16 as a whole. Although dependent upon three psalms also found in the Hebrew Psalter, the composite nature of the Chronicler's song gives it a structure and message all its own.[16] The reconfiguration of the material borrowed from the three source songs is skillful and shows the same intentional care that the Chronicler's use of source material demonstrates elsewhere.[17] From Psalm 105, the Chronicler takes only the

---

[14]Mark Throntveit, "Songs in a New Key: The Psalmic Structure of the Chronicler's Hymn (1 Chr 16:8–36)," in *A God So Near: Essays on Old Testament Theology in Honor of Patrick D. Miller* (ed. Brent Strawn and Nancy Bowen; Winona Lake, Ind.: Eisenbrauns, 2003), 153–70. The chiastic structure proposed by Throntveit commends itself, since the same structure can also be found incorporated in various narrative passages of Chronicles. See Leslie Allen, "Kerygmatic Units in 1 and 2 Chronicles," *JSOT* 41 (1988): 21–36.

[15]Throntveit, "Songs in a New Key," 168.

[16]Butler, "A Forgotten Passage from a Forgotten Era," 143.

[17]See N. Na'aman, "Sources and Redaction in the Chronicler's Genealogies of Asher and Ephraim," *JSOT* 49 (1991): 99–111; Andrew Hill, "Patchwork Poetry or Reasoned Verse? Connective Structures in 1 Chronicles XVI," *VT* 33 (1983): 97–101; John Kleinig, *The Lord's Song: The Basis, Function, and Significance of Choral Music in Chronicles* (JSOTSup 156; Sheffield: JSOT Press, 1993), 91–95; Steven

beginning, a call to praise and statements of God's protection. These affirmations of God's protection in the psalm are applied to the patriarchs and to those participating in the exodus from Egypt. The Chronicler, however, does not include those distant figures in the song but instead applies the assurances of God's protection to "a new generation, few in number, wandering between world powers, but armed with God's eternal covenant and his warning to the nations not to harm his designated leaders."[18] The selection from the second psalm used by the Chronicler continues the process of character formation. The Chronicler takes a selection from Psalm 96 that presses home Yahweh's universal claim of sovereignty among all the nations. This call for the whole earth to sing to Yahweh must certainly have given confidence to the postexilic few of Jerusalem, the "anointed ones" (1 Chr 16:22 NRSV), to join the chorus and offer praise to Yahweh for his protection over them and his "prophets" (i.e., their leaders). The third selection used by the Chronicler to conclude the rendition is taken from a psalm that concludes the fourth book of the Psalter. Psalm 106 is full of warnings stemming from the negative examples provided by generations of those who had forgotten God, their savior (Ps 106:21), and had despised the pleasant land (v. 24) or who had angered Yahweh (v. 32). Psalm 106 concludes with a plea for help and a call for praise. Skillfully the Chronicler uses this psalm to create a powerful, if muted, conclusion to the newly crafted song. The note of praise and thanksgiving that dominated the middle part of the Chronicler's song changes to a plea for deliverance and the recognition that dangerous enemies are all around. Quite out of character if placed in the context of the Chronicler's narrative about David's triumphal Jerusalem, this plea makes perfect sense as a description of the postexilic few.[19]

In addition to the changes effected by the Chronicler's selective and partial use of source psalms, he made subtle changes in the borrowed texts themselves.[20] These changes indicate that the Chronicler's use of the

---

McKenzie, "The Chronicler as Redactor," in *The Chronicler as Theologian: Essays in Honor of Ralph W. Klein* (ed. M. Patrick Graham, Steven McKenzie, and Gary Knoppers; JSOTSup 371; New York: T&T Clark, 2003), 70–90; William Schniedewind, "The Chronicler as an Interpreter of Scripture," in *The Chronicler as Author: Studies in Text and Texture* (ed. M. Patrick Graham and Steven McKenzie; JSOTSup 263; Sheffield: Sheffield Academic, 1999), 158–80.

[18] Butler, "A Forgotten Passage from a Forgotten Era," 144.

[19] J. P. Weinberg, *The Citizen-Temple Community* (trans. D. L. Smith-Christopher; JSOTSup 151; Sheffield: JSOT Press, 1992).

[20] Butler, "A Forgotten Passage from a Forgotten Era," 142, identifies forty-five "textual differences between Chronicles and Pss cv 1–15, xcvi 1b–13a, and cvi 1, 47f., on which it depends."

song was quite intentional and that it was important to get it right if the desired effect was to be achieved.[21] And it does seem that the Chronicler had a specific purpose in mind when inserting the song into the narrative. The prose introduction to the song (1 Chr 16:1–3) is based upon 2 Sam 6:16–19. Likewise the narrative resumption (1 Chr 16:43) after the song in 1 Chronicles 16 is very similar to 2 Sam 6:19–20. The 2 Samuel account makes no mention of the song, and so it seems clear that the song in 1 Chronicles 16 is the idea of the Chronicler. There was some benefit to be had by adding the song to the narrative material.[22]

The Chronicler's Editorial Changes

One of the dynamics investigated by performance criticism is the interplay between spectator, actor, and character. A powerful outcome of the interaction between these three is the formation of a social identity or the propagation of a shared belief that becomes owned by the spectator. The power of a performance is often judged by the ability of the performance to move an audience, to enable the audience to think, believe, or act differently. The Chronicler's appropriation of the psalms and the resulting lyrics seem to have been intended to help shape a social identity by moving the spectator into the role of character. The editorial changes made by the Chronicler when appropriating the source psalms reveal the dramatic intent.

Butler makes a sweeping judgment concerning the text of 1 Chronicles 16: "The often-studied textual problems show little that is of real theological significance."[23] From a performance-critical viewpoint, his judgment does not hold, for the editorial activity of the Chronicler does lead to significant theological insights. It is true that some of the variations between the song in 1 Chronicles and the source psalms are relatively minor: the use of the copulative "we," variations in spellings, prepositional variations, the addition or subtraction of the sign of the direct object, and variations in phrase construction. These changes do not alter the meaning or thrust of the quoted material. Other changes made by the Chronicler, however,

---

[21] R. Braun, 1 Chronicles (WBC; Waco: Word, 1986), xxv.
[22] The same can be said for the other psalmic insertions made by the Chronicler: 1 Chr 16:34, 41; 2 Chr 5:13; 7:3, 6; 20:21; 2 Chr 6:41–42. See Shipp, "'Remember His Covenant Forever,'" 30–32, 37–39: "I suggest that Chr displayed a great deal of conscious literary art in the construction *and the placement* of the Chronistic Psalm" (p. 37, emphasis added).
[23] Butler, "A Forgotten Passage from a Forgotten Era," 143.

seem to be more significant.[24] One of the more notable is the use of the word "Israel" in 16:13 in place of "Abraham," which appears in the source material Ps 105:6.[25] Although the Chronicler favors the name "Israel"[26] over the pseudonym "Jacob," the substitution of "Israel" for "Abraham," especially in quoting a psalm most likely familiar to his readers, could only have a surprise effect. This unexpected mention of "Israel" would have drawn attention. It drew the audience into the performance of the song as they—those now reading or listening to the Chronicler's work and considering themselves "Israel"—suddenly found the song to be about them.[27]

This audience participation of a sort seems to also be the effect of the next variation introduced by the Chronicler. In 1 Chr 16:15 the Chronicler uses the imperative, "you remember" (*zikru*), in place of "He remembers" (*zakar*) in Ps 105:8. The psalm reads, "He remembers his covenant forever," whereas 1 Chronicles reads, "Remember his covenant forever." This declarative statement, with God as the subject, in the psalm is turned into a command directed at the Chronicler's audience (whether listening or reading). In this way an identity, a sense of being, is enjoined upon the audience. They are made up of those who remember the covenant with Yahweh.

Once again, the Chronicler's edits in 1 Chr 16:19 have the effect of drawing the audience into the work. He writes, "when you were few in number," (*bihyotekem*) instead of "when they were few in number" (*bihyotam*) in Psalm 105:12. In Chronicles the audience is thus addressed directly. The psalm's story of generations gone by becomes the audience's story in Chronicles. And quite explicitly, the Chronicler's insertion of the plural imperative "say" in 1 Chr 16:35 before the quotation of Psalm 106 makes the words of the psalm the words of the audience at hand.

---

[24]In his use of the psalmic material, the Chronicler was functioning as an interpreter of a tradition. His act of interpretation had an impact on the tradition no less intentionally than on the reading or listening audience. See Schniedewind, "The Chronicler as an Interpreter of Scripture," 179.

[25]The RSV emends the text of 1 Chronicles here and elsewhere in the song to agree with the MT of the various source psalms. This emendation seems to be without warrant. See Butler, "A Forgotten Passage from a Forgotten Era," 143. The NIV presents a different selection, retaining "Israel" in v. 13 but reverting back to the verbal forms found in the source psalms in its presentation of vv. 15 and 19. The NJPS translates the MT of 1 Chr 16 so as to preserve all the Chronicler's edits.

[26]Howard Wallace, "What Chronicles Has to Say about Psalms," in *The Chronicler as Author: Studies in Text and Texture* (ed. M. Patrick Graham and Steven McKenzie; JSOTSup 263; Sheffield: Sheffield Academic, 1999), 267–91, here 269–70.

[27]William Rudolph, *Chronikbücher* (Tübingen: Mohr, 1955), 120.

A pair of changes in 1 Chr 16:27 and 29 also seem intent on making the Chronicler's rendition of the song more applicable to the immediate audience. In verse 27, the Chronicler renders the song as "strength and joy are in his place" whereas Ps 96:6, from which he is quoting, reads, "strength and beauty are in his sanctuary." In a similar vein, 1 Chr 16:29 reads, "come before him," whereas the source, Ps 96:8, reads, "come into his courts." If the Jerusalem temple planned by David and built by Solomon no longer existed, as was the case in the time of the Chronicler, the alteration of references to the sanctuary and the courts was a necessary condition if the Chronicler's audience was to feel part of the song and to have the ability to *enter the song* as participants.

In the next two verses, 1 Chr 16:30–31, a phrase is repositioned with the result that a new sense is given when compared with the original in Ps 96:10a.[28] In the psalm it is the families of the peoples, that is, neighboring countries (96:7), that are to ascribe to Yahweh glory and strength and to bring an offering and worship Yahweh. These worshiping people declare, "The LORD reigns!" (96:10). In 1 Chronicles 16, it is the heavens and the earth that make the declaration. Given the political domination experienced by the Chronicler's audience, it only makes sense that since they can no longer speak to their neighbors, nature itself will pick up the refrain[29] and continue the song begun in verse 23. A similar comment on the lived experience of the Chronicler's audience may be evident in verse 35, where the Chronicler inserts an explicit appeal for deliverance that is not found in the source verse, Ps 106:47. The plea is strangely out of place within the story line surrounding the song of 1 Chronicles 16. In the Chronicler's narrative, David has been victorious over all his enemies (14:17), and no one appears on the horizon to offer a serious threat. Yet the appeal for deliverance is quite appropriate if placed in the fourth or sixth century B.C.E. Surrounded by powerful and menacing nations that threatened to impose on their way of life, the Chronicler's audience of postexilic Jerusalem would have found the plea for deliverance appropriate and a natural conclusion to the celebration of Yahweh's presence articulated in the song.[30]

---

[28]Contra Butler, "A Forgotten Passage from a Forgotten Era," 143; and Leslie Allen, *The Greek Chronicles: The Relation of the Septuagint of I and II Chronicles to the Massoretic Text* (2 vols.; VTSup 25, 27; Leiden: Brill, 1974), 1:217.

[29]Wallace, "What Chronicles Has to Say about Psalms," 270.

[30]See John Endres, "Theology of Worship in Chronicles," in *The Chronicler as Theologian: Essays in Honor of Ralph W. Klein* (ed. M. Patrick Graham, Steven McKenzie, and Gary Knoppers; JSOTSup 371; New York: T&T Clark, 2003), 165–88, here 171–72; Zipora Talshir, "Several Canon-Related Concepts Originating in Chronicles," *ZAW* 113 (2001): 386–403, here 398.

The Chronicler also changed the ending of the last psalm quoted. Psalm 106:48 ends with an imperative, "Praise the LORD!" (106:48), and a jussive, "let all the people say" (106:48). The Chronicler transforms both into descriptive statements that form a narrative conclusion after the recitation of the song, ending in 1 Chr 16:36a.[31] Indeed, for the Chronicler, everyone performed her or his part.

The chart offers a handy summary of the major editorial changes just discussed. The cumulative effect of these subtle changes is quite striking.

The Chronicler's Editorial Changes

Source psalms	Song of Asaph
105:6 Abraham *zeraᶜ ᵓabraham ᶜabdo*	16:13 Israel *zeraᶜ yisraᵓel ᶜabdo*
105:8 He remembers *zakar leᶜolam beriyto*	16:15 You remember (plural imperative) *zikro leᶜolam beriyto*
105:12 They were few in number *bihyotam metey mispar*	16:19 You (plural) were few in number *bihyotekem metey mispar*
96:6 in his sanctuary *bemiqdasho*	16:27 in his place *bimqomo*
96:8 come into his courts *uboᵓu lexatsrotayw*	16:29 come before him *uboᵓu lepanyw*
96:10 Let neighboring countries declare: YHWH reigns! *ᵓimru baggoyim YHWH malak*	16:31 Let them [Heaven and earth] declare among the nations: YHWH reigns! *weyoᵓmeru baggoyim YHWH malak*
106:48 Let all the people say *weᵓamar kol-haᶜam ᵓamen*	16:36 All the people said (authors' translation) *wayyoᵓmeru kol-haᶜam ᵓamen*

Through editorial changes, the Chronicler's listening or reading audience is absorbed into the text of the song, and then, by turning the ending of the psalm into a narrative description, the Chronicler inserts this audience into the story being told. He transforms an audience of spectators into characters within the story. This observation has been made before. "One gets the impression that the psalm text has been constructed to address

---

[31] Watts, *Psalm and Story*, 161, contends that the song is designed to create continuity between the Chronicler's audience and the cult in David's time.

the audience of Chr.'s day."[32] This manipulation of the source text allows the Chronicler to turn audiences into active participants. "The Chronicler's theological strengths lie less in his direct presentation of the great events of the people's history than in his creative use of existing traditions, of making them appropriate and relevant to the situation of the community for which he wrote."[33] And this "creative use," this manipulation of a performed text (psalms) in order to create active participants, moves us into the realm of performance criticism.

Active Audience

The movement that occurs when a performance changes a passive audience into active participants has been identified as the unique contribution made by the song of 1 Chronicles 16: "The poetic text addresses the reader and makes the reader contemporary with the arrival of the ark in Jerusalem. It thus draws the reader into the everlasting song of praise in a way that makes it impossible simply to replace the poetry with a piece of prose."[34] Although this audience formation, enhanced by the Chronicler's psalmic selections and his editing of these selections, has been widely recognized, the dynamics of this audience formation have yet to be explored.[35]

The Chronicler assumes a communal audience, that is, a group of "people whose total social experience is at one with each other and the

---

[32] Wallace, "What Chronicles Has to Say about Psalms," 288. Leslie Allen, "Aspects of Generational Commitment and Challenge in Chronicles," in *The Chronicler as Theologian: Essays in Honor of Ralph W. Klein* (ed. M Patrick Graham, Steven McKenzie, and Gary Knoppers; JSOTSup 371; New York: T&T Clark, 2003), 123–32, also notes the importance of generational continuity in the Chronicler's theology.

[33] R. J. Coggins, "Theology and Hermeneutics in the Books of Chronicles," in *In Search of True Wisdom: Essays in Old Testament Interpretation in Honour of Ronald E. Clements* (ed. Edward Ball; JSOTSup 300; Sheffield: Sheffield Academic, 1999), 263–78, here 265.

[34] Kirsten Nielson, "Whose Song of Praise? Reflections on the Purpose of the Psalm in 1 Chronicles 16," in *The Chronicler as Author: Studies in Text and Texture* (ed. M. Patrick Graham and Steven McKenzie; JSOTSup 263; Sheffield: Sheffield Academic, 1999), 327–36, here 336.

[35] Sara Japhet, "Exile and Restoration in the book of Chronicles," in *The Crisis of Israelite Religion: Transformation of Religious Tradition in Exilic and Post-exilic Times* (ed. Bob Becking and Marjo Korpel; Leiden: Brill, 1999), 33–44, argues a similar point in her characterization of the Chronicler's manner of depicting the history of all Israel. She writes that in the story of Chronicles, "'All Israel,' in the true meaning of this term for the Chronicler, had never been exiled and never left the land!" That is, a stream of continuity is established by the Chronicler, uniting the fourth-century audience to the experiences of the past in the land promised by God (p. 42).

presenters."[36] In the fully formed communal audience, the values, language, and thoughts of all involved in the theatrical experience are identical or as close to identical as possible. This kind of community makes multiple communication possible. A common ground must be established between presenter, presentation, and spectator.[37]

The common ground between Chronicler and audience, materials, history, and memory of the Chronicler's text, creates this active, communal relationship between the two. The spectator is engaged on multiple levels—indeed is required to be engaged. As Marco De Marinis suggests about the process of spectatorship, "There is no doubt that the sensory faculties of the perceiving subject are called upon to sustain an effort, to which, for both quantity and quality, there is no equivalent in any other artistic field."[38] At the very core of drama (as it occurs for an audience) there is a continuous give-and-take, or interplay, between audience and presentation along a spectrum that can be from the emotional and intellectual to full participation.

> Initially, the give-and-take occurs between the physical activity of presentation and the sensitized organs of perception in an audience. Gradually the sensory response expands into the imaginative. Entertainment is thus a precondition to other specific responses. Something must be held between the presenter and the receiver. Such and such an action, being entertained, should effect entertainment in the audience.[39]

This is precisely what Goldman refers to as the important connections between drama and life and those features of life "we're likely to regard as intensely difficult, issues that bear on self and meaning, on persons and texts, on identity and community."[40] This give-and-take leads to our active participation in the performative aspects of the drama. In the case of 1 Chronicles, a postexilic Jerusalemite audience becomes both *singer* of the song and the *Israel* described in the song.

Power of Performance

The creation of an active audience, a situation in which the Chronicler's readers and listeners are drawn into the story, is one of the effects

---

[36] Bernard Beckerman, *Dynamics of Drama: Theory and Method of Analysis* (New York: Drama Book Specialists, 1979), 135.

[37] Doan and Giles, *Prophets, Performance, and Power,* 101.

[38] Marco De Marinis, "Dramaturgy of the Spectator," *Drama Review* 31.2 (1987): 100–14, here 107.

[39] Beckerman, *Theatrical Presentation,* 145.

[40] Goldman, *On Drama,* 6–7.

of the song in 1 Chronicles 16. The power of the song, inset into the Chronicler's narrative, is enhanced if his audience is already familiar with the song. It is quite probable that the Chronicler's readers and listeners knew the psalms that are now borrowed by him. In this case, the audience would have been able to sing along and so become part actor (reader of the song) in addition to being an audience. Further, by means of the strategic changes made by the Chronicler, this audience would have recognized themselves as a character within the song. The song establishes a fluid dynamic in which the reader/listener becomes all three:

Performer ◄————————► Audience ◄————————► Character

The character, or persona, that the audience adopts is in part defined by the prose narrative that introduces the song. This song is introduced by the notation that "on that day David first appointed that thanksgiving be sung to the LORD by Asaph" (1 Chr 16:7). The difficulty is that it is more than likely that the Chronicler's audience knew this was not true—not true at least in terms of the composite song presented in 1 Chronicles 16. None of the psalms used by the Chronicler are attributed in the Psalter to either Asaph or David.[41] Psalm 106 has a heading identifying it as a hallelujah psalm. Psalm 105 has a heading only if prefaced by the last phrase from Psalm 104. And Psalm 96 has no heading at all. The reading or listening audience would have known the source songs from which the composite was formed and would have easily recognized the Chronicler's song for what it was—a composite created for its affect in the Chronicle's narrative. This means that in entering into the spirit of the song—in adopting the persona of the song—the audience is forced to assume a fiction.[42] The audience enters a willful suspension of disbelief in order to achieve some greater good. In the same way that a modern audience suspends disbelief when the house lights go down—in order to enter the world of the play— the Chronicler's audience was required to suspend disbelief as well. And this suspension of disbelief is especially appropriate to the song, for it is in the nature of song to suspend time. Song functions as a pause in the normal space-time we occupy. As soon as the singers begin, the narrative

---

[41] Butler, "A Forgotten Passage from a Forgotten Era," 143.

[42] Ehud Ben Zvi has observed a similar dynamic at work in Chronicles, suggesting that the Chronicler asked of his reading audience that they bracket "out questions of narrow historical referentiality and focus(ed) on ideological and typological messages" (*History, Literature, and Theology in the Book of Chronicles* [London: Equinox, 2006], 51).

stops, only to be resumed when the song concludes.[43] This suspension of disbelief allows an audience to choose to adopt an identity rather than passively accept that identity. In other words, the song has an iconic function that stresses *being* rather than *becoming*, and in the Chronicler's view of history, this is exactly what his audience needs.

Being and Becoming

The song of 1 Chronicles 16 contains the major themes that appear throughout the Chronicler's history. The covenant with God, Davidic kingship, prophets, God's sovereignty, the kingship of God, and a call for judgment are major theological themes occupying the song and the whole of the Chronicler's history.[44] In terms of performance criticism, there is a wonderful agreement between the "becoming" presented in the Chronicler's narrative and the "being" found in the Chronicler's song. Both narrative and song advocate an audience identity in a way that is unique to each and yet complementary to both.[45]

In this section of 1 Chronicles, the author uses narrative as a dialectic and song as an iconic mode of presentation. An understanding of both iconic and dialectic modes of presentation is critical when performance criticism is applied to the Hebrew Bible. In the context of dramatic performances and presentations, an audience usually encounters a mixture of both the iconic and the dialectic, although the balance between the two can differ radically from one historical period to another or from one theatrical genre to another. The boundaries of iconic and dialectic modes of presentation are permeable, and the skillful combination of the two is mainly responsible for the dynamics of a performance, especially in audience formation and participation.

Iconic modes of presentation (e.g., the Song of Asaph, the Song of Deborah, the Song of the Sea), stress being whereas dialectic modes of presentation (the surrounding narrative) stress becoming. In terms of dramatic or theatrical events, the clearest examples of an iconic mode of presentation are to be found in shows of celebration, where past and present, achievements, identity, and stability are celebrated and presented in

---

[43]The same point is made by Nielson, "Whose Song of Praise?" 333.

[44]See Butler, "A Forgotten Passage from a Forgotten Era," 147–49. Although Butler includes Ezra-Nehemiah in his comparison, the same themes can be identified when one limits oneself to 1 and 2 Chronicles.

[45]Audience identity is a theme that recurs throughout Chronicles, beginning with the opening genealogies. See Manfred Oeming, *Das wahre Israel: Die 'genealogische Vorhalle' 1 Chronik 1–9* (Beiträge zur Wissenschaft vom Alten und Neuen Testament 128; Stuttgart: Kohlhammer, 1990), 1–11.

formal ways. As Beckerman stresses, iconic modes of presentation are rooted in idealism.[46]

Dialectic modes of presentation, dominated by tension and resistance, or conflict and change, represent inherent risks to characters and performers. Tension results from a struggle to overcome some kind of resistance located either in the plot of the drama itself or in the audience, whose inertia, disbelief, or skepticism the performer must overcome.[47] "Resistance . . . is the factor that the performer needs to overcome in order to realize a performance. It is the focus of the risk that resides in the act, and overcoming it produces an elemental pleasure for the spectators."[48] As already stated, elements of dialectic modes of presentation would more appropriately be applied to the narrative surrounding the Song of Asaph. A general example is the structure of many classical operas where the recitative, adopting the rhythms of ordinary speech, allows characters to confront each other, to engage in conflict and exchange, for generating emotion and influencing the "life" of another character, as opposed to the aria, which tends more toward the iconic, emphasizing and presenting the character's current "state," or status.

Iconic modes of presentation, as we have seen, are dominated by the three features of being over becoming, the ritualized enactment of prescribed movements, and the sense of things falling into place as they should be.[49] Within the Song of Asaph of 1 Chronicles 16, these distinguishing features observed by Beckerman are clearly present. In the Chronicler's editing changes alone, being is established for the spectators: "you remember" (v. 15), "you were few in number" (v. 19), "you say" (v. 35) [authors' translations]. Earlier, in verses 13–14, by addressing the offspring of Israel, an identity is named and made concrete. There is no trial or test to overcome (conflict and resistance) as in dialectic modes of presentation. The spectators are Yahweh's chosen ones. The ritual enactment of prescribed movements, the second feature of iconic presentation, permeates the song. The expressions "Give thanks to the LORD," "Sing to him," "Glory in his holy name," and "tell of all his wonderful works" are all directives or actions that take place in the song itself. Repetition of these actions functions to sustain the spectators' identity. The third feature, which focuses on the effect of demonstrative events, clearly occurs at the end of the song. The

---

[46]Bernard Beckerman, *Theatrical Presentation: Performer, Audience, and Act* (ed. Gloria Brim Beckerman and William Coco; New York: Routledge, 1990), 43.

[47]See ibid., 53–72.

[48]Ibid., 57.

[49]See chapter 1, above, for a full description of the elements of iconic presentation.

repetitive pattern of prescribed actions—thanking, praising, worshiping—is brought to a unified (communal) conclusion in verses 35–36. Singing collectively, "Save us, O God of our salvation" (NRSV), the characters in the song end the performance with an act that simply and precisely makes everything fall into place: "Then all the people said 'Amen!' and praised the LORD."

In the context of the narrative dialectic, the Chronicler presents in song an iconic interlude, one that allows the spectators to embrace an identity and a history. Their participation in the song allows his audience to claim the identity of past heroes as their own identity.

Conclusion

For the Chronicler, audience formation is of prime importance.[50] By applying insights from performance criticism, we gain a fresh appreciation for the skillful way in which the Chronicler uses the iconic nature of the Song of Asaph to help construct audience identity in a way not possible in narrative alone. He carefully chose selections of specific psalms and skillfully edited these selections, presenting a composite song at just the right spot in the narrative to maximize the iconic value of the song for audience formation. And it is the formation of audience identity that gets to the very heart of what the Chronicler was all about.

The Song of Asaph

The following translation is based on the English translation of the RSV, but it has been modified by the authors to reflect their understanding of the Hebrew of the MT of 1 Chronicles.

Song of Asaph

8 O give thanks to the LORD,
Call on his name,
Make known his deeds among the peoples!
9 Sing to him,
Sing praises to him,
Tell of all his wonderful works!

---

[50] Ben Zvi, *History, Literature, and Theology in the Book of Chronicles,* 32, describes this audience formation as "the enlargement of the main social memory." This social memory is the foundation of group identity.

10 Glory in his holy name;
Let the hearts of those who seek the Lord reioice!
11 Seek the Lord and his strength,
Seek his presence continually!
12 Remember the wonderful works that he has done,
The wonders he wrought,
The judgments he uttered,
13 O offspring of Israel his servant,
Sons of Jacob, his chosen ones!

14 He is the Lord our God;
His judgments are in all the earth.
15 You remember his covenant for ever.
Of the word that he commanded,
For a thousand generations,
16 The covenant which he made with Abraham,
His sworn promise to Isaac,
17 Which he confirmed as a statute to Jacob
As an everlasting covenant to Israel,
18 Saying, "To you I will give the land of Canaan,
As your portion for an inheritance."

19 When you were few in number,
And of little account,
And sojourners in it,
20 Wandering from nation to nation,
From one kingdom to another people,
21 He allowed no one to oppress them;
He rebuked kings on their account,
22 Saying, "Touch not my anointed ones,
Do my prophets no harm!"

23 Sing to the Lord, all the earth!
Tell of his salvation from day to day.
24 Declare his glory among the nations,
His marvelous works among all the peoples!
25 For great is the Lord, and greatly to be praised,
And he is to be held in awe above all gods.
26 For the gods of the peoples are idols;
But the Lord made the heavens.
27 Honor and majesty are before him;
Strength and joy are in his place.

28 Ascribe to the Lord,
O families of the peoples,
Ascribe to the Lord glory and strength!
29 Ascribe to the Lord the glory due his name;

Bring an offering,
And come before him!
Worship the LORD in holy array;
30 Tremble before him,
All the earth;
Yea, the world stands firm,
Never to be moved.
31 Let the heavens be glad,
And let the earth rejoice,
And let them [heaven and earth] say among the nations, "The LORD reigns!"
32 Let the sea roar,
And all that fills it,
Let the field exult,
And everything in it!
33 Then shall the trees of the wood sing for joy,
Before the LORD,
For he comes to judge the earth.
34 O give thanks to the LORD,
For he is good;
For his steadfast love endures for ever!
35 [You pl] Say also:

"Deliver us, O God of our salvation,
And gather and save us from among the nations,
That we may give thanks to thy holy name,
And glory in thy praise.
36 Blessed be the LORD, the God of Israel,
From everlasting to everlasting!"

All the people said, "Amen!"

Chapter 6: **Songs Not Sung**

A Song Not Sung

This chapter moves to a type of twice-used song different from those in earlier chapters. So far all the songs that we've surveyed were songs sung (or quoted from a songbook [Josh 10; 2 Sam 1; and 1 Kgs 8]). Unlike all these others, the Song of Moses in Deuteronomy 32 and the Song of David in 2 Samuel 22 are both recited—spoken and taught by the characters in the narratives but not sung. The way in which the songs are introduced in their respective narratives suggests two important matters. First, the identification and presence of the composer of the song are an important feature of the narrative. Second, the assignment of these particular words of the song (and perhaps not some variant rendition) to that composer is also important to the point being made by the narrator. The projection of the presence of the song's composer or commissioner into the lived reality of the audience sets these twice-used songs apart from the rest.

The Song of Moses (Deuteronomy 32:1–43)

The Song of Moses in Deut 32:1–43 is a song not sung. We are given not only the text of the song but also a method of interpreting the song. Deuteronomy 31:19–22 provides narrative background to the song and indicates the reason for composing the song and the purpose for teaching it to succeeding generations. In that the song is intended to be taught by one generation to the next, it is quite comfortable in its Deuteronomic setting, for the book as a whole shares an interest in passing a story and way of life to generations yet to come. A number of literary forms and methods are used to accomplish this didactic goal, not by enforcement techniques characteristic of law but by persuasion and conviction.[1] *Teaching* and *learning* are a particularly important concern of Deuteronomy.[2] And it is within this context of teaching and learning that we are introduced to the song.

In an editorial comment in 31:21, the narrator acknowledges that the song enjoys widespread familiarity among the narrative's audience ("it [the song] will live unforgotten") and that presumably the audience recognized the song's great antiquity with quite probably a traditional attribution to Moses as the author. The audience knew the song independently of its present location in Deuteronomy.[3] If, then, as most scholars agree, the text of Deuteronomy reached its present shape by at least the sixth or fifth century B.C.E., we can assume that the song enjoyed a lengthy history prior to its incorporation in Deuteronomy, for it seems quite likely that the song was composed in the monarchic period, perhaps early in that period.[4] The placement of the song at the end of the book of Deuteronomy may well have been the result of the work of the last Deuteronomic redactor, who appended chapters 31–34 by borrowing from previously known but quite independent prose and poetic sources.

---

[1] Patrick Miller, "Constitution or Instruction? The Purpose of Deuteronomy," in *Constituting the Community: Studies on the Polity of Ancient Israel in Honor of S. Dean McBride Jr.* (ed. John T. Strong and Steven S. Tuell; Winona Lake, Ind.: Eisenbrauns, 2005), 133. See also Dennis Olson, *Deuteronomy and the Death of Moses: A Theological Reading* (Minneapolis: Fortress, 1994); Joachim Schaper, "A Theology of Writing: The Oral and the Written, God as Scribe and the Book of Deuteronomy," in *Anthropology and Biblical Studies: Avenues of Approach* (ed. Louise Lawrence and Mario Aguilar; Leiden: Deo, 2005), 97–111.

[2] The verb *lmd* is used seventeen times in the book of Deuteronomy but nowhere else in the Pentateuch.

[3] Gerhard von Rad, *Deuteronomy* (OTL; Philadelphia: Westminster, 1966), 195; S. Driver, *Deuteronomy* (ICC; New York: Charles Scribner's Sons, 1906), 338; James Watts, *Psalm and Story: Inset Hymns in Hebrew Narrative* (JSOTSup 139; Sheffield: JSOT Press, 1992), 79. It may be that the intertextual connections between the song of Deut 32 and the text of Second and perhaps Third Isaiah also provide evidence of the widespread familiarity the song enjoyed.

[4] Some scholars have argued for a very early date of composition. W. F. Albright, "Some Remarks on the Song of Moses in Deuteronomy 32," *VT* 9 (1959): 339–46, thinks that the song was composed in the eleventh century. Driver, *Deuteronomy*, 345–46, advocates a date of composition in the late monarchy. Others place its date in the exilic or early postexilic period: von Rad, *Deuteronomy*, 200; A. D. Mayes, *Deuteronomy* (London: Marshall, Morgan & Scott, 1981), 382; J. Tigay, *Deuteronomy* (JPS Torah Commentary; Philadelphia: Jewish Publication Society, 1996), 293–316; Richard Nelson, *Deuteronomy* (OTL; Philadelphia: Westminster John Knox, 2002), 369. Solomon Nigosian, "Linguistic Patterns of Deuteronomy 32," *Biblica* 78 (1997): 206–24, makes a compelling argument for dating the song between the tenth and the eighth century; if indeed this is accurate, the song circulated for centuries before finding a home in the prose of Deuteronomy.

The redactor in Deut 31:16–22 describes the connection between the song and the narrative to which it was added. In this narrative introduction to the song, the redactor recounts a conversation between Yahweh and Moses in which Yahweh describes a coming apostasy and the consequences to be visited on the wayward people.[5] The song is to be a warning for now and the future. It is to be written down and taught to the people so that it may be a witness for Yahweh against the people of Israel. This witness function makes the song parallel in function to the law,[6] the focus of attention in 31:1–15 and again in 31:24–29.[7] The "law" is to be deposited next to the ark of the covenant and to constitute an official shrine. In similar fashion, the song, too, is deposited—not in a shrine but in the popular imagination. If this part of Deuteronomy was fixed late in the monarchy, it may well be that the song was known much more widely and had much greater popular authority than the official Deuteronomic law. The song lent its authority and popularity to the law and so provided an effective witness, making Yahweh present (in the explicit commissioning of the song) in the popular imagination of a generation much later than Moses. If the book of Deuteronomy as a whole functions as a witness, to future generations, of the need to maintain fidelity with Yahweh, God of Israel, then the song in Deuteronomy 32 majestically captures this same intent and draws the audience into the story.

It has been suggested that the law and the song mentioned in Deuteronomy 31 are, in fact, the same text simply put to different presentations: one as an iconic legal text and the other as a popular lyric.[8] Certainly, the song is complementary to the intended function of the book of Deuteronomy as a whole and to the stated function of the law in Deuteronomy 31. In addition, numerous indicators point to the conclusion that the book

---

[5]H. Huffmon, "The Covenant Lawsuit in the Prophets," *JBL* 78 (1959): 285–95, was the first to suggest that the song fits a lawsuit pattern. G. E. Wright, "The Lawsuit of God: A Form-Critical Study of Deuteronomy 32," in *Israel's Prophetic Heritage: Essays in Honor of James Muilenburg* (ed. Bernhard Anderson and Walter Harrelson; New York: Harper, 1962), 26–67, proposed a ninth-century date of composition for the song on the basis of his understanding of the lawsuit pattern.

[6]Steven Weitzman, *Song and Story in Biblical Narrative: The History of a Literary Convention in Ancient Israel* (Bloomington: Indiana University Press, 1997), 44, argues that "law" is not a good term to use in this case; he suggests instead "instruction." Certainly, Weitzman's suggested translation, "instruction," aptly describes what the author of Deut 31 had in mind, but regardless of which term is employed, it needs to describe the object that is inscribed and envisioned on display next to the ark (Deut 31:26).

[7]A similar event is attested in Isa 30:8–9.

[8]Weitzman, *Song and Story in Biblical Narrative*, 44.

presumes an oral presentation. Sermons, speeches, teaching, and preaching throughout the book use immediate language and a frequent reliance upon explicit motivational clauses.[9] It is within this context of immediate presentation that the song provides an opportunity for audience interaction that is absent in the prose alone.[10] In the song, warnings against infidelity and hope for the future are woven into one relatively short and fast-paced literary piece that requires no one specific historical or narrative context for its application. Through the song, the generations to come, no less than those written about in the prose, can be led into the immediate presence of Yahweh, God of Israel, and form part of the didactic chain stretching *dor ledor,* from generation to generation.

Composed and Commissioned by God

The placement of the song here in Deuteronomy 32 requires a suspension of disbelief. In the story line, the song is God's song. God teaches the song to Moses, and Moses in turn teaches it to all the people. Yet the song references events and places from a later time, long after Moses has left the scene. An acknowledgment of the historical misplacement of the song is held in suspension, and instead the writer of the narrative asks the reader to agree that the song was composed by God and given to Moses just before his death. This suspension of disbelief allows for a very important component of the narrative. God composes and commissions the song. Commissioning is an important characteristic of the prose introduction to the song in Deuteronomy 31. Not only does God compose and commission the song; Joshua, too, is commissioned by God (Deut 31:23) to function as Moses' successor with the guarantee that Yahweh will be present with Joshua just as Yahweh was with Moses.

This composing and commissioning by God make the song of Deuteronomy 32 unique. It is God's song. And only here in the whole of the Hebrew Bible does God compose lyrics. The song does not allow the voice of God in the first person until 32:20, and its most natural singer is a representative of the people of Israel performing to an audience of the people of Israel. But despite these obvious difficulties, the composition and commissioning are an important feature of the narrative introduction to the song.

Composition and commissioning are processes whereby the presence of the composer and commissioner is extended to audiences of the

---

[9]Miller, "Constitution or Instruction?" 136.

[10]Weitzman, *Song and Story in Biblical Narrative,* 53, characterizes the song as filled with intellectual pessimism that "cuts across the grain of much of the rest of the book."

future.[11] The same dynamic is present in the Song of Asaph of 1 Chronicles 16. The Chronicler identified David as commissioner of the Song of Asaph to ensure that David—and, more to the point, what David represented in the social imagination—would be a present component of the communal identity that the Chronicler wanted to form. Likewise the Deuteronomic narrative writer wants to make sure that his audience is mindful of God's presence, and so he made Yahweh the author of the song about to be recited. Even more than Moses, who simply repeated the words of the song, it is God who is brought near to the Deuteronomic audience through the presentation of this song. And this is an important point, for, in a sense, the song functions as a didactic climax to the teaching of the book. If, indeed, the "ultimate goal" of the teaching of the book of Deuteronomy within the Israelite community is to "instill a proper fear and worship of YHWH their God,"[12] then the song of Deuteronomy 32 provides a masterful culmination by drawing God, the author of the song, into the performance.

A related issue regarding the authorial attribution to the song concerns Moses and his part in delivering the song. In 31:22 we are told that Moses wrote the song. Yet when it comes time to deliver the song to the people, Moses does not read his composition, as we might suppose, but simply speaks it (31:30). Unlike the pattern of writing and reading found in Exod 24:4, 7, here Moses speaks the song. In Deuteronomy, reading is an act that takes place in the future, after Israel is settled in the promised land.[13] As long as Moses is alive, no reading takes place; he performs his composition unmediated. It is an oral performance without the aid of written helps. And it is a complete oral performance. The song is introduced in 31:30 by the notation that Moses spoke the song "completely" or "to the end" (ʿad tamim). Reinforced by the mention of "all the words of this song" in 32:44, this explicit reference to the whole song must be designed to counter any doubts that the surprise ending of 32:43 may have engendered or to emphasize that the song is complete and, as now positioned in Deuteronomy, also makes another act complete: the giving of the torah (32:46).

---

[11] It is common practice for a commissioned work to be published, performed, and/or presented with acknowledgment of the details of the commissioning. In essence, the details of the commissioning become part of the narrative of the song. Even after significant time passes, it is common to hear the phrase "Originally commissioned by . . ." as part of a verbal introduction to the piece and to see a printed acknowledgment in a program. Clearly, the facts of the commissioning can raise or lower the status of a piece or, at the very least, signal the work's significance to an audience, exerting an impact on the reception of the piece.

[12] Miller, "Constitution or Instruction?" 140.

[13] Jean-Pierre Sonnot, *The Book within the Book: Writing in Deuteronomy* (New York: Brill, 1997), 173.

A Gemstone

The Song of Moses in Deuteronomy 32 has been characterized as one of those "gemstones that occur in a rough matrix."[14] This description is meant to draw attention to the quite distinct literary characteristics that poems (songs) display when compared with the prose contexts in which they now find themselves. Some of these characteristics include the density of verbs, the frequent use of imperatives, and the terseness of the language. All of these characteristics are commonly found in immediate forms of communication, as contrasted with a more formal and distant communicative form, and they are to be expected in songs.[15] And it seems quite certain that this song, although not sung by Moses, was intended to be sung by others.[16] The shifts in person resident in the lyrics "indicate that the song was not merely to be read but was to be performed. The changes in person may well mark off speeches of different people in the performance of the song."[17]

The form of the song has been characterized in several different fashions. Some scholars see the song's structure as reminiscent of a prophetic lawsuit[18] whereas others find the comparison to a hymn more appropriate.[19] Still others consider the song most appropriately characterized as a "last-words" literary piece[20] or part of a treaty pattern characteristic of the book as a whole.[21] The song begins with a call for attention and then provides a litany of images in which the faithfulness of God is contrasted with the faithlessness of his people, Israel. Contrary to what might be expected, the song does not mention the events of the exodus, even though it is now situated to rehearse these episodes in a powerful fashion. Instead the song

---

[14]David Peterson and Kent Richards, *Interpreting Hebrew Poetry* (Minneapolis: Fortress, 1992), 67.

[15]William Doan and Terry Giles, *Prophets, Performance, and Power: Performance Criticism of the Hebrew Bible* (New York: T&T Clark, 2005), 5–10.

[16]Dan Vogel, "Moses as Poet: Ha azinu as Poem," *Jewish Bible Quarterly* 31 (2003): 211–18, suggests that the song is powerful, at least in part, because poetic imagery is more memorable than prose.

[17]Matthew Thiessen, "Form and Function of the Song of Moses," *JBL* 123: 401–24, here 408–9.

[18]Wright, "The Lawsuit of God."

[19]Nelson, *Deuteronomy,* 369.

[20]Weitzman, *Song and Story in Biblical Narrative,* 37–39.

[21]M. G. Kline, *Treaty of the Great King: The Covenant Structure of Deuteronomy* (Grand Rapids: Eerdmans, 1963); Peter Craigie, *The Book of Deuteronomy* (New International Commentary on the Old Testament; Grand Rapids; Eerdmans, 1976), 373.

presupposes a national existence in which "Jacob" and "Jeshurun"[22] (both pseudonyms for the people of Israel) took for granted the loving care and protection offered by Yahweh, turning rather to gods that were in reality nongods. In response Yahweh will raise the sword of protection against Israel. Disasters and terrors lie in store for Jeshurun, who has spurned the "rock" and sought refuge in gods who could provide no protection. Yet Israel's destruction will not be complete, for Yahweh will once again take compassion on them. The sword of Yahweh will devour God's enemies, and the blood of his children will be avenged. For the chastened children of Yahweh, hope is not abandoned. He has wounded but he will heal. There is a future and there is reason to raise a shout of joy. And this message of chastisement, hope, and joy becomes all the more powerful when delivered first person, through the familiar words of a song composed by God.

The Song of David (2 Samuel 22:2–51)

The Song of David in 2 Samuel 22 is also a song not sung, at least as presented in 2 Samuel. Fortunately, two renditions of this song are preserved in the Hebrew Bible, since it also appears as Psalm 18.[23]

According to the prose introduction to the song (2 Sam 22:1), the song was composed and recited "on the day when the LORD delivered him from the hand of all his enemies, and from the hand of Saul." The implication is that there was one identifiable event or circumstance that provoked the creation of the lyric. The song itself, however, gives a different impression. It is devoid of historical specificity and can easily be applied to a variety of contexts.[24] Indeed, if it were not for the editorial notes of 22:1

---

[22] "Jeshurun" is a term used by Isaiah. Other Isaiah-like language and metaphors appear in the song. See Hyun Chul Paul Kim, "The Song of Moses (Deuteronomy 32:1–43) in Isaiah 40–55," in *God's Word for Our World* (ed. J. Harold Ellens, Deborah Ellens, Rolf Knierim, and Isaac Kalimi; 2 vols.; JSOTSup 388–89; New York: T&T Clark, 2004), 1:147–71. Similarities between the song of Deut 32 and the language of the prophets leads to the speculation that the song had a wide circulation and impact. "The preponderance of the Song's linguistic features playing compositional roles in the literary units within these important Isaianic chapters [1, 5, 28 and 30] . . . leads to the conclusion that the former work was well known by the author and by those to whom the prophecies were addressed" (Ronald Bergey, "The Song of Moses [Deuteronomy 32:1–43] and Isaianic Prophecies: A Case of Early Intertextuality?" *JSOT* 28 [2003]: 53).

[23] The Song of Asaph in 1 Chronicles preserves material culled from three independent psalms and so is not quite like 2 Sam 22 in this regard.

[24] Watts, *Psalm and Story*, 106, notes that the links between the song in 2 Sam 22 and its narrative context are "sparse," especially when compared with

and 51, there would be nothing in the song itself to suggest that David was the author or in any way associated with the song.[25] Considerable debate has taken place as to whether the song is a literary unity or was (as posited by the current scholarly consensus), at some earlier stage, two separate compositions (the first composed of vv. 2–20 and the second lyric preserved in vv. 29–51 except for the insertion of verse 32)[26] with a connective segment (vv. 21–28) in between.[27] The connective (vv. 21–28) is often thought to be the composition of an editor or perhaps even the prose narrator, who took older lyrics and combined them, giving the song its present structure.[28] The conclusion appears correct that the song is a composite whose literary strands are older (by perhaps more than two hundred years) than its current prose context[29] and only in its twice-used function associated with David. The orthography of the version in 2 Samuel appears to be older than the version preserved in Psalm 18.[30] H. W. Hertzberg contends that even though the song(s) were not originally written about David, the combined song is appropriate here, at the end of David's career, because it provides "a theological commentary on the history of David. The history of

---

the verbal and thematic links to the Song of Hannah at the opening to the books of Samuel.

[25] A. A. Anderson, *2 Samuel* (WBC 11; Dallas: Word, 1989), 261. Notice also that of the psalms associated with David in the Psalter (Pss 3, 7, 18, 34, 51, 52, 54, 56, 57, 59, 60, 63, 142), only Ps 18 is general, lacking any specific incident or occasion for composition.

[26] P. Kyle McCarter, *II Samuel* (AB 9; Garden City, N.Y.: Doubleday, 1984), 473–75. The composite nature of the song in 2 Sam 22 is also supported by D. Michel, *Tempora und Satzstellung in den Psalmen* (Abhandlungen zur evangelischen Theologie 1; Bonn: H. Bouvier, 1960), 49, but not concluded to be so by Hertzberg, *I and II Samuel*, 392, and is left undecided by Frank Moore Cross and David N. Freedman, "A Royal Song of Thanksgiving: II Samuel 22–Psalm 18," *JBL* 72 (1953): 21.

[27] The Song of Asaph, formed from selections culled from three independent psalms, offers ample illustration of this kind of process at work.

[28] Anderson, *2 Samuel*, 262; McCarter, *II Samuel*, 474–75.

[29] The combined poem is often dated to the seventh century (McCarter, *II Samuel*, 474) whereas the two halves of the poem are recognized as having been composed much earlier (Anderson, *2 Samuel*, 262).

[30] McCarter, *II Samuel*, 464, has amassed convincing evidence for the probable identification. Whether one is dependent upon the other or both Ps 18 and 2 Sam 22 are variants of a common older source is difficult to tell. Cross and Freedman, "A Royal Song of Thanksgiving," 15, suggest that the two renditions, as we have them now, show "a strong tendency toward harmonization"—a process that was never completed. But it can be argued that the psalm instead had a lengthy prehistory as two independent pieces (a deliverance song [vv. 2–20] and a royal victory song [vv. 29–31, 32–50]) that only later became associated with David when they were formed into one single composition with the addition of the material in vv. 21–28.

David is to be read and heard in the light of this psalm."[31] In other words, the song is twice-used, and the manner in which it is twice-used invites performance-critical analysis.

And so the question presents itself: what was the hoped-for effect of inserting into the narrative of 2 Samuel a song that was apparently widely known (either in whole or in part) and only lately associated with David? If the song (or its recognizable composite parts) had a long tradition in ancient Israel, with people from a variety of circumstances singing the lyrics for their own purposes, how does its recontextualization into the life of David change the 2 Samuel narrative or change the way in which people heard and read the 2 Samuel narrative? More seems to be going on than a poetic theological commentary.

The Song of David Compared with Psalm 18

Both the 2 Samuel narrator and the editor of the Psalms invite a comparison between Psalm 18 and the Song of David in 2 Samuel 22. The introduction to the Song of David in 2 Sam 22:1 is repeated almost word for word as an introductory note to the "choirmaster" in Ps 18:1. The differences between the two renditions have been characterized as "scribal in origin and correspond to the categories of change that take place in the transmission of any ancient text (modernization of grammar and spelling, scribal errors, glosses, etc.)."[32] And certainly this does seem to be a fair description of most of the variations between the Song of David and Psalm 18. Several differences, however, that appear slight do have a measure of significance from a performance-critical perspective.

Some scholars have considered the phrase *umenusi moshi‘i mekhamas toshi‘eni*, "you save me from violence" (NRSV), which appears in 2 Sam 22:3b but not in Psalm 18, "superfluous."[33] McCarter argues that this phrase, addressing Yahweh in the second person—the only second-person address in the first part of the song—should be emended to a third-person address.[34] This need not be the case. The presence of the phrase in the second person helps make the song twice-used. The phrase, in David's mouth,

---

[31] Hertzberg, *I and II Samuel*, 393.

[32] McCarter, *II Samuel*, 473. Watts, *Psalm and Story*, 99, characterizes the variations as minor.

[33] H. P. Smith, *The Books of Samuel* (ICC; New York: Charles Schribner's 1909), 379. The same verb (*ysh‘*), however, appears in "David's last words" (2 Sam 23:4) and may be part of the verbal linkage, further tying the Song of David to its 2 Samuel narrative context.

[34] McCarter, *II Samuel*, 456.

makes perfect sense given the narrative context established by the narrator in the introduction to the song in 2 Sam 22:1.[35] The song is being spoken to Yahweh. Some moment of immediate address certainly fits the scene created by the introductory note.

But how does our observation about 22:3b mesh with a second variation, in which Psalm 18 NRSV reads, "at your rebuke, O LORD" (second person), whereas the rendition in 2 Sam 22:16 NRSV reads, "at the rebuke of the LORD" (third person). Does not this nullify the observations made about the manner of address in 22:3? Not necessarily. This third-person address in 22:16 does seem most appropriate in the Song of David, for the action described is distant, not immediate for the singer (David); making the phrase third person makes the song more applicable to David. The second person in Psalm 18, on the other hand, allows a greater variety of application and so permits more singers access to the song, each applying the lyrics to their own circumstance, time, and place.

Both of these variations between second- and third-person address have, at their core, a common concern with actor, character, and audience. In the Song of David, the actor and the character are both identified as David, and the *imagined audience* is Yahweh, imagined only in the sense that others in attendance could not see Yahweh in the same way they could see each other. As imagined audience, Yahweh, too, becomes a character in the drama unfolding in the song. The Song of David comes alive if imagined as a dramatic performance in which the actor, David, addresses at times Yahweh and at other times the attending audience. In the Psalm 18 rendition, the audience is still Yahweh and the character remains David (or an assumed Davidic persona); the actor or singer is anyone willing to take up the song. Actor, character, and audience provide the framework by which to understand the changes in person evident between the Song of David and Psalm 18.

Actor, Character, and Audience

This interplay between actor, character, and audience, seen in the text of the Song of David, gives us an insight into understanding why the

---

[35]The absence of the direct-address statement that opens the Ps 18 rendition of the song does not negate this observation, particularly if Ps 18 is the later of the two renditions and the opening address was not part of the version known to the narrator of Samuel. J. Vesco, "Le psaume 18, lecture davidique," *Revue biblique* 94 (1987): 54, 56, and Gerald Sheppard, *Wisdom as a Hermeneutical Construct* (BZAW 151; Berlin: de Gruyter, 1980), 149, argue, however, in the opposite direction, that the narrative placement of the song was the last stage of development.

Song of David appears in 2 Samuel (and perhaps why the Song of Asaph does not).[36] The Samuel narrative presents David[37] as a man of the people. This David character begins as a shepherd, young and impetuous but with a pure trust in Yahweh. He is at times naïve in his reliance on the providence of God, yet he is clearly capable of intrigue and deception, especially when it comes to his enemies and the enemies of Israel. The Samuel narrative presents David as a talented character whose abilities propel him into the national spotlight and equally threaten to undo him. He is "a favored figure who rises to power almost in spite of himself."[38] He is spared none of the difficulties common to life and is himself the cause of his greatest heartaches. David is favored by God and commended for his repentant and hopeful trust in Yahweh.[39] From the spectators' point of view, these are the given circumstances of David's character. They are the "social and temperamental"[40] features that allow for an empathic relationship to the character. In other words, they are the performative boundaries of David's character, rooted in the social conditions of the spectators' world.

The David created in Samuel knows lust and anger, fear and joy. He is at times bold but often timid. David shows great pride in his children but must flee for his life when threatened by several of them. In some important ways, David is, for the readers of Samuel, all of us writ large. Brueggemann refers to this projected identity: "The appendix [2 Sam 21–24] is a dramatic invitation to go back across that threshold to an egalitarian covenantal mode of life."[41] That is, as the character of David is developed

---

[36]K. Budde, *Die Bücher Samuel* (Kurzer Hand-Commentar zum Alten Testament 8; Tübingen: Mohr, 1902), 314, argued, on the other hand, that had the Chronicler been aware of the Song of David, he would undoubtedly have used it. But there is good reason that this is not the case.

[37]The Samuel narrator uses four large blocks of material, identified in modern scholarship as the History of David's Rise (1 Sam 16 to 2 Sam 5), the Ark Narrative (1 Sam 4–5 and 2 Sam 6), the Succession Narrative (2 Sam 9–20 and 1 Kgs 1–2), and the Appendices (2 Sam 21–24), of which the Song of David is a part. Within the Appendices, a pairing of material occurs in a chiastic pattern: a famine story (21:1–14) is paired with a census story (24:1–25) around David's exploits (21:15–22; 23:8–38), which in turn surround the Song of David (22:1–51) and David's Last Words (23:1–7). See H. P. Smith, *The Books of Samuel* (ICC; New York; Charles Scribner's Sons, 1909), xxvii.

[38]David Howard, "David," *ABD* 2:46.

[39]Walter Brueggemann, "2 Samuel 21–24: An Appendix of Deconstruction?" *CBQ* 50 (1988): 389, makes similar observations about the Appendices as a whole but does not apply these observations to a character development as is done here.

[40]Bernard Beckerman, *Dynamics of Drama: Theory and Method of Analysis* (New York: Drama Book Specialists, 1979), 211.

[41]Brueggemann, "2 Samuel 21–24," 395.

in Samuel, he is a character approachable by the audience and to some degree available to the audience for their own identification. In the Samuel narrative, the audience reads about a character. In the Song of David, this audience, already familiar with the song, can become the actor of the song and iconically identify with the character of the narrative.[42] The narrator of Samuel wishes upon his audience a reliance on Yahweh just like that shown by David. In the narrator's wish we find the very essence of the performed nature of the theatrical experience: "a simultaneous awareness of something previously experienced and of something being offered in the present that is both the same and different, which can only be fully appreciated by a kind of doubleness of perception in the audience."[43] The character qualities of David as developed by Samuel provide a point of contact between the narrative and the audience.[44]

What we find in the literary presentation of David's character are the three fundamental dimensions of theatrical character described by Beckerman: width, length, and depth,[45] essential to audience reception of the character. From the outset, the width of David's character is developed with a full range of possibilities in terms of action and activity (he is impetuous, capable of intrigue and deception, talented, repentant, and hopeful and knows lust, anger, fear, and joy). The width of his character encompasses both physical and social features, which are key elements to audience/spectator reception because of their ability to connect directly to a spectator's emotions, attitudes, and beliefs. He has the potential for complexity. It is the width of David's character, or its complexity, that helps sustain audience interest in him. As "a favored figure who rises to power almost in spite of himself,"[46] David's humanness compels spectators to become empathically involved with him as he speaks.

The length of the character refers to the passage of the character through the action of the drama. Obviously, some characters have greater

---

[42] Although differing in the specifics from the presentation here, Watts begins to encourage us to think of the function of the song as character development. He sees that in the song the "characterization of the speaker assumes a predominant role. . . . In 2 Samuel 22 all thematic links with the narrative serve the overriding purpose of characterizing David" (*Psalm and Story*, 109, 115). It is important also to recognize that although the song presents David as vulnerable, it contains no elements of David's dark side, so openly portrayed in the preceding narrative. This may be a function of the iconic nature of character portrayal in the song.

[43] Marvin Carlson, *The Haunted Stage: The Theatre as Memory Machine* (Ann Arbor: University of Michigan Press, 2001), 51.

[44] A quite different dynamic is at work in Chronicles, as is evident in the different character development presented in the Song of Asaph.

[45] Beckerman, *Dynamics of Drama*, 215.

[46] Howard, "David," 2:46.

length than others. Those who pass through the action of the drama quickly have little time for development. Those, like David, who pass through the length of the drama provide opportunities for intensification and revelation, elements critical to audience perception and response. "Thus, we can speak of development through change, through intensification, or through revelation. It is possible that a single individual may exhibit all of these kinds of development although one will tend to be accentuated."[47]

What Beckerman means by "depth" refers to the relationship between what a character does and that character's inner life. These dimensions of character are not only literary concepts but performative aspects of character critical to the way character resonates with spectators. "In simplest terms depth is concerned with how the inner life of a character continues or counterpoints the outer."[48] How do the character's actions (what he or she does) coincide with his or her thoughts, feelings, and desires. Is there continuity between the inner and the outer life? Are there contradictory impulses lurking beneath the surface? What is most interesting for us, in terms of the David in Samuel versus the David in Chronicles, is the difference in the depth of the character. As seen below, the depth of David's character is deeply affected by the editorial changes of the Chronicler.

A similar audience-actor-character dynamic occurs with the Song of Asaph of 1 Chronicles. Chronicles, however, offers a much more idealized presentation of David. There the character of David is "completely flawless, and very much concerned with religious matters."[49] And so the Song of Asaph, as already seen, requires editorial changes in order to allow a different sort of audience identification. In Chronicles the narrative becomes the vehicle by which the participating (singing) audience can reaffirm their identification with the postexilic sanctuary of Jerusalem. They are given access to an idealized past by singing the song. The Song of Asaph allows a present audience to identify with an idealized past. In Samuel the Song of David allows David to become one of us, part of the audience's shared identity. The songs work, as it were, in opposite directions. The Song of Asaph would be totally out of place in Samuel, just as the Song of David would be out of place in Chronicles. Both the Samuel narrator and the Chronicler are using song to assist in their own projects, in each case the formation of an audience identity. In essence each author chose a song to assist in a particular audience formation. For that reason the songs are not interchangeable.

---

[47] Beckerman, *Dynamics of Drama*, 216.
[48] Ibid., 216–17.
[49] Howard, "David," 2:46.

Strategic Placement in the Narrative

Besides the fact that both the Song of Moses and the Song of David are recited (not sung) by the characters in the story, these two songs share several other literary characteristics.[50] Both lyrics form material that is like an appendix to the preceding narrative. The positions of both songs within their respective contexts are strikingly similar. Both are spoken by two of Israel's greatest heroes just before their deaths. A second song immediately follows each. And both share a common lexicon of significant terms. These clues raise the question whether, from a performance-critical viewpoint, the twice-used purpose of each song is the same or nearly the same. The Song of Moses makes present the character of Yahweh as a vital member of the audience, and the Song of David makes present the character of David and provides a meeting place for the inner and the outer lives of both the character and the spectators. Both songs help shape the formation of an audience by inserting a cherished person or Person as a member of that group identity.

---

[50]See Watts, *Psalm and Story,* 107. Some earlier commentators have noted the same: Hertzberg, *I and II Samuel,* 399; R. A. Carlson, *David, the Chosen King* (Stockholm: Almqvist & Wiksell, 1964), 227–28; Peter Ackroyd, *The Second Book of Samuel* (CBC; Cambridge: Cambridge University Press, 1977), 203.

Chapter 7: **Short Choruses**
The Pop Music of Hebrew Narrative

Introduction

Scattered throughout the biblical literature, from the earliest to the latest, are a handful of short choruses. They are not bound together (as are the songs in the *Song Scroll*), nor do they resemble each other in form, theme, or provenance. What is common to all these choruses, as well as to the other songs inserted into prose, is that the songs predate the narratives in which they are now placed. Although this observation, on the face of it, may seem quite insignificant, this use of preexisting songs by prose writers may give us a clue to their function within the prose narratives. Without exception, the narrators use songs that people already knew. In other words, it was not enough for the narrator to include a song, a little ditty that he or she may have just made up; what was important was to insert a song already familiar to the narrator's reading or listening audience. It is not just the song that is added to the narrative; the narrative writer is appropriating the song's reputation and social influence. It is what the song represents that is important to the narrator. And this "social presence" of the song takes us into the realm of performance criticism. This chapter examines the short choruses, the pop music of biblical narrative.

Roman Jakobson made a fascinating observation about group narrative that Masao Sekine applies to the way in which epic and lyric operate. Sekine claims that epic is motivated by a group consciousness whereas lyric involves the "maturity" of the individual consciousness.[1] If this is

---

[1]Masao Sekine, "Lyric Literature in the Davidic-Solomonic Period in the Light of the History of Israelite Literature," in *Studies in the Period of David and Solomon and Other Essays* (ed. Tomoo Ishida; Winona Lake, Ind.: Eisenbrauns, 1982), 1–2.

so—and it apparently is—a wonderful dynamic is unleashed when epic and lyric are combined. When lyric is inserted into epic or group narrative, the individual consciousness or identity is in some fashion applied to the group consciousness or identity. The lyric becomes "popular" in that it is readily applicable to a variety of individuals or groups in a number of circumstances; this makes the lyric prime material for recycling, or reuse. The dynamic is evident in the Israelite choruses.

The recycling dynamic that makes a chorus twice-used, particularly as it concerns applicability to changing audiences, is one of the most significant effects of theatre and drama's practice of recycling material from age to age. Indeed, as Carlson points out, recycling and providing variations to a narrative "encourages audiences to compare varying versions of the same story, leading them to pay closer attention to how the story is told and less to the story itself."[2] Netta Zagagi observes,

> Variations on a given theme were far more likely to stimulate the imagination, and the more complex and comprehensive the link between the individual work and the literary tradition from which it sprang, the greater were the prospects of the writer winning praise and recognition for his work.[3]

The Song of Miriam (Exodus 15:21)

Song of Miriam

Sing to the LORD!
For he has triumphed gloriously
The horse and his rider
He has thrown into the sea.

The most obvious question regarding this chorus, called the Song of Miriam, in Exod 15:21 is, Why is the song there?[4] It repeats verbatim (less the prefacing, "I will sing," which is replaced with the imperative "Sing!")

---

[2] Marvin Carlson, *The Haunted Stage: The Theatre as Memory Machine* (Ann Arbor: University of Michigan Press, 2001), 27. The applicability of Carlson's observation to the stories of the patriarchs in Genesis is evident.

[3] Netta Zagagi, *The Comedy of Menander: Convention, Variation, and Originality* (Bloomington: Indiana University Press, 1995), 15–16, quoted in Carlson, *The Haunted Stage,* 27. Zagagi is a leading authority on Menander and classical Greek New Comedy.

[4] Brevard S. Childs, *The Book of Exodus* (OTL; Philadelphia: Westminster, 1974), 246, simply concludes that the relation of these verses "remains a problem." Frank Moore Cross and David N. Freedman, "The Song of Miriam," *Journal of Near*

the opening of the Song of the Sea in 15:1b–18.[5] Moreover, the insertion of Miriam (v. 20) and then the song (v. 21) into the narrative seems to interrupt its flow. It appears that the plot of the story could go much more smoothly if these two verses were not present. The Song of Miriam with its introduction is quite likely a later insertion into an already developed narrative.

The whole passage (15:1–21) has been seen as a fitting end for the larger literary unit extending from Exodus 1 to Exodus 15. Part of the evidence adduced for the appropriateness of the passage is the observation that women are actors only at the very beginning (1:15–2:10) and at the very end of the literary unit (15:19–21). Thus the Song of Miriam functions as part of this literary balance in which women are actors.[6] Yet even this observation of literary balance does not seem compelling in explaining the function of the Song of Miriam. The balance could be achieved just as well by concluding with verse 20 and leaving out the song altogether. John Durham takes a slightly different tack, considering the section (vv. 19–21) a transitional summary moving the reader forward from the sea to conquest and settlement.[7] Still, the same weakness is present. The song is not necessary to propel the story forward. Balance and forward movement could be accomplished just as well, perhaps even better, without the recitation of the Song of Miriam. There must be an additional reason the Exodus narrator chose to insert the Song of Miriam.

Since neither of the above explanations for the presence of the Song of Miriam is convincing, we must look elsewhere for the reason. Could it be that the song is present in the narrative not so much for what the song itself contributes as for what the song represents? Could it be that the song represents a line of social power and influence, a performative event, that the narrator wanted to appropriate and add to the persuasive power of the story being told?[8] Apparently, the Song of the Sea was not enough.

Eastern Studies 14 (1955): 237, argue that the poem of v. 21 is simply a title for the longer song in vv. 1–18.

[5] A common explanation for the presence of the two songs is that the Song of Miriam is an antiphonal response song by the women of Israel and that it follows every stanza of the longer song of verses 1b–18. See U. Cassuto, *A Commentary on the Book of Exodus* (trans. I. Abrahams; Jerusalem: Magnes, 1967), 182; James Watts, *Psalm and Story: Inset Hymns in Hebrew Narrative* (JSOTSup 139; Sheffield: JSOT Press, 1992), 43; Terence Fretheim, *Exodus* (Louisville: John Knox, 1991), 161.

[6] Watts, *Psalm and Story*, 49. See also P. Trible, "Bringing Miriam out of the Shadows," *BRev* 5 (1989): 14–25, 34.

[7] John Durham, *Exodus* (WBC; Waco: Word, 1987), 209.

[8] Carol Meyers, "Miriam the Musician," in *A Feminist Companion to Exodus to Deuteronomy* (ed. Athalya Brenner; Feminist Companion to the Bible 6;

And even though the words of the Song of Miriam are almost identical to those of the Song of the Sea, the inclusion of this short chorus associated with Miriam added influence to the narrative. Could this influence have been in the form of an additional social segment that was now engaged through the Song of Miriam and that, without the song, would have been outside the arena of active audience?

This may be why the song is introduced by the phrase "and Miriam answered" (ᶜnh), followed by an imperative, "Sing!" which begins the song. The Song of Miriam functions to extend an invitation to the reading—or, better, to the listening—audience. Reminded of the song through the recitation of the Song of the Sea, the listening audience is invited to take its part, to sing aloud and so make the story their own. If so, the Song of Miriam is not an awkward duplicate but a necessary cue, signaling the audience that now is the time to make the song their own by singing aloud and so assist in telling the story they are now actively participating in.[9]

The Song of Wells (Numbers 21:17–18)

Song of Wells

Spring up, O well!—
Sing to it!—
The well which the princes dug,
Which the nobles of the people delved
With the scepter and with their staves.

Numbers 21:10–22:40 has presented many difficulties for modern interpreters; not least is the presence of the songs embedded in the narrative. This section of Numbers contains three pieces of poetry, two of which (21:14–15 and 21:17–18a) are generally considered ancient songs. That all three poems predate the compilation of this complex narrative seems assured.[10] The first poem, not identified as song by the Numbers narrator, is said to come from the "Book of the Wars of the LORD." The sec-

---

Sheffield: Sheffield Academic, 1994), 207–30, points out that in most biblical narratives, when women display musical skills, it is a moment of social power and status.

    [9]Watts, *Psalm and Story*, 55, begins to anticipate this theme of audience participation but applies the dynamic to the whole of 15:1–21 and not to the special role played by the Song of Miriam.

    [10]George Gray, *Numbers* (ICC; Edinburgh: T&T Clark, 1903), 279.

ond poem is explicitly identified as song, is sung in the narrative, but does not have an identified source. This song has been variously identified as a "work song,"[11] a "court song,"[12] or a form of incantation in which "word and song were not only aids to labor, but also endowed with a power of their own, which it was believed would bring success."[13] Regardless of the relative merits of each of these descriptions, the matter under discussion is why the songs now appear in this narrative. Why is it important for the narrator not only to tell us that the Israelites sang but also to give us the words that were sung?

Philip Budd answers these questions by suggesting that the narrator "does not have much traditional material from which to construct a Transjordanian journey" and so must resort "to fill this out" with whatever is at hand and that the narrator has "only the ancient songs"[14] by which to fill out the story. In other words, the songs are there only because the narrator had nothing else to use. Performance criticism can lead us to a more satisfying conclusion.

Within its present literary context, the Song of the Well must have a function that is related to the Victory Ballad recited a few short verses later. Songs are so rare in Numbers that it cannot be simply accidental that two (perhaps three if vv. 14b–15 are allowed as song) of them appear in such close proximity. The songs communicate in a way that is quite different from the way the prose narrative does. As examples of performative material, these songs represent a way of thinking and articulating thoughts to others that cannot be conveyed through prose alone. Something must be at work here that requires the songs to be present.[15]

The Song of the Well seems to have been a popular chorus[16] that could be sung in a number of contexts. Nothing within the song necessitates its application to only this particular story or requires its origination at this point in Israel's sojourn. The song encourages the singers

---

[11] Otto Eissfeldt, *The Old Testament: An Introduction* (trans. Peter Ackroyd; Oxford: Blackwell, 1965), 88; R. K. Harrison, *Numbers* (Chicago: Moody, 1990), 282.

[12] J. Sturdy, *Numbers* (CBC; Cambridge: Cambridge University Press, 1972), 152.

[13] Philip Budd, *Numbers* (WBC; Waco: Word, 1984), 239.

[14] Ibid.

[15] Watts, *Psalm and Story,* 174, suggests that the songs appearing in narrative contexts tend to either end a particular narrative section or further the plot of the section. But this judgment is muted when he writes, "Writers and editors of ancient Hebrew literature seem to have had the freedom to use poetry in either of these narrative roles, or neither" (p. 175). In other words, there is no obvious and persuasive narrative role for the songs.

[16] Gray, *Numbers,* 289.

(whoever they may be) to address in song a well, asking it to give its wa-
ters as was intended by the "princes" and "nobles." The song may have
assumed something akin to *folksong* status by the time the Numbers narrative was written. The presumed readers of the narrative would have
known the song and been well prepared to sing along at this point in the
Numbers narrative. The inclusion of the Song of the Well cast a wide net
by not specifying the identity of the singers (and so allowed the greatest possible participation); at the same time, it affirmed a group loyalty
to the princes and nobles by recognizing their benefactions in producing
the much-needed supply of water. And the assistance of the princes and
nobles was needed for the completion of this "public works" endeavor,
since the digging and maintaining of a well formed a project that required
community cooperation.

The Song of the Well possesses key qualities similar to those identified by Eli Rozik in his exploration of choral storytelling and the performance of dithyrambic choruses of ancient Greece.[17] The song seems
to be a reminder of, and point to, a past that has folkloric qualities connected to princes, nobles, and heroic deeds. It employs a serious and
lofty style, poetic in nature, compact but powerful in its immediacy. As
a medium, the song contains direct speech, possibly enacted, and could
accommodate dance and song together.[18] Again we find the basic formula
of performance: A (the Numbers narrator) enacts B (the lead singer for
the Song of Wells) while C (hearers, spectators) look on or momentarily
participate.

Those now invited to join in the singing (the readers or listeners of
the Numbers narrative) echo their own identification with this sojourn
from the distant past and also affirm solidarity with their own generation of princes and nobles, who will, through their leadership and in like
fashion, provide for the well-being of this generation of people amid a
new and dangerous group of surrounding enemy nations. And for an exilic
or postexilic audience, for which threats are real and immediate, the Song of
the Well provides a welcome glimpse of security and protection. Security
and protection, communicated powerfully through the medium of song,
are also the point of the Victory Ballad, the next song appropriated by the
Numbers narrator.

---

[17]Chapter 2, above, takes a closer look at Rozik's analysis of choral storytelling and dithyrambic choruses.

[18]These qualities or aspects of the dithyramb are adapted from Eli Rozik,
The Roots of Theatre: Rethinking Ritual and Other Theories of Origin (Iowa City:
University of Iowa Press, 2002), 150–51.

The Victory Ballad (Numbers 21:27–30)

Victory Ballad

Come to Heshbon,
Let it be built
Let the city of Sihon be established.
For fire went forth from Heshbon,
Flame from the city of Sihon.
It devoured Ar of Moab,
The lords of the heights of the Arnon.
Woe to you, O Moab!
You are undone, O people of Chemosh!
He has made his sons fugitives,
And his daughters captives,
To an Amorite king, Sihon.
So their posterity perished from Heshbon,
As far as Dibon,
And we laid waste until fire spread to Medeba.

The narrator's introduction to the Victory Ballad acknowledges its widespread and contemporary performance: "That is why the ballad singers say" (Num 21:27, authors' translation). The narrator states clearly that the song is currently being performed by the ballad singers, presumably heard by many, if not all, of the readers. The narrator thus borrows from the ballad singers and uses their ballad to enhance the narrative now being told. The identity and function of the ballad singers (*moshelim*) is uncertain, as attested by the variety of ways in which *moshelim* has been translated in Num 21:27.[19] The word is a participial form of the noun *mashal,* more familiar to readers of English as "proverb." The noun, when used to describe a literary genre, refers to a poetic literary form that contains a comparison between similar ideas or objects. The participial form refers to those who characteristically compose or recite such pieces of poetry. The translation "ballad singers" in Numbers 21 recognizes that the piece they are said to recite (21:27–30) is a song of some sort that needs no further introduction by the narrator.

Commentators have not given a great deal of attention to these "ballad singers," but securing their identity and function may be of help in

---

[19]The RSV translates "ballad singers"; the NIV, "poets." Commentators likewise offer their own varieties. Baruch Levine, *Numbers 21–36* (AB 4A; New York: Doubleday, 2000), 102, has "composers of *mesalim*"; Gray, *Numbers,* 299, has "reciters of poems"; Budd, *Numbers,* 246, has "ballad singers"; Jacob Milgrom, *Numbers* (JPS Torah Commentary; Philadelphia: Jewish Publication Society, 1989), 181, has "bard."

piecing together the social location in which the twice-used songs were first performed. Gray identifies the group mentioned in Numbers 21 as "reciters of poems" and suggests that it would be easy to imagine a "class of people" who "went about in Israel and, especially in time of war, by reciting poems like the present (see Isa 14:4–11; also Hab 2:6), and thus recalling former victories, stimulated and encouraged the people (see Judg 5:31)."[20]

This class of people deserves further attention. Groups of people matching the description given by Gray have played important roles in other cultures. Historians of western theatre indicate that in ancient times there was a strong tradition of individual oral storytelling that was sung.

> In both the *Iliad* and the *Odyssey*, stories from the present and the past are related by a bard or minstrel. A major, if not decisive, factor in the development of Greek tragedy may have been the manner in which social entertainment, rather than religious expression, supplied a performance convention.[21]

The bard, or rhapsode, is associated with lyric and choral practices, predating the formal practices of Greek drama, that make the bard a central component to more than one origin narrative about the roots of the theatre medium.[22] Later, from about the fifth to the seventh or eighth century C.E., another type of performer flourished with roots in the same tradition: the scop. "The Scop was a singer and teller of tales about the deeds of Teutonic heroes. As the principle preserver of the tribe's history and chronology, he was prized and awarded a place of honor in society. His songs and stories were major features of feasts and other great occasions."[23]

Both Rozik and J. Michael Walton acknowledge that choral storytelling is not drama proper, and this is correct. The performative practices of the bard, rhapsode, or ballad singer are, however, closely associated with drama proper—most notably, direct speech, characterization, and an implicit audience, or group of hearers. Perhaps the ballad singers of Numbers 21 filled a similar function in ancient Israel. Granted, in order to form a firmer conclusion, more explicit reference to ballad singers throughout the Hebrew Bible would be desirable; still, comparing the kind of material performed by the ancient Greek bard or rhapsode with the Victory Ballad

---

[20]Gray, *Numbers*, 299. Milgrom, *Numbers*, 181, adds to the list of examples: Mic 2:4; Ezekiel's allegories (Ezek 17:2–12); the discourse in Job; and the contents of Proverbs.

[21]J. Michael Walton, *Greek Theatre Practice* (Westport, Conn.: Greenwood, 1980), 46.

[22]Rozik, *The Roots of Theatre*, 153.

[23]Oscar G. Brockett and Franklin J. Hildy, *History of the Theatre* (9th ed.; Boston: Allyn & Bacon, 2000), 74.

of Numbers 21 may be fruitful.[24] In any case, the ballad singers of Numbers 21 were obviously both recognized and respected by the writer and audience of the Numbers narrative.

As many scholars have noted, the Victory Ballad of Heshbon adds nothing to the narrative development of the story in Numbers 21 but functions simply to end the account of the defeat of the Amorites.[25] But what a way to end it! The song provides the narrator the opportunity to take on the character of the ballad singer and to connect directly to the audience by compelling them to "come to Heshbon" and cast out curses against Moab and Chemosh. The narrative is suddenly lifted out of the ordinary by the character of the ballad singer, who gives the hearers a glimpse of the extraordinary. Levine describes this part of Numbers 21 as "singular" because of the appearance of the "Heshbon Ballad, a poem of dramatic quality."[26] The songs of Numbers 21 ascend in intensity, climaxing with the Victory Ballad. The songs are celebrations; they give what would otherwise be an intense and violence-ridden narrative a touch of joy and celebration. The conflict is still present in the narrative, but the songs diminish the air of uncertainty that might hang over the account and infuse the narrative with a more triumphal and celebratory flavor. And if the songs were indeed familiar to the readers or listeners of the narrative, as seems to be the case, then the inclusion of the songs in the narrative gives the audience something to cheer about. Once again, the songs allow the readers or listeners to "sing along" and so make the story their own by participating in the telling. Once again, the audience is placed in a position to "possess [the] land" (21:35).

The origin of this song is a matter of some dispute and most likely lost to antiquity. Its Israelite origin can in no manner be assured,[27] and although the relationship to Jer 48:45–46 is clear, the exact nature of this relationship has yet to be explored. Here it is enough to recognize that the song predates its inclusion in the narrative[28] and that it is likely that various renditions of

---

[24]Several linkages deserve further investigation. Could the function of the bard also be fulfilled by the "sons of the prophets"? Or could the *moshelim* be related to the "men of Hezekiah" and others given credit for gathering together some of the Proverbs (*mashal*)?

[25]Watts, *Psalm and Story,* 174; J. R. Bartlett, "The Historical Reference of Numbers XXI. 27–30," *PEQ* 101 (1969): 94.

[26]Levine, *Numbers 21–36,* 99.

[27]Norman Gottwald, *Tribes of Yahweh: A Sociology of the Religion of Liberated Israel, 1250–1050 B.C.E.* (Maryknoll, N.Y.: Orbis, 1979), 215. Gray, *Numbers,* 300, however, is convinced that the song has a Hebrew origin and celebrates a victory over Moab but that everything else about the poem is "more or less uncertain."

[28]John Van Seters concludes that Num 21:21–35 is a post-Deuteronomic and late-exilic composition that borrows a taunt song against Moab that was "reworked

the song were available to the ballad singers.[29] Indeed, it may be the case
that the narrator was influenced by the song to form the narrative, adding
material found in no other known tradition (Num 21:14–21) and so con-
forming the narrative to the story line of the well-known taunt song (i.e., a
short song that further celebrates a victory by demeaning or ridiculing the
vanquished enemy).[30] The song raises historical difficulties associated with
assigning to Moab control of territory north of the Arnon, and there are a
number of campaigns vying for recognition as the one "against Moab which
might conceivably be reflected in the poem of Num. 21:27b–30."[31] Although
certainly a worthwhile question, our concern is not with identifying the precise historical antecedent to the song, for the narrative quality of the song is
not its chief contribution to the Numbers account. Nor does the song seem
to be an "illustration of the narrative."[32]

Rather, the mention of the ballad singers (hammoshelim) is an important clue about the function of the song in the Numbers account. The ballad
singers are certainly a respected group for both the narrator and the presumed listening or reading audience. Otherwise there would be no point
in mentioning them. By placing the song into the repertoire of the ballad singers and invoking the song at this point in the story, the narrator
makes use of the social status accorded to the ballad singers to enhance
the credibility of his story. The Numbers narrator does not dispute or challenge the social influence granted to the ballad singers' performance but,
rather, uses this influence to enhance the persuasive power of the tale
now being told. It is enough to see the song as a celebration of the Israelite
community's supremacy over their historical or contemporary adversaries.
Whether the song mocks the addressed Amorites or simply celebrates an
Israelite triumph over the Moabites, the result is the same. It celebrates
an Israelite identity, and this identity can now be shared by those attentive
to the narrator's story.

---

and fitted into his account" ("The Conquest of Sihon's Kingdom: A Literary Examination," *JBL* 91 [1972]: 195).

[29] Budd, *Numbers*, 245, suggests that both the Numbers version of the song
and the Jeremiah version are influenced by a "common tradition behind both
texts."

[30] Ibid., 247. See also Van Seters, "The Conquest of Sihon's Kingdom," 197.
Bartlett, "The Historical Reference of Numbers XXI. 27–30," 96, contests the
description of the song as a taunt song.

[31] Bartlett, "The Historical Reference of Numbers XXI. 27–30," 99–100. Bartlett goes on to suggest a tenth-century date for the song, so that it originates from
Jerusalem and celebrates the glories of the Davidic era. Gray, *Numbers*, 301, cites
other estimates, placing the poem's composition in the early 900s B.C.E., but then
suggests that the poem may in fact be much older.

[32] Gray, *Numbers*, 299.

We are now in a position to address the question asked at the beginning of our consideration of Numbers 21: why is there such a concentration of songs here when they appear nowhere else in Numbers? Numbers 20–21 introduces people groups that stand or stood in opposition to the Israelite readers or listeners of the narrative. Conflict abounds in the narrative, and a strong "we"-versus-"they" dichotomy is established. To some degree, the "we," or group identity of the Israelite community, is established by using the other people groups as boundaries. "We" are not these others. The songs function in a remarkably appropriate way to complement the formation of group identity. Not just the words of the songs but their social presence and influence are an important dynamic of group formation in the communities of the readers or listeners of the narrative. And so the songs appear here in Numbers not because the narrator was desperate to include anything remotely relevant but because the songs are uniquely able to assist in the rhetorical purpose of the narrator: to create a sense of community identity. If, as Levine suggests, the narrative of Numbers 21 is the work of the JE writers (those biblical writers who employed the terms "Yahweh" and "Elohim" in the Pentateuch and who are thought by many biblical scholars to have performed editorial work on the Pentateuch in the eighth century B.C.E.) and was "aimed primarily at legitimizing Israelite sovereignty, or hegemony, over most of the area east of the Jordan and north of the Arnon," this narrative can be dated in the middle of the ninth century B.C.E., probably at the time of Omri and Ahab.[33] These were violent years, marked by military excursions into Transjordan and conflict with Moab. Shifting alliances, clashes with Moab and Ammon, and the darkening shadow of the Assyrian Empire all provide ample reason for the existence of a state-supported troupe of bards making popular a social identity of use to the state.

The Song of David's Honor (1 Samuel 18:7; 21:12; 29:5)

Song of David's Honor

Saul has slain his thousands,
And David his ten thousands.

The Song of David's Honor is introduced in 1 Sam 18:7, presented as part of the celebration conducted by Israelite women commemorating

---

[33] Levine, *Numbers 21–36*, 40.

David's victory over the Philistines. In the last two occurrences of the chorus (21:12; 29:5), Philistine personnel recite the song in order to remind their superiors of David's reputation for military prowess. The women recite the song in celebration, but others recite it as a warning. In all cases, the chorus is woven well into the narrative but is not essential for the development of the narrative. The repeated use of this chorus shows its versatility to elicit a number of responses. First, among Israelite women, the song is part of a celebration and becomes shorthand for communicating the many laudable qualities of their hero David. Quickly, however, the song is used quite differently (18:8) when, now placed in the mouth of Saul, the song becomes a way to express jealousy. Later, in the David story, the song reappears (21:12 and 29:5), this time spoken by Philistines (the servants of Achish and the Philistine commanders), and both times the song becomes a warning of treachery and duplicity.

And so, like a proverb that can be applied in a number of settings for a number of purposes, this chorus is capable of assuming a variety of meanings. Just as the phrase "You got to know when to hold 'em and know when to fold 'em" can be used to celebrate the success of a strategy or, on the other hand, to warn against pressing your luck, so, too, the Song of David's Honor may have become a common, versatile, and effective refrain, used now by the Samuel narrator. And the reader not only imports the sentiment of the chorus's words into the narrative that is being read but also brings a number of prior applications of the chorus into the reading. The narrative gains a breadth and depth far beyond the mere words of the chorus.

On the level of performance, something very complex occurs even in the brief confines of these two lines. If the gathered spectators or hearers suddenly perform the chorus by joining in its singing, a split-second transformation occurs in which they assume the "character" behind the lines and are able to embody an identity, complete with its emotions and passions, providing direct entrance into the world of the song and its context in Samuel.

The Song of David's Honor gives the impression of a chorus that could easily have been at home in a longer ballad sung in honor of the hero of Israel. Indeed, the chorus appears to need a ballad to provide supporting material, like that supplied by the narrative in which the chorus appears in 1 Samuel 18. Since the structure of this chorus (a *mashal*) is similar to that of the choruses in the Book of Proverbs, perhaps it, too, was performed by ballad singers (the *moshelim*) like those mentioned in Numbers 21.

The Temple Dedication Chorus (2 Chronicles 5:13; 7:3; 7:6)

Temple Dedication Chorus

For he is good,
For his steadfast love endures for ever.

The Temple Dedication Chorus occurs repeatedly in a key section of 2 Chronicles, but it is not found at all in the 1 Kings 8 counterpart to 2 Chronicles 5 or in the 1 Kings 8 counterpart to 2 Chronicles 7. Second Chronicles 5:12 introduces the chorus as a song sung by the Levitical singers, who are accompanied by musicians, including a powerful display of 120 trumpeters. The chorus is sung during the procession of the priests out of the holy place as a cloud fills the temple, signifying the presence of the glory of Yahweh. The Temple Dedication Chorus is repeated twice, this time sung by "all the people," at the conclusion of Solomon's prayer in 2 Chr 7:3; 7:6.

It seems most likely that the Chronicler, when writing the Solomon temple narrative, relied heavily on the account found in 1 Kings.[34] Consequently, that the chorus appears three times (5:13; 7:3; 7:6) in the 2 Chronicles account (and once, in variant form, as part of a prayer in 2 Chr 6:13) and not at all in the 1 Kings rendition makes its appearance Chronicles quite conspicuous.[35] John Kleinig concludes that these choral passages "together present the most complete statement in Chronicles on the nature and significance of liturgical song at the temple."[36] And they appear at a very strategic location in the narrative. This is the very climax of the temple story, and so the repeated appearance of this chorus is not to be taken lightly. The chorus is woven into a description of how the authorized temple functionaries perform their duties, how God appears in glory, and how the whole "people of Israel" voice their commitment to Yahweh through sacred ritual.

A comparison between Kings and Chronicles, particularly the Chronicler's use of song in 2 Chronicles 5–7, yields several fascinating

---

[34]"More than for any other section of Chronicles, Kings is the ultimate source for the Chronicler's history of Solomon" (Sara Japhet, *I and II Chronicles* [OTL; Louisville: Westminster /John Knox, 1993], 16–17).

[35]R. Dillard, *2 Chronicles* (WBC; Waco: Word, 1987), 5–7, attempts to account for the material in 2 Chr 1–9 by asserting a chiastic structure, but the arguments are less than convincing, particularly as applied to 2 Chr 5–7.

[36]John Kleinig, *The Lord's Song: The Basis, Function, and Significance of Choral Music in Chronicles* (JSOTSup 156; Sheffield: JSOT Press, 1993), 161.

observations.[37] First, whereas in Kings the appearance of Yahweh's glory is associated with the entrance of the ark, in Chronicles the glory of God is evoked by the performance of song. In the postexilic Jerusalem of the Chronicler—a Jerusalem to which the ark is long lost—song remained a viable accompaniment for the presence of God. And it was not due simply to the power of the music, the trumpets and cymbals, as powerful as that may have been. It was due also to the presentation of the refrain that the glory of God was known. Indeed, the refrain itself seems to have been the catalyst. Second, the refrain does not appear to be a special composition for this very special occasion, nor is it used only as a divine processional. The chorus is equally at home whether sung by the functionaries (5:13; 7:6), as part of a prayer (6:14), as a response of all the people (7:3), or as part of a war processional (20:21). A common link among these narratives is the song itself. And so it is appropriate to focus our investigation upon the performance of the song.

Second Chronicles 5–7 is not the only place where the chorus appears in the Hebrew Bible; the chorus makes an appearance in a variety of narrative contexts.[38] This repeated use of the chorus suggests that it enjoyed a widespread usage, particularly among a postexilic Judean audience.[39] If this is so, then the insertion of the chorus in 2 Chronicles 5–7, though not in the Kings version of the temple dedication, would have given the Chronicler's narrative a familiar ring to it, a familiarity that would have brought new life into the story from the distant past. The Chronicler's audience, most likely located in postexilic Jerusalem, could well have found

---

[37] Ibid., 164–67.

[38] 1 Chr 16:34, 41; 2 Chr 20:21; Ezra 3:11; Ps 100:5; 106:1; 107:1; 118:1–4, 29; 136:1–26. Jeremiah 33:11 is built upon the chorus as well and is introduced in many English translations as a lyric sung by those bringing thank offerings to the temple. The MT, however, does not say that is was sung but simply states that the lyric was said. But if Jeremiah meant the singing of the chorus, his use of the chorus is important. He acknowledges the use of the chorus in happy times, as an appropriate expression of national and personal joy. In Jeremiah the chorus becomes the fitting expression of joy's return. In place of waste and desolation (33:10), gladness will reign, the kind of joy evident in the voices of a bride, the bridegroom, and the invited guests present to share in their happiness. This appearance of the chorus in Jeremiah is significant for our overall understanding of the use of the chorus. Looking for the best expression of joy and gladness, an expression widely and immediately understood by a desperate Israelite audience, the writer settled on this chorus. And unlike in its other uses, the chorus is here separated from its temple moorings. The joy spoken of by the Jeremiah writer is like that of those bringing thank offerings to the house of the Lord, but the joy expressed by the song will be occasioned by the return of good fortune to *all* the land.

[39] Most of the song's occurrences are in Chronicles, Ezra, Nehemiah, and Psalms.

in the chorus a link binding themselves, as those who may had sung the song many times, with the characters in the story of Jerusalem's glorious past, singing the same song and worshiping the same God. In the chorus, Yahweh and his people met. The song was the vehicle by which "the singers presented the LORD to his assembled people."[40] At the same time, the sacred song served to articulate the response of the people to the Lord's presence with them.[41]

The Temple Foundation Chorus (Ezra 3:11)

Temple Foundation Chorus

For he is good,
For his steadfast love endures for ever toward Israel.

Only in Ezra 3 is the phrase "toward Israel"[42] added to what is otherwise a familiar and oft-repeated chorus used by the writers of Chronicles and Ezra-Nehemiah.[43] The addition of this phrase, which is certainly no accident, seems to be consistent with the Chronicler's, and now the Ezra-Nehemiah compiler's, intent to establish the postexilic Jerusalemite audience as the "Israel" of both now and the future. The addition of this phrase, "toward Israel," confirms the function of the chorus within its narrative setting. The chorus provides a means of audience identity. In the narratives of Ezra and Nehemiah, a community is described—an "Israel" that, in the mind of the compiler, will project into the future. The chorus of Ezra 3 provides a very explicit iconic means of binding the projected future community to its idealized roots from the past, with the temple at its very core. It is not just the means for audience identity but also an opportunity for the physical embodiment of this identity. The massed voices, gathered at a state or religious function, become the reality they declare. The performance is an act of belief, embodied by the whole assemblage and experienced communally by those past, present, and future.

---

[40]Kleinig, *The Lord's Song*, 180.

[41]Ibid., 181.

[42]Ps 100:5 adds the phrase "to all generations."

[43]Joseph Blenkinsopp comments that this chorus is a "favorite of C [the Chronicler], and he brings it in whenever he can" (*Ezra-Nehemiah* [OTL; Philadelphia: Westminster, 1988], 101).

Chapter 8: **Conclusion**

T wice-used songs constitute an important element in the narratives contained in the Hebrew Bible. The songs are present in both some of the oldest prose found in the Hebrew Bible and some of the most recent. The practice of including songs in narrative—of twice-using the songs—is firmly embedded in the Hebrew literary tradition. They rarely add to the narrative detail of the story being told by the prose writer and often conflict with the details found in the narrative. And since the songs do not add to the plot of the story, their presence in the narrative must be explained some other way.

The songs in the narratives provide a bridge of sorts from the story to the audience, drawing the reader or listener into the tale and encouraging the reading or listening audience to become an active part of the story; they accomplish this by giving to the audience a part to play—a way to sing along with the characters in the narrative. This dynamic of active participation means that the songs also provide a window into appreciating the purpose of the narrator. They provide clues to what the narrator wanted to accomplish with the story and how he or she hoped to affect the audience. By giving the audience a chance to sing along, with all the emotion and communal identity formation that accompanies group participation, the songs provide an occasion for the audience to accept for themselves the kind of self-identification that the narrator hoped to achieve through the presentation of the story. The songs are thus not at cross purposes with the narratives but, rather, form a symbiotic relationship with them in order to make a tradition (the story being told) part of the living reality for the reading and listening audience.

This examination of twice-used songs is certainly not the end of performance-critical analysis in the Hebrew Bible. It is not the last word. Performance criticism, as applied to the Hebrew Bible, is in its early and formative stages, and performance-critical studies can be applied to other

portions of the Hebrew Bible. The Song of Songs is an obvious candidate
for a performance-critical analysis, but there are other texts also. For example, the grand, sweeping story of Genesis 1–11 may well be served by an
examination that highlights the iconic and dialectic elements of the story
as a means of providing evidence pointing to a performative dynamic at
work and to the presence of various literary sources. And the short stories
woven together in the patriarchal cycles, appearing later in Genesis, offer
opportunities to examine audience formation techniques through the use
of character development.

The Hebrew prophets are perhaps attracting the greatest amount
of attention from performance critics.[1] Isaiah, Jeremiah, and Ezekiel provide rich fields for the application of performance criticism. The reported
speech events, iconic prophetic dramas, and twice-used songs appearing
in the poetic sections of these books may yield important new insights
when they are considered through a performance mode of thought. Prophetic and nonprophetic books such as Jonah, Ruth, Esther,[2] and Hosea
construct intricate dramatic tensions and, when examined through the
constructs of act-schemes and character formation, come to life in a whole
new way.

In addition to the examination of specific biblical texts, performance
criticism may offer insights for social-science studies of ancient Israel. For
example, the identity and the social function of the *moshelim,* or ballad
singers (Num 21:27), deserve greater attention. The existence of travel-
ing bards or preliterate newscasters identified as *moshelim* may shed new
light on the function of the "men of Hezekiah" (Prov 25:1) as well as on
the identity of Agur (30:1) and Lemuel (31:1). If the model of bard or
rhapsode is applicable to Hebrew literature, there may be additional significance to be explored in the Solomonic association with Proverbs. Does
the presence of state-sponsored *moshelim* imply that sections of Proverbs
originated as state-sponsored literature with the interest and agenda of
a centralized government in mind? If so, is the rich tradition of political
theatre in the form of either protest or propaganda drama applicable to
our understanding of the Proverbs collection? Additional application to
the social background of the prophetic literature may also be in order. The
use of music within ancient prophetic circles has long been recognized.
Often the music has been considered under the rubric of ecstatic behavior,
part of the prophet's display as diviner. But perhaps an additional dynamic

---

[1]An early example is Paul House, *Zephaniah: A Prophetic Drama* (Sheffield:
Almond, 1989).

[2]See Michael Fox, *Character and Ideology in the Book of Esther* (Grand Rapids:
Eerdmans, 1991).

is at work. The presence of lyric may also provide a lens by which to view some of the Hebrew prophets (1 Sam 10:11–12) and the sons of the prophets (2 Kgs 3:15; 6:1–7) as serving a function similar to the socially respected and sometimes state-sponsored bards known to us from slightly later Greek culture.

As with any emerging methodology, the application of performance criticism will include starts and stops, moments of insight and false turns as performance-critical ideas are applied to the text of the Hebrew Bible. During the last ten to fifteen years, a dialogue has begun among groups of biblical scholars concerning the applicability of performance criticism to the biblical text. Articles employing performance criticism are making their way into the professional journals, and several books applying performance criticism to the Hebrew Bible and the Christian New Testament test the limits of the method's applicability. Out of these discussions, the best ideas will become apparent, gain acceptance, and begin to affect the way all of us read the Bible. The performance has just begun.

Glossary

The sustained relationship between the spectator and the activity of the drama is at the core of this exploration of the Hebrew Bible's twice-used songs. The key drama and performance concepts presented here help navigate this exploration. The authors are indebted to the work of Bernard Beckerman and in several instances have quoted his terminology directly.[1] Over time, however, they have developed their own nuances for many of these terms and concepts in relation to a performance-critical approach to the biblical text.

active audience: This term is a variation of Beckerman's communal audience.[2] Like the communal audience, the active audience shares a common ground between presenter, presentation, and spectators. The values, language, and thoughts of all involved are as identical as possible, making multiple communications not only possible but also effective on physical, verbal, and aural levels. Additionally the active audience participates in the performance.

actor: The actor is the agent of presentation in the theatre and the drama. In the drama, the actor is always engaged in a double effort: the demonstration of actual skill and the portrayal of virtual existence.

act-scheme: The act-scheme is the structural organization of the drama's activity. Historically, dramatic structure is governed by a process of selection and feedback resulting in recognizable literary and performance

---

[1] See Bernard Beckerman: *Dynamics of Drama: Theory and Method of Analysis* (New York: Drama Book Specialists, 1979); and idem, *Theatrical Presentation: Performer, Audience, and Act* (ed. Gloria Brim Beckerman and William Coco; New York: Routledge, 1990).

[2] Beckerman, *Dynamics of Drama*, 135–36.

structures shared by both performers and spectators. This pattern of organization facilitates the presentation of the drama.

audience: The audience is an essential ingredient in performance. If there is no audience, there is no theatre or drama. Performance is heightened by the very fact that it is on display for an audience. For the drama to be realized in performance, something must be held between the performers and spectators: an interplay that requires both as participants. Modes of presentation (iconic/dialectic) can be fully understood only when one considers the presence of an audience.

character: The medium of the drama is human presence, not just language or even a combination of thought and diction (Aristotle). In performance terms, character is the *result* of a human presence (actor) engaged in portraying a virtual existence. More than the Aristotelian notion of "good and/ or bad" qualities, character emerges from the pursuit of goals or intentions; character is a kind of energy.

code: A code is a pattern or system of conventions that is culturally determined and that makes communication in a performance setting possible on a large scale. Codes are formed out of cultural needs and understanding: What is the context for this performance? What are the political, social, and/or religious forces influencing this context? What do the spectators need to hear, to see?

cultural memory: Cultural memory is a concept constructed by the reusable texts, images, rituals, and so forth, that are specific to certain periods in the life of a culture and that are critical to conveying that culture's self-image. Cultural memory is articulated by those who own the cultural forms and reflect upon past expressions of cultural values and significant events.

dialectic mode of presentation: According to Beckerman, the dialectic mode of presentation is the "nothing" we respond to during performance: "The air that crackles from the interchange between one actor and another, between one moment and another. The sensory response of what can be seen and heard turns into the imaginative response of what is felt, intuited, and interpreted."[3] It is what results from the exchange between the performance, the space and time of the performance, and the witnesses to the performance.

---

[3] Beckerman, *Theatrical Presentation,* 73–74.

direct address: Direct address, or direct presentation, occurs when the performer acknowledges the presence of the audience and makes this knowledge explicit during the presentation. Direct address creates the here-and-now relationship between presenter and spectator.

drama: "Drama occurs when one or more human beings, isolated in time and space, present themselves in imagined acts to another or others."[4]

dramaturgy: Dramaturgy is the set of techniques and/or theories governing the composition of a theatrical text. Critics such as Marco De Marinis have also explored the concept of a dramaturgy of the spectator, arguing that performance itself generates a "text" that is the construction of both the performers and the spectators. Some of the tools of dramaturgical analysis contribute to performance criticism.

embodied action: Embodied actions are the ways in which we re-present our perceptions of the world, contributing to the enactment of that world. Singing, dancing, preaching, and prophesying are all examples of embodied action that contribute to creating our world and giving it meaning.

iconic mode of presentation: According to Beckerman, the iconic mode of presentation is the "something" a performance gives the audience to respond to: that which is offered for display. Sound, color, movement—all of these are part of what is given to the audience. Dramas that are primarily iconic in nature (parades, shows of glorification, etc.) emphasize the static nature of what is.[5]

implicit audience: When a text is clearly speaking to an audience outside the text itself, the presence of that audience is implied. Analyzing how the implied audience is addressed can provide insight into the performative context. This is particularly important to our consideration of twice-used songs embedded in new narratives.

magnetic song: A magnetic song is used to persuade individuals, both emotionally and intellectually, to join a movement or at least to support a specific movement. The song is constructed to create solidarity and an intense feeling of membership in a group or movement.

performance: This complicated term runs the gamut of disciplines in the humanities, social sciences, and fine arts. Pageant, dance, magic, play making,

---

[4] Beckerman, *Dynamics of Drama*, 21.
[5] Ibid., 55.

parade, rally—all share a common feature as examples of public display: they involve the human being as both producer and product and offer a gift of sorts to spectators. Performances seem to be essential to the creation, sustenance, and transformation of culture.

performance criticism: This term has a wide range of meanings, from the traditional practice of critically analyzing performance histories, through the study of the presentation of theatre and drama, to the anthropological and sociological study of identity, politics, and power.

performative scheme: A performative scheme is a sequence of perceptible signs created by the performer. These signs are visual and/or auditory. The schematic emerges from the presentational idea that forms the core of the act itself. The activity must, then, be appropriate to the idea of the presentation.

performative mode of thought: The performative mode of thought is the peculiar type of orality evidenced in the prophetic literature of the Hebrew Bible. It is a way of thinking that engages both the cognitive and the imaginative aspects of thought to conceive of reality not in propositions but in actions and being. Similar to the notion of a dramatic imagination, it is the shared imaginative space of performance where both actors and spectators are transformed.

performance studies: Performance studies, a relatively new academic discipline, focuses on aspects of performance (presentation); it incorporates, for example, theories of dance, art, anthropology, philosophy, and cultural studies, investigating how we ourselves perform in individual, social, political, religious, gendered, and other contexts.

recycled songs: Recycled songs are songs that are reused, for a variety of reasons—for example, identity making, cultural transmission, consciousness raising, celebration, and cultural preservation.

rhetorical song: The rhetorical song is written to describe a particular social situation. Unlike a magnetic song, this song does not ask for action or seek to create a unified response but to pose a question or a position of dissent regarding the social situation. It asks for reflection upon the dominant understanding of a particular social situation.

spectator: The spectator is the cocreator of the theatrical or dramatic experience. Since theatre and drama occur only when presented to another or others, the spectator is both observer and participant in the experience.

In the case of the drama, the imagined act must be realized between the performers and the spectators. It is the spectator for whom the inner life of the drama is revealed.

speech act: In the grammar of performance, the speech act can be seen as the most basic, irreducible unit. It is thought, language, and action all rolled into one. In very simple terms, J. L. Austin teaches us that when saying something, we *do* something—most famously exemplified by the "I do" pronouncements made at the time of marriage.

suspension of disbelief: Suspension of disbelief is the practice of accepting something as "real" for a limited time within a specific context. We know the actor playing Hamlet is not really Hamlet, but we agree to believe that he is Hamlet for the duration of the performance.

theatre: "Theater occurs when one or more human beings isolated in time and space present themselves to another or others."[6] Theatre is the larger framework for acts of presentation. Drama is a form or subset of theatre.

---

[6]Beckerman, *Dynamics of Drama*, 10.

Bibliography

Ackroyd, Peter. *I and II Chronicles, Ezra, Nehemiah*. London: SCM, 1973.

———. *The Chronicler in His Age*. Journal for the Study of the Old Testament: Supplemental Series 101. Sheffield: JSOT Press, 1991.

———. "The Composition of the Song of Deborah." *Vetus Testamentum* 2 (1952): 160–62.

———. *The Second Book of Samuel*. Cambridge Bible Commentary. Cambridge: Cambridge University Press, 1977.

Albright, W. F. "Some Remarks on the Song of Moses in Deuteronomy 32." *Vetus Testamentum* 9 (1959): 339–46.

Allen, Leslie. *1, 2 Chronicles*. Waco: Word, 1987.

———. "Aspects of Generational Commitment and Challenge in Chronicles." Pages 123–32 in *The Chronicler as Theologian: Essays in Honor of Ralph W. Klein*. Edited by M. Patrick Graham, Steven McKenzie, and Gary Knoppers. Journal for the Study of the Old Testament: Supplement Series 371. New York: T&T Clark, 2003.

———. *The Greek Chronicles: The Relation of the Septuagint of I and II Chronicles to the Massoretic Text*. 2 vols. Supplements to Vetus Testamentum 25, 27. Leiden: Brill, 1974.

———. "Kerygmatic Units in 1 and 2 Chronicles." *Journal for the Study of the Old Testament* 41 (1988): 21–36.

Alter, Robert. *The Art of Biblical Poetry*. New York: Basic Books, 1985.

Anderson, A. A. *2 Samuel*. Word Biblical Commentary 11. Dallas: Word, 1989.

Assmann, Jan. "Collective Memory and Cultural Identity." Translated by John Czaplicka. "Cultural History/Cultural Studies," special issue, *New German Critique* 65 (spring–summer 1995): 125–33.

———. *Das kulturelle Gedächtnis: Schrift, Erinnerung, und politische Identität in frühen Hochkulturen*. Munich: Beck, 1992.

————. "Kulturelle und literarische Texte." Pages 76–77 in *Ancient Egyptian Literature: History and Forms*. Edited by A. Loprieno. Leiden: Brill, 1996.

Auld, Graeme. "What If the Chronicler Did Use the Deuteronomistic History?" *Biblical Interpretation* 8 (2000): 137–50.

Austin, J. L. *How to Do Things with Words*. Cambridge: Harvard University Press, 1962.

Bal, M. *Murder and Difference: Gender, Genre, and Scholarship on Sisera's Death*. Translated by M. Gumpert. Bloomington: Indiana University Press, 1988.

Balentine, S. *Prayer in the Hebrew Bible*. Minneapolis: Augsburg Fortress, 1993.

Barthes, Roland. *Image, Music, Text*. Translated by Stephen Heath. New York: Hill & Wang, 1977.

Bartlett, J. R. "The Historical Reference of Numbers XXI. 27–30." *Palestine Exploration Quarterly* 101 (1969): 94–100.

Beckerman, Bernard. *Dynamics of Drama: Theory and Method of Analysis*. New York: Drama Book Specialists, 1979.

————. *Theatrical Presentation: Performer, Audience, and Act*. Edited by Gloria Brim Beckerman and William Coco. New York: Routledge, 1990.

Ben Zvi, Ehud. *History, Literature, and Theology in the Book of Chronicles*. London: Equinox, 2006.

Bender, A. "Das Lied Exodus 15." *Zeitschrift für die alttestamentliche Wissenschaft* 23 (1903): 1–48.

Bergey, Ronald. "The Song of Moses [Deuteronomy 32:1–43] and Isaianic Prophecies: A Case of Early Intertextuality?" *Journal for the Study of the Old Testament* 28 (2003): 33–54.

Bleek, F. *Einleitung in das Alte Testament*. Berlin: Reimer, 1878.

Blenkinsopp, Joseph. *Ezra-Nehemiah*. Old Testament Library. Philadelphia: Westminster, 1988.

Boling, Robert, and G. Ernest Wright. *Joshua*. Anchor Bible 6. New York: Doubleday, 1982.

Braun, R. *1 Chronicles*. Word Biblical Commentary. Waco: Word, 1986.

Brenner, Martin. *The Song of the Sea: Ex 15:1–21*. Beiheft zur Zeitschrift für die alttestamentliche Wissenschaft 195. Berlin and New York: de Gruyter, 1991.

Brockett, Oscar G., and Franklin J. Hildy. *History of the Theatre*. 9th ed. Boston: Allyn & Bacon, 2000.

Brueggemann, Walter. "2 Samuel 21–24: An Appendix of Deconstruction?" *Catholic Biblical Quarterly* 50 (1988): 383–97.

————. "Samuel, Book of 1–2." Pages 965–73 in vol. 5 of *Anchor Bible Dictionary*. Edited by David N. Freedman. New York: Doubleday, 1992.

Budd, Philip. *Numbers.* Word Biblical Commentary. Waco: Word, 1984.

Budde, K. *Die Bücher Samuel.* Kurzer Hand-Commentar zum Alten Testament 8. Tübingen: Mohr, 1902.

Butler, Judith. *Excitable Speech.* New York: Routledge, 1997.

———. "Performative Acts and Gender Constitution: An Essay in Phenomenology and Feminist Theory." *Theatre Journal* 40 (1988).

Butler, Trent. "A Forgotten Passage from a Forgotten Era 1 (Chr. XVI 8–36)." *Vetus Testamentum* 28 (1978): 142–50.

———. *Joshua.* Word Biblical Commentary. Waco: Word, 1983.

Carlson, Marvin. *The Haunted Stage: The Theatre as Memory Machine.* Ann Arbor: University of Michigan Press, 2001.

———. *Performance: A Critical Introduction.* New York: Routledge, 1996.

Carlson, R. A. *David, the Chosen King.* Stockholm: Almqvist & Wiksell, 1964.

Carr, David. *Writing on the Tablet of the Heart: Origins of Scripture and Literature.* Oxford: Oxford University Press, 2005.

Carroll, Robert. *Jeremiah.* Philadelphia: Westminster, 1986.

Cassuto, U. *A Commentary on the Book of Exodus.* Translated by I. Abrahams. Jerusalem: Magnes, 1967.

Childs, Brevard S. *The Book of Exodus.* Old Testament Library. Philadelphia: Westminster, 1974.

Coggins, R. J. "Theology and Hermeneutics in the Books of Chronicles." Pages 263–78 in *In Search of True Wisdom: Essays in Old Testament Interpretation in Honour of Ronald E. Clements.* Edited by Edward Ball. Journal for the Study of the Old Testament: Supplement Series 300. Sheffield: Sheffield Academic, 1999.

Coogan, M. "A Structural and Literary Analysis of the Song of Deborah." *Catholic Biblical Quarterly* 40 (1978): 143–66.

Craigie, Peter. *The Book of Deuteronomy.* New International Commentary on the Old Testament. Grand Rapids: Eerdmans, 1976.

———. "The Song of Deborah and the Epic of Tukulti-Ninurta." *Journal of Biblical Literature* 88 (1969): 253–65.

Crane, Mary Thomas. "What Was Performance?" *Criticism* 43.2 (2002): 16–87.

Cross, Frank Moore. *From Epic to Canon: History and Literature in Ancient Israel.* Baltimore: Johns Hopkins University Press, 1998.

———. "A Reconstruction of the Judean Restoration." *Journal of Biblical Literature* 94 (1975): 4–18. Repr. pages 167–69 in *From Epic to Canon: History and Literature in Ancient Israel.* Baltimore: Johns Hopkins University Press, 1998.

———. "The Song of the Sea and Canaanite Myth." Pages 112–44 in *Canaanite Myth and Hebrew Epic.* Cambridge: Harvard University Press, 1973.

Cross, Frank Moore Jr., and David N. Freedman. "A Royal Song of Thanksgiving: II Samuel 22–Psalm 18." *Journal of Biblical Literature* 72 (1953): 15–34.

———. "The Song of Miriam." *Journal of Near Eastern Studies* 14 (1955): 237–50.

De Marinis, Marco. "Dramaturgy of the Spectator." *Drama Review* 31.2 (1987): 100–14.

De Vries, Simon. *1 and 2 Chronicles*. Forms of Old Testament Literature 11. Grand Rapids: Eerdmans, 1989.

Denisoff, R. Serge. "Songs of Persuasion: A Sociological Analysis of Urban Propaganda Songs." *Journal of American Folklore* 79, no. 314 (October–December 1966): 581–89.

Diamond, Elin. *Writing Performances*. London: Routledge, 1995.

Dillard, R. *2 Chronicles*. Word Bible Commentary. Waco: Word, 1987.

Doan, William, and Terry Giles. *Prophets, Performance, and Power: Performance Criticism of the Hebrew Bible*. New York: T&T Clark, 2005.

———. "The Song of Asaph: A Performance Critical Analysis of 1 Chronicles 16:8–36." *Catholic Biblical Quarterly* 70 (2008): 29–43.

Doane, Alger N. "The Ethnography of Scribal Writing and Anglo-Saxon Poetry: Scribe as Performer." *Oral Tradition* 9 (1994): 420–39.

Dolan, Jill. *Utopia in Performance: Finding Hope at the Theater*. Ann Arbor: University of Michigan Press, 2005.

Dozeman, Thomas. "The Song of the Sea and Salvation History." Pages 96–113 in *On the Way to Nineveh*. Edited by Stephen Cook and S. C. Winter. Atlanta: Scholars Press, 1999.

Driver, S. *Deuteronomy*. International Critical Commentary. New York: Charles Scribner's Sons, 1906.

Durham, John. *Exodus*. Word Bible Commentary. Waco: Word, 1987.

Eissfeldt, Otto. *The Old Testament: An Introduction*. Translated by Peter Ackroyd. Oxford: Blackwell, 1965.

Endres, John. "Theology of Worship in Chronicles." Pages 165–88 in *The Chronicler as Theologian: Essays in Honor of Ralph W. Klein*. Edited by M. Patrick Graham, Steven McKenzie, and Gary Knoppers. Journal for the Study of the Old Testament: Supplement Series 371. New York: T&T Clark, 2003.

Eskenazi, Tamara. "A Literary Approach to Chronicles' Ark Narrative in 1 Chronicles 13–16." Pages 258–74 in *Fortunate the Eyes That See: Essays in Honor of David Noel Freedman in Celebration of His Seventieth Birthday*. Edited by Astrid Beck et al. Grand Rapids: Eerdmans, 1995.

Flanagan, James. "Samuel, Book of 1–2." Pages 957–65 in vol. 5 of *Anchor Bible Dictionary*. Edited by David N. Freedman. New York: Doubleday, 1992.

Fowke, Edith, and Joe Glazer. *Songs of Work and Freedom*. Chicago: Labor Education Division, Roosevelt University, 1960.

Fox, Michael. *Character and Ideology in the Book of Esther*. Grand Rapids: Eerdmans, 1991.

Freedman, David N. "The Chronicler's Purpose." *Catholic Biblical Quarterly* 23 (1961): 436–42.

———. "Divine Names and Titles in Early Hebrew Poetry." Pages 55–107 in *Magnalia Dei, the Mighty Acts of God: Essays on the Bible and Archaeology in Memory of G. Ernest Wright*. Edited by Frank Moore Cross, Werner Lembke, and Patrick Miller. Garden City, N.Y.: Doubleday, 1976.

———. "Early Israelite Poetry." Pages 167–78 in *Pottery, Poetry, and Prophecy: Studies in Early Hebrew Poetry*. Winona Lake, Ind.: Eisenbrauns, 1980.

———. "The Refrain in David's Lament over Saul and Jonathan." Pages 115–26 in vol. 1 of *Ex orbe religionum: Studia Geo Widengren oblata*. Edited by C. J. Bleeker et al. Leiden: Brill, 1972.

———. "The Song of the Sea." Pages 179–86 in *Pottery, Poetry, and Prophecy: Studies in Early Hebrew Poetry*. Winona Lake, Ind.: Eisenbrauns, 1980.

———. "Strophe and Meter in Exodus 15." Pages 187–227 in *Pottery, Poetry, and Prophecy: Studies in Early Hebrew Poetry*. Winona Lake, Ind.: Eisenbrauns, 1980.

Fretheim, Terence. *Exodus*. Louisville: John Knox, 1991.

Giles, Terry, and William Doan. "Peformance Criticism of the Hebrew Bible." *Religion Compass* 6.3 (2008).

Globe, A. "The Literary Structure and Unity of the Song of Deborah." *Journal of Biblical Literature* 93 (1974): 493–512.

Goldman, Michael. *On Drama: Boundaries of Genre, Borders of Self*. Ann Arbor: University of Michigan Press, 2000.

Goody, Jack. *The Interface between the Written and the Oral*. Cambridge: Cambridge University Press, 1987.

Gottwald, Norman. *Tribes of Yahweh: A Sociology of the Religion of Liberated Israel, 1250–1050 B.C.E.* Maryknoll, N.Y.: Orbis, 1979.

Graham, M. Patrick, ed. *The Chronicler as Historian*. Sheffield: Sheffield Academic, 1997.

Graham, M. Patrick, Steven McKenzie, and Gary Knoppers, eds. *The Chronicler as Theologian: Essays in Honor of Ralph W. Klein*. Journal for the Study of the Old Testament: Supplement Series 371. New York: T&T Clark, 2003.

Gray, George. *Numbers*. International Critical Commentary. Edinburgh: T&T Clark, 1903.

Gray, John. *I and II Kings*. Old Testament Library. Philadelphia: Westminster, 1970.

Green, Archie. "A Discography (LP) of American Labor Union Songs." *New York Folklore Quarterly* 17 (1961): 187–93.

Greenway, John. *American Folksongs of Protest*. Philadelphia: University of Philadelphia Press; London: Oxford University Press, 1953.

Gunkel, H. *The Psalms: A Form Critical Introduction*. Translated by T. Horner. Philadelphia: Fortress, 1967.

Halpern, Baruch. "Doctrine by Misadventure: Between the Israelite Source and the Biblical Historian." Pages 41–73 in *The Poet and the Historian: Essays in Literary and Historical Biblical Criticism*. Edited by Richard Elliott Friedman. Harvard Semitic Series 26. Chico, Calif.: Scholars Press, 1983.

———. *The First Historians: The Hebrew Bible and History*. San Francisco: Harper & Row, 1988.

———. "The Resourceful Israelite Historian: The Song of Deborah and Israelite Historiography." *Harvard Theological Review* 76 (1983): 379–401.

Harrison, R. K. *Numbers*. Chicago: Moody, 1990.

Hauser, Alan. "Two Songs of Victory: A Comparison of Exodus 15 and Judges 5." Pages 265–84 in *Directions in Biblical Hebrew Poetry*. Edited by Elaine Follis. Sheffield: JSOT Press, 1987.

Hausmann, J. "Gottesdienst als Gotteslob: Erwägungen zu 1 Chr 16, 8–36." Pages 83–92 in *Spiritualität: Theologische Beiträge*. Edited by H. Wagner. Stuttgart: Calwer, 1987.

Hendel, Ronald. "A Book of Memories." *Bible Review* 18 (2002): 38–45, 52–53.

Herder, Johann G. von. *The Spirit of Hebrew Poetry*. 2 vols. Burlington, Vt.: Edward Smith, 1833. Repr., Naperville, Ill.: Aleph, 1971.

Hertzberg, H. W. *I and II Samuel*. Translated by J. Bowden. Old Testament Library. Philadelphia: Westminster, 1964.

Hill, Andrew. "Patchwork Poetry or Reasoned Verse? Connective Structures in 1 Chronicles XVI." *Vetus Testamentum* 33 (1983): 97–101.

Holladay, John. "The Day(s) the *Moon* Stood Still." *Journal of Biblical Literature* 88 (1968): 166–78.

Holladay, William. "Form and Word-Play in David's Lament over Saul and Jonathan." *Vetus Testamentum* 20 (1970): 153–89.

House, Paul. *Zephaniah: A Prophetic Drama*. Sheffield: Almond, 1989.

Houston, Walter. "Misunderstanding or Midrash? The Prose Appropriation of Poetic Material in the Hebrew Bible." *Zeitschrift für die alttestamentliche Wissenschaft* 109 (1997): 342–48.

Huffmon, Herbert. "The Covenant Lawsuit in the Prophets." *Journal of Biblical Literature* 78 (1959): 285–95.

Hurvitz, Avi. "Dating the Priestly Source in Light of the Historical Study of Biblical Hebrew a Century after Wellhausen." *Zeitschrift für die alttestamentliche Wissenschaft* 100 Supplement (1988): 88–99.

Jackson, Shannon. *Professing Performance: Theatre in the Academy from Philology to Performativity.* Cambridge: Cambridge University Press, 2004.

Japhet, Sara. *I and II Chronicles.* Old Testament Library. Louisville: Westminster/John Knox, 1993.

———. "Exile and Restoration in the Book of Chronicles." Pages 33–44 in *The Crisis of Israelite Religion: Transformation of Religious Tradition in Exilic and Post-exilic Times.* Edited by Bob Becking and Marjo Korpel. Leiden: Brill, 1999.

———. "The Historical Reliability of the Book of Chronicles." *Journal for the Study of the Old Testament* 33 (1985): 83–107.

———. *The Ideology of the Book of Chronicles and Its Place in Biblical Thought.* Translated by A Barber. Frankfurt am Main: Peter Lang, 1989.

———. "The Relationship between Chronicles and Ezra-Nehemiah." Pages 298–313 in *Congress Volume: Leuven, 1989.* Edited by J. A. Emerton. Leiden: Brill, 1991.

Jauss, Hans Robert. *Toward an Aesthetic of Reception.* Translated by Timothy Bahti. Minneapolis: University of Minnesota Press, 1982.

Johnstone, W. *1 and 2 Chronicles.* Sheffield: Sheffield Academic, 1997.

Keel, Othmar. "Der salomonische Tempelweihspruch: Beobachtungen zum religionsgeschichtlichen Kontext des ersten Jerusalemer Tempels." Pages 9–24 in *Gottesstadt und Gottesgarten: Zur Geschichte und Theologie des Jerusalemer Tempels.* Edited by Othmar Keel and Erich Zenger. Quaestiones disputatae 191. Freiburg im Breisgau: Herder, 2002.

Keil, C. *Die Bücher der Chronik.* Vol. 5 of *Biblischer Commentar über das Alte Testament.* Leipzig: Dorffling & Franke, 1861.

Kim, Hyun Chul Paul. "The Song of Moses (Deuteronomy 32:1–43) in Isaiah 40–55." Pages 147–71 in *God's Word for Our World.* Edited by J. Harold Ellens, Deborah Ellens, Rolf Knierim, and Isaac Kalimi. 2 vols. Journal for the Study of the Old Testament: Supplement Series 388–89. New York: T&T Clark, 2004.

Klein, Ralph W. "Psalms in Chronicles." *Currents in Theology and Mission* 32 (2005): 264–75.

Kleinig, John. "The Divine Institution of the Lord's Song in Chronicles." *Journal for the Study of the Old Testament* 55 (1992): 75–83.

———. *The Lord's Song: The Basis, Function, and Significance of Choral Music in Chronicles.* Journal for the Study of the Old Testament: Supplement Series 156. Sheffield: JSOT Press, 1993.

———. "Recent Research in Chronicles." *Currents in Research: Biblical Studies* 2 (1994): 43–76.

Kline, M. G. *Treaty of the Great King: The Covenant Structure of Deuteronomy.* Grand Rapids: Eerdmans, 1963.

Kraft, C. F. "Jashar, Book of." Page 803 in vol. 2 of *The Interpreter's Diction-ary of the Bible.* Edited by George A. Buttrick et al. 4 vols. New York: Abingdon, 1962.

Kugel, James. *The Idea of Biblical Poetry: Parallelism and Its History.* New Haven: Yale University Press, 1981.

Kuntzmann, Raymond. "Dieu vient vers son lieu de repos (2 Ch 6, 41)." Pages 203–13 in *Ce Dieu qui vient: Études sur l'Ancien et le Nouveau Testament offertes au professeur Bernard Renaud à l'occasion de son soix-ante-cinquième anniversaire.* Edited by Raymond Kuntzmann. Paris: Cerf, 1995.

Levine, Baruch. *Numbers 21–36.* Anchor Bible 4A. New York: Doubleday, 2000.

Levy, Shimon. *The Bible as Theatre.* Portland, Oreg.: Sussex Academic, 2002.

Lichtheim, Miriam. *Ancient Egyptian Literature: A Book of Readings.* 3 vols. Los Angeles: University of California Press, 1973–1980.

Loader, J. A. "Redaction and Function of the Chronistic 'Psalm of David.'" Pages 69–75 in *Studies in the Chronicler.* Edited by W. C. van Wyk. Johannesburg: Weeshuipers, 1976.

Lowth, Robert. *Lectures on the Sacred Poetry of the Hebrews.* Translated by G. Gregory. London: Chadwick, 1847.

Margalit, Baruch. "The Day the Sun Did Not Stand Still: A New Look at Joshua X 8–15." *Vetus Testamentum* 42 (1992): 466–91.

Mathys, Hans-Peter. *Dichter und Beter: Theologen aus spätalttestamentlichen Zeit.* Orbis biblicus et orientalis 132. Freiburg, Switz.: Universitäts-verlag, 1994.

Mayes, A. D. *Deuteronomy.* London: Marshall, Morgan & Scott, 1981.

McCarter, P. Kyle. *II Samuel.* Anchor Bible 9. Garden City, N.Y.: Doubleday, 1984.

McKenzie, Steven. "The Chronicler as Redactor." Pages 70–90 in *The Chronicler as Theologian: Essays in Honor of Ralph W. Klein.* Edited by M. Patrick Graham, Steven McKenzie, and Gary Knoppers. Journal for the Study of the Old Testament: Supplement Series 371. New York: T&T Clark, 2003.

———. *The Chronicler's Use of the Deuteronomistic History.* Atlanta: Scholars Press, 1985.

Meyers, Carol. "Miriam the Musician." Pages 207–30 in *A Feminist Com-panion to Exodus to Deuteronomy.* Edited by Athalya Brenner. Feminist Companion to the Bible 6. Sheffield: Sheffield Academic, 1994.

Meyers, J. M. *1 Chronicles.* Anchor Bible 12. New York: Doubleday, 1965.

Michel, D. *Tempora und Satzstellung in den Psalmen*. Abhandlungen zur evangelischen Theologie 1. Bonn: H. Bouvier, 1960.

Milgrom, Jacob. *Numbers*. JPS Torah Commentary. Philadelphia: Jewish Publication Society, 1989.

Miller, Patrick. "Constitution or Instruction? The Purpose of Deuteronomy." Pages 125–41 in *Constituting the Community: Studies on the Polity of Ancient Israel in Honor of S. Dean McBride Jr*. Edited by John T. Strong and Steven S. Tuell. Winona Lake, Ind.: Eisenbrauns, 2005.

Montgomery, James. *The Book of Kings*. International Critical Commentary. Edinburgh: T&T Clark, 1951.

Mowinckel, S. "Hat es ein israelitisches Nationalepos gegeben?" *Zeitschrift für die alttestamentliche Wissenschaft* 53 (1935): 130–52.

Muilenburg, James. "A Liturgy on the Triumphs of Yahweh." Pages 233–51 in *Studia biblica et semitica*. Wageningen, Neth.: H. Veenman, 1966.

Na'aman, N. "Sources and Redaction in the Chronicler's Genealogies of Asher and Ephraim." *Journal for the Study of the Old Testament* 49 (1991): 99–111.

Nelson, Richard. *Deuteronomy*. Old Testament Library. Philadelphia: Westminster John Knox, 2002.

———. *Joshua*. Old Testament Library. Louisville: Westminster John Knox, 1997.

Newsom, Carol. "Joshua, Book of." Pages 1002–15 in vol. 3 of *Anchor Bible Dictionary*. Edited by David N. Freedman. New York: Doubleday, 1992.

Newsome, James. "Toward a New Understanding of the Chronicler and His Purposes." *Journal of Biblical Literature* 94 (1975): 4–18.

Nielson, Kirsten. "Whose Song of Praise? Reflections on the Purpose of the Psalm in 1 Chronicles 16." Pages 327–36 in *The Chronicler as Author: Studies in Text and Texture*. Edited by M. Patrick Graham and Steven McKenzie. Journal for the Study of the Old Testament: Supplement Series 263. Sheffield: Sheffield Academic, 1999.

Nigosian, Solomon. "Linguistic Patterns of Deuteronomy 32." *Biblica* 78 (1997): 206–24.

———. "The Song of Moses (Dt 32): A Structural Analysis." *Ephemerides theologicae lovanienes* 72 (1996): 5–22.

Noth, Martin. *The Chronicler's History*. Translated by H. G. M. Williamson. Journal for the Study of the Old Testament: Supplement Series 50. Sheffield: Sheffield Academic, 1987.

O'Connor, M. *Hebrew Verse Structure*. Winona Lake, Ind.: Eisenbrauns, 1980.

Oeming, Manfred. *Das wahre Israel: Die 'genealogische Vorhalle' 1 Chronik 1–9*. Beiträge zur Wissenschaft vom Alten und Neuen Testament 128. Stuttgart: Kohlhammer, 1990.

Olson, Dennis. *Deuteronomy and the Death of Moses: A Theological Reading.* Minneapolis: Fortress, 1994.

Patterson, Richard. "Victory at Sea: Prose and Poetry in Exodus 14–15." *Bibliotheca sacra* 161 (2004): 42–54.

Peltonen, Kai. "Function, Explanation, and Literary Phenomena: Aspects of Source Criticism as Theory and Method in the History of Chronicles Research." Pages 18–69 in *The Chronicler as Author: Studies in Text and Texture.* Edited by M. Patrick Graham and Steven McKenzie. Journal for the Study of the Old Testament: Supplement Series 263. Sheffield: Sheffield Academic, 1999.

Peterson, David, and Kent Richards. *Interpreting Hebrew Poetry.* Minneapolis: Fortress, 1992.

Phythian-Adams, W. J. "A Meteorite of the Fourteenth Century." *Palestine Exploration Quarterly* 78 (1946): 116–24.

Rad, Gerhard von. *Deuteronomy.* Old Testament Library. Philadelphia: Westminster, 1966.

Reventlow, H. G. *Gebet im Alten Testament.* Stuttgart: Kohlhammer, 1986.

Roach, Joseph, and Janelle Reinelt. *Critical Theory and Performance.* Ann Arbor: University of Michigan Press, 1992.

Rozik, Eli. *The Roots of Theatre: Rethinking Ritual and Other Theories of Origin.* Iowa City: University of Iowa Press, 2002.

Rudolph, William. *Chronikbücher.* Tübingen: Mohr, 1955.

———. "Problems of the Book of Chronicles." *Vetus Testamentum* 4 (1954): 401–9.

Sailhamer, John. *First and Second Chronicles.* Chicago: Moody, 1983.

Sanders, P. *The Provenance of Deuteronomy 32.* Leiden: Brill, 1996.

Schaper, Joachim. "A Theology of Writing: The Oral and the Written, God as Scribe and the Book of Deuteronomy." Pages 97–111 in *Anthropology and Biblical Studies: Avenues of Approach.* Edited by Louise Lawrence and Mario Aguilar. Leiden: Deo, 2005.

Schechner, Richard. *Between Theater and Anthropology.* Philadelphia: University of Pennsylvania Press, 1985.

———. *Performance Studies: An Introduction.* New York: Routledge, 2002.

Schmuttermayr, Georg. *Psalm 18 und 2 Samuel 22: Studien zu einem Doppeltext.* Munich: Kosel, 1971.

Schniedewind, William. "The Chronicler as an Interpreter of Scripture." Pages 158–80 in *The Chronicler as Author: Studies in Text and Texture.* Edited by M. Patrick Graham and Steven McKenzie. Journal for the Study of the Old Testament: Supplement Series 263. Sheffield: Sheffield Academic, 1999.

———. *How the Bible Became a Book.* Cambridge: Cambridge University Press, 2004.

Schokel, Alonso. *A Manual of Hebrew Poetics*. Rome: Pontifical Biblical Institute, 1988.

Sekine, Masao. "Lyric Literature in the Davidic-Solomonic Period in the Light of the History of Israelite Literature." Pages 1–11 in *Studies in the Period of David and Solomon and Other Essays*. Edited by Tomoo Ishida. Winona Lake, Ind.: Eisenbrauns, 1982.

Sheppard, Gerald. *Wisdom as a Hermeneutical Construct*. Beiheft zur Zeitschrift für die alttestamentliche Wissenschaft 151. Berlin: de Gruyter, 1980.

Shipp, R. Mark. "'Remember His Covenant Forever': A Study of the Chronicler's Use of the Psalms." *Restoration Quarterly* 35 (1993): 31–39.

Smith, H. P. *The Books of Samuel*. International Critical Commentary. New York: Charles Scribner's Sons, 1909.

Smith, Mark. "The Poetics of Exodus 15 and Its Position in the Book." Pages 26–29 in *Imagery and Imagination in Biblical Literature: Essays in Honor of Aloysius Fitzgerald, F.S.C.* Edited by Lawrence Boadt and Mark Smith. Catholic Biblical Quarterly Monograph Series 32. Washington, D.C.: Catholic Biblical Association of America, 2001.

Soggin, J. Alberto. *Joshua*. Old Testament Library. Philadelphia: Westminster, 1972.

———. *Judges*. Translated by John Bowden. Old Testament Library. Philadelphia: Westminster, 1981.

Sonnot, Jean-Pierre. *The Book within the Book: Writing in Deuteronomy*. New York: Brill, 1997.

States, Bert O. *Dreaming and Storytelling*. Ithaca, N.Y.: Cornell University Press, 1993.

Sternberg, Meir. *The Poetics of Biblical Narrative: Ideological Literature and the Drama of Reading*. Bloomington: Indiana University Press, 1987.

Stulman, Louis. *Jeremiah*. Nashville: Abingdon, 2005.

Sturdy, J. *Numbers*. Cambridge Bible Commentary. Cambridge: Cambridge University Press, 1972.

Talshir, Zipora. "Several Canon-Related Concepts Originating in Chronicles." *Zeitschrift für die alttestamentliche Wissenschaft* 113 (2001): 386–403.

Thackeray, H. "New Light on the Book of Jasher (a Study of 3 Regn.VIII 53b LXX)." *Journal of Theological Studies* 11 (1910): 518–32.

Thiessen, Matthew. "Form and Function of the Song of Moses." *Journal of Biblical Literature* 123 (2004): 401–24.

Throntveit, Mark. "Songs in a New Key: The Psalmic Structure of the Chronicler's Hymn (1 Chr 16:8–36)." Pages 153–70 in *A God So Near: Essays on Old Testament Theology in Honor of Patrick D. Miller*. Edited by Brent Strawn and Nancy Bowen. Winona Lake, Ind.: Eisenbrauns, 2003.

Tigay, J. *Deuteronomy*. JPS Torah Commentary. Philadelphia: Jewish Publication Society, 1996.

Trible, P. "Bringing Miriam out of the Shadows." *Bible Review* 5 (1989): 13–25, 34.

Turner, Victor. *The Anthropology of Performance*. New York: PAJ, 1986.

———. *Dramas, Fields, and Metaphors*. Ithaca, N.Y.: Cornell University Press, 1974.

———. *From Ritual to Theatre*. New York: PAJ, 1982.

Van Seters, John. "The Conquest of Sihon's Kingdom: A Literary Examination." *Journal of Biblical Literature* 91 (1972): 182–97.

Varela, Francisco, Evan Thompson, and Eleanor Rosch. *The Embodied Mind: Cognitive Science and Human Experience*. Cambridge: MIT Press, 1993.

Velikovsky, Immanuel. *Worlds in Collision*. New York: Macmillan, 1950.

Vesco, J. "Le psaume 18, lecture davidique." *Revue biblique* 94 (1987): 5–62.

Vogel, Dan. "Moses as Poet: Ha azinu as Poem." *Jewish Bible Quarterly* 31 (2003): 211–18.

Wallace, Howard. "What Chronicles Has to Say about Psalms." Pages 267–91 in *The Chronicler as Author: Studies in Text and Texture*. Edited by M. Patrick Graham and Steven McKenzie. Journal for the Study of the Old Testament: Supplement Series 263. Sheffield: Sheffield Academic, 1999.

Walton, J. Michael. *Greek Theatre Practice*. Westport, Conn.: Greenwood, 1980.

Watson, Wilfred G. *Classical Hebrew Poetry: A Guide to Its Techniques*. Journal for the Study of the Old Testament: Supplement Series 26. Sheffield: JSOT Press, 1984.

Watts, James. "Biblical Psalms outside the Psalter." Pages 288–309 in *The Book of Psalms: Composition and Reception*. Edited by Peter Flint and Patrick Miller. Vetus Testamentum Supplements 99. Leiden: Brill, 2004.

———. *Psalm and Story: Inset Hymns in Hebrew Narrative*. Journal for the Study of the Old Testament: Supplement Series 139. Sheffield: JSOT Press, 1992.

———. "Psalmody in Prophecy: Habakkuk 3 in Context." Pages 209–23 in *Forming Prophetic Literature: Essays on Isaiah and the Twelve in Honor of John D. W. Watts*. Edited by James Watts and Paul House. Journal for the Study of the Old Testament: Supplement Series 235. Sheffield: Sheffield Academic, 1996.

———. "Song and the Ancient Reader." *Perspectives in Religious Studies* 22 (1995): 135–47.

————. "'This Song': Conspicuous Poetry in Hebrew Prose." Pages 345–58 in *Verse in Ancient Near Eastern Prose.* Edited by J. C. de Moor and Wilfred G. Watson. Alter Orient und Altes Testament 42. Neukirchen-Vluyn: Neukirchener Verlag, 1993.

Webb, B. G. *The Book of Judges: An Integrated Reading.* Journal for the Study of the Old Testament: Supplement Series 46. Sheffield: JSOT Press, 1972.

Weinberg, J. P. *The Citizen-Temple Community.* Translated by D. L. Smith-Christopher. Journal for the Study of the Old Testament: Supplement Series 151. Sheffield: JSOT Press, 1992.

Weiskopf, A. "Artists Remake Classic Song to Benefit Sept. 11, AIDS Victims." *The Heights: The Independent Student Newspaper of Boston College* (January 15, 2002): 2.

Weitzman, Steven. *Song and Story in Biblical Narrative: The History of a Literary Convention in Ancient Israel.* Bloomington: Indiana University Press, 1997.

Wellhausen, J. *Die Composition des Hexateuchs und der historischen Bücher des Alten Testaments.* 3d ed. Berlin: Georg Reimer, 1899. Repr., Berlin: de Gruyter, 1963.

Williamson, H. G. M. *1 and 2 Chronicles.* New Century Bible. Grand Rapids: Eerdmans, 1982.

————. "History." Pages 25–38 in *It Is Written—Scripture Citing Scripture: Essays in Honour of Barnabas Lindars, SSF.* Edited by D. A. Carson and H. G. M. Williamson. Cambridge: Cambridge University Press, 1988.

Wright, G. E. "The Lawsuit of God: A Form-Critical Study of Deuteronomy 32." Pages 26–67 in *Israel's Prophetic Heritage: Essays in Honor of James Muilenburg.* Edited by Bernhard Anderson and Walter Harrelson. New York: Harper, 1962.

Wright, John. "The Founding Father: The Structure of the Chronicler's David Narrative." *Journal of Biblical Literature* 117 (1998): 45–59.

Performance Criticism Bibliography

The following bibliography is by no means exhaustive. The entries selected are those we have found useful in developing a Performance Critical approach to the Hebrew Bible and give to the reader a point of entry to the literature on both the theory and application of Performance Criticism to the biblical text.

Theatre

Bennett, Susan. *Theatre Audiences: A Theory of Production and Reception.* 2d ed. New York: Routledge, 1997.

Bieber, Margaret. *The History of the Greek and Roman Theater.* Princeton, N.J.: Princeton University Press, 1961.

Carlson, Marvin. *The Haunted Stage: The Theatre as Memory Machine.* Ann Arbor: University of Michigan Press, 2001.

———. *Performance: A Critical Introduction.* New York: Routledge, 1996.

Kirsch, Gesa, and Duane H. Roen, eds. *A Sense of the Audience in Written Communication.* Written Communication Annual 5. Newbury Park, Calif.: Sage, 1990.

Levy, Shimon. *The Bible as Theatre.* Portland, Oreg.: Sussex Academic, 2002.

———. *Theatre and Holy Script.* Brighton, U.K.: Sussex Academic, 1999.

Maclean, Marie. *Narrative as Performance: The Baudelairean Experiment.* New York: Routledge, 1988.

McNeill, David. *Gesture and Thought.* Chicago: University of Chicago Press, 2005.

Orality

Bauman, Richard. *Story, Performance, and Event: Contextual Studies of Oral Narrative*. Cambridge: Cambridge University Press, 1986.

———. *Verbal Art as Performance*. Rowley, Mass.: Newbury House, 1978.

Becker, John E. "Orality and Literacy." *Worldview* 26 (1983): 8–10.

Ben Amos, D., and K. Goldstein, eds. *Folklore: Performance and Communication*. The Hague: Mouton, 1975.

Bright, William. "Literature: Written and Oral." Pages 271–83 in *Analyzing Discourse—Text and Talk: Georgetown University Round Table on Languages and Linguistics, 1981*. Edited by Deborah Tannen. Washington, D.C.: Georgetown University Press, 1982.

Chafe, Wallace L. "Integration and Involvement in Speaking, Writing, and Oral Literature." Pages 35–53 in *Spoken and Written Language: Exploring Orality and Literacy*. Edited by Deborah Tannen. Advances in Discourse Processes 9. Norwood, N.J.: Ablex, 1982.

Coward, Harold G. "The Spiritual Power of Oral and Written Scripture." Pages 111–37 in *Silence, the Word, and the Sacred*. Edited by E. D. Blodgett and H. G. Coward. Waterloo, Ont.: Wilfrid Laurier University Press, 1989.

Farrell, Thomas. "An Overview of Walter Ong's Work." Pages 25–43 in *Media, Consciousness, and Culture: Exploration of Walter Ong's Work*. Edited by Bruce E. Gronbeck, Thomas J. Farrell, and Paul Soukop. Newbery Park, Calif.: Sage, 1991.

Fine, Elizabeth, and Jean Haskell Speer, eds. *Performance Culture and Identity*. Westport, Conn.: Praeger, 1992.

Finnegan, Ruth. *Literacy and Orality Studies in the Technology of Communication*. New York: Blackwell, 1998.

———. *Oral Poetry: Its Nature, Sign, and Social Context*. Bloomington: Indiana University Press, 1992.

Foley, John Miles. *The Singer of Tales in Performance*. Bloomington: Indiana University Press, 1995.

———. *The Theory of Oral Composition: History and Methodology*. Bloomington: Indiana University Press, 1988.

Fumiss, Graham. *Orality: The Power of the Spoken Word*. New York: Palgrave Macmillan, 2004.

Goody, Jack. *Domestication of the Savage Mind*. Cambridge: Cambridge University Press, 1977.

———. *The Interface between the Written and the Oral*. Cambridge: Cambridge University Press, 1987.

———. *The Logic of Writing and the Organization of Society*. Cambridge: Cambridge University Press, 1986.

———. *The Power of the Written Tradition*. Washington, D.C.: Smithsonian Institution Press, 2000.

———, ed. *Literacy in Traditional Societies*. Cambridge: Cambridge University Press, 1968.

Goody, Jack, and Ian Watt. "The Consequence of Literacy." *Comparative Studies in Society and History* 5 (1963): 304–45.

Graham, William. *Beyond the Written Word: Oral Aspects of Scripture in the History of Religion*. Cambridge: Cambridge University Press, 1987.

———. "Scripture as Spoken Word." Pages 129–69 in *Rethinking Scripture*. Edited by Miriam Levering. Albany: State University of New York Press, 1989.

Gray, Bennison. "Repetition in Oral Literature." *Journal of American Folklore* 84 (1971): 289–303.

Green, Laurie. "Oral Culture and the World of Words." *Theology* 102 (1999): 328–35.

Havelock, Eric A. *The Muse Learns to Write: Reflections on Orality and Literacy from Antiquity to the Present*. New Haven: Yale University Press, 1986.

———. "Oral Composition in the *Oedipus Tyrannus* of Sophocles." *New Literary History* 16 (1984): 175–97.

Jaffee, Martin S. "Oral Culture in Scriptural Religion: Some Exploratory Studies." *Recherches de science religieuse* 24.3 (1998): 223–30.

Jahandarie, Khosrow. *Spoken and Written Discourse: A Multi-disciplinary Perspective*. Stamford, Conn.: Ablex, 1999.

Joubert, A. *The Power of Performance*. Berlin: Mouton de Gruyter, 2004.

Lord, Albert Bates. *Epic Singers and Oral Tradition*. Ithaca, N.Y.: Cornell University Press, 1991.

———. *The Singer of Tales*. Cambridge: Harvard University Press, 1960.

Mazamisa, Welile. "Reading from This Place: From Orality to Literacy/Textuality and Back." *Scriptura* 9 (1991): 67–72.

Murray, Denise E. "The Context of Oral and Written Language: A Framework for Mode and Medium Switching." *Language and Society* 17 (1988): 351–73.

Niditch, Susan. *Oral World and Written Word*. Louisville: Westminster John Knox, 1996.

O'Donnell, Roy C. "Syntactic Differences between Speech and Writing." *American Speech* 49 (1974): 102–10.

Olson, David R. "From Utterance to Text: The Bias of Language in Speech and Writing." *Harvard Educational Review* 47 (1977): 257–81.

———. *The World on Paper: The Conceptual and Cognitive Implications of Writing and Reading*. Cambridge: Cambridge University Press, 1994.

Olson, David R., and Nancy Torrance. *Literacy and Orality*. Cambridge: Cambridge University Press, 1991.

Ong, Walter J. *Interfaces of the Word: Studies in the Evolution of Consciousness and Culture*. Ithaca, N.Y.: Cornell University Press, 1977.

———. "Oral Remembering and Narrative Structures." Pages 12–24 in *Analyzing Discourse: Text and Talk: Georgetown University Round Table on Languages and Linguistics, 1981*. Edited by Deborah Tannen. Washington, D.C.: Georgetown University Press, 1982.

———. *Orality and Literacy: The Technologizing of the Word*. London: Routledge, 1988.

———. *The Presence of the Word: Some Prolegomena for Cultural and Religious History*. Minneapolis: University of Minnesota Press, 1967.

———. "Text as Interpretation: Mark and After." *Semeia* 39 (1987): 7–26. Repr., pages 191–210 in vol. 2 of *Faith and Contexts*. Edited by Walter Ong, T. J. Farrell, and P. A. Soukup. Atlanta: Scholars Press, 1992.

———. "Writing Is a Technology That Restructures Thought." Pages 23–50 in *The Written Word: Literacy in Transition*. Edited by Gerd Baumann. Oxford: Clarendon, 1986.

Schlain, Leonard. *The Alphabet versus the Goddess: The Conflict between Word and Image*. New York: Penguin, 1998.

Simms, Norman. *The Humming Tree: A Study in the History of Mentalities*. Urbana: University of Illinois Press, 1992.

Tannen, Deborah. "The Myth of Orality and Literacy." Pages 37–50 in *Linguistics and Literacy*. Edited by William Frawley. New York: Plenum, 1982.

———, ed. *Spoken and Written Language: Exploring Orality and Literacy*. Advances in Discourse Processes 9. Norwood, N.J.: Ablex, 1982.

Hebrew Bible Interpretation

Coote, Robert. 1976. "The Application of Oral Theory to Biblical Hebrew Literature." *Semeia* 5 (1976): 1–64.

———. "Tradition, Oral, OT." Pages 914–16 in *Interpreter's Dictionary of the Bible: Supplementary Volume*. Nashville: Abingdon, 1976.

Doan, William, and Terry Giles. "Masking God: The Application of Drama Theory to Biblical Texts." *Proceedings: Eastern Great Lakes and Midwest Biblical Societies* 22 (2002): 127–45.

———. "Masking God: The Role of Ritual Masks in the Religion(s) of Ancient Israel." *Text and Presentation: Journal of the Comparative Drama Conference* 23 (2002): 1–15.

———. "Prophecy and Theater." *Journal of Religion and Society* 2 (2000). No pages. Cited January 27, 2008. Online: http://moses.creighton. edu/JRS/2000/2000-2.html.

———. *Prophets, Performance, and Power: Performance Criticism of the Hebrew Bible*. New York: T&T Clark, 2005.

———. "The Songs of Israel: Exodus 15:1–18." *Proceedings: Eastern Great Lakes and Midwest Bible Societies* 25 (2005): 29–42.

Gitay, Yehoshua. "Deutero-Isaiah: Oral or Written?" *Journal of Biblical Literature* 99.2 (1980): 185–97.

Greene, John T. *The Role of the Messenger and Message in the Ancient Near East: Oral and Written Communication in the Ancient Near East and in the Hebrew Scriptures—Communicators and Communiqués in Context*. Atlanta: Scholars Press, 1989.

Jaffe, Martin. "Figuring Early Rabbinic Literary Culture." *Semeia* 65 (1994): 67–73.

Long, Burke O. "Recent Field Studies in Oral Literature and Their Bearing on OT Criticism." *Vetus Testamentum* 26.2 (1976): 187–98.

Person, R. F. "The Ancient Israelite Scribe as Performer." *Journal of Biblical Literature* 117 (1998): 601–9.

Rebera, Basil. "Translating a Text to Be Spoken and Heard: A Study of Ruth 1." *Bible Today* 43 (1992): 230–36.

Silver, Daniel Jeremy. *The Story of Scripture: From Oral Tradition to the Written Word*. New York: Basic Books, 1990.

Stacey, David. *Prophetic Drama in the Old Testament*. London: Epworth, 1990.

New Testament Cultural Context

Alexander, Loveday. "Ancient Book Production and the Circulation of the Gospels." Pages 71–111 in *The Gospels for All Christians*. Edited by Richard Bauckham. Grand Rapids: Eerdmans, 1998.

———. "The Living Voice: Skepticism towards the Written Word in Early Christian and in Greco-Roman Texts." Pages 221–47 in *The Bible in Three Dimensions*. Edited by D. A. Clines. Sheffield: JSOT Press, 1990.

Bar-ilan, Meir. "Scribes and Books in the Late Second Commonwealth and Rabbinic Period." Pages 21–37 in *Mikra: Text, Translation, Reading, and Interpretation of the Hebrew Bible in Ancient Judaism and Early Christianity*. Edited by Martin Jan Mulder. Compendia rerum iudaicarum ad Novum Testamentum 1. Philadelphia: Fortress, 1988.

Botha, Pieter. "Greco-Roman Literacy as Setting for New Testament Writings." *Neotestamentica* 26 (1992): 195–215.

————. "Letter Writing and Oral Communication in Antiquity: Suggested Implications for the Interpretation of Paul's Letter to the Galatians." *Scriptura* 42 (1992): 17–34.

————. "Mute Manuscripts: Analyzing a Neglected Aspect of Ancient Communication." *Theologia evangelica* 23 (1990): 35–47.

Downing, F. Gerald. "Word-Processing in the Ancient World: The Social Production and Performance of Q." *Journal for the Study of the New Testament* 64 (1996): 29–48.

Draper, Jonathan A., ed. *Orality, Literacy, and Colonialism in Antiquity*. Atlanta: Society of Biblical Literature, 2004.

Gamble, Harry Y. *Books and Readers in the Early Church: A History of Early Christian Texts*. New Haven: Yale University Press, 1995.

Haines-Eitzen, Kim. *Guardians of Letters: Literacy, Power, and the Transmitters of Early Christian Literature*. New York: Oxford University Press, 2000.

Horsley, Richard, ed. *Oral Performance, Popular Tradition, and Hidden Transcript in Q*. Semeia Studies 60. Atlanta: Society of Biblical Literature, 2006.

Lord, Albert B. "The Gospels as Oral Traditional Literature." Pages 33–91 in *The Relationships among the Gospels: An Interdisciplinary Dialogue*. Edited by William O. Walker. San Antonio: Trinity University Press, 1978.

Millard, Alan. *Reading and Writing in the Time of Jesus*. New York: New York University Press, 2000.

Murphy-O'Connor, Jerome. *Paul the Letter-Writer: His World, His Options, His Skills*. Collegeville, Minn.: Liturgical Press, 1995.

Noakes, Susan. "Gracious Words: Luke's Jesus and the Reading of Sacred Poetry at the Beginning of the Christian Era." Pages 38–57 in *The Ethnography of Reading*. Edited by Jonathan Boyarin. Berkeley: University of California Press, 1992.

Olson, David R. *The World on Paper: The Conceptual and Cognitive Implications of Writing and Reading*. Cambridge: Cambridge University Press, 1994.

Slusser, Michael. "Reading Silently in Antiquity." *Journal of Biblical Literature* 111 (1992): 499.

Starr, Raymond J. "Reading Aloud: *Lectores* and Roman Reading." *Classical Journal* 86.4 (1991): 337–43.

Stirewalt, M. Luther. *Paul, the Letter Writer*. Grand Rapids: Eerdmans, 2003.

Stock, Brian. *Listening for the Text: On the Uses of the Past*. Philadelphia: University of Pennsylvania Press, 1996.

Thomas, Rosalind. *Oral Tradition and Written Record in Classical Athens*. Cambridge Studies in Oral and Literate Culture 18. Cambridge: Cambridge University Press, 1990.

Tolbert, Mary Ann. *Sowing the Gospel: Mark's World in Literary Historical Perspective.* Philadelphia: Fortress, 1989.

Yaghjian, Lucretia B. "Ancient Reading." Page 206–30 in *The Social Sciences and New Testament Interpretation.* Edited by Richard Rohrbaugh. Peabody, Mass.: Hendrickson, 1996.

New Testament Interpretation

Anderson, Oivind. "Oral Tradition." Pages 17–58 in *Jesus and the Oral Gospel Tradition.* Edited by Henry Wansbrough. Sheffield: Sheffield Academic, 1991.

Bailey, Kenneth E. "Informal Controlled Oral Tradition and the Synoptic Gospels." *Asia Journal of Theology* 5 (1991): 34–54.

———. "Middle Eastern Oral Tradition and the Synoptic Gospels." *Expository Times* 106 (1995): 363–67.

———. "Recovering the Poetic Structure of 1 Cor. i 17–ii 2: A Study in Text and Commentary." *Novum Testamentum* 17 (1973): 265–96.

Barr, David. "The Apocalypse of John as Oral Enactment." *Interpretation* 40 (1986): 243–56.

Bartholomew, Gilbert. "Feed My Lambs: John 2 1:15–19 as Oral Gospel." *Semeia* 39 (1987): 69–86.

Barton, Stephen C. "New Testament Interpretation as Performance." *Scottish Journal of Theology* 52.2 (1999): 179–208.

Beavis, Mary Ann. *Mark's Audience: The Literary and Social Setting of Mark 4.11–12.* Journal for the Study of the New Testament: Supplement Series 33. Sheffield: Sheffield Academic, 1989.

Bilezekian, Gilbert. *The Liberated Gospel: A Comparison of the Gospel of Mark and Greek Tragedy.* Grand Rapids: Baker, 1977.

Boomershine, Thomas. "Peter's Denial as Polemic or Confession: The Implication of Media Theory for Biblical Hermeneutics." *Semeia* 39 (1987): 47–68.

Botha, Pieter. "The Historical Setting of Mark's Gospel: Problems and Possibilities." *Journal for the Study of the New Testament* 51 (1993): 27–55.

———. "Letter Writing and Oral Communication in Antiquity: Suggested Implications for the Interpretation of Paul's Letter to the Galatians." *Scriptura* 42 (1992): 17–34.

———. "Mark's Story as Oral Traditional Literature: Rethinking the Transmission of Some Traditions about Jesus." *Hervormde teologiese studies* 47 (1991): 304–31.

———. "Paul and Gossip: A Social Mechanism in Early Christian Communities." *Neotestamentica* 32 (1998): 267–88.

———. "The Verbal Art of the Pauline Letters: Rhetoric, Performance, and Presence." Pages 409–28 in *Rhetoric and the New Testament: Essays from the 1992 Heidelberg Conference.* Edited by Stanley E. Porter and T. H. Olbricht. Sheffield: Sheffield Academic, 1993.

Bryan, Christopher. *A Preface to Mark: Notes on the Gospel in Its Literary and Cultural Context.* Oxford: Oxford University Press, 1993.

Byrskog, Samuel. *Story as History—History as Story: The Gospel Tradition in the Context of Ancient Oral History.* Leiden: Brill, 2000.

Callahan, Allan Dwight. "The Language of the Apocalypse." *Harvard Theological Review* 88 (1995): 453–70.

Carter, Warren. *Matthew: Storyteller, Interpreter, Evangelist.* Peabody, Mass.: Hendrickson, 1996.

Chapell, Bryan. "The Incarnate Voice: An Exhortation for Excellence in the Oral Reading of Scripture." *Presbyterion* 14 (1988): 42–57.

Crafton, Jeffrey. *The Agency of the Apostle: A Dramatistic Analysis of Paul's Responses to Conflict in 2 Corinthians.* Journal for the Study of the New Testament: Supplement Series 51. Sheffield: Sheffield Academic, 1991.

Davis, Casey W. *Oral Biblical Criticism: The Influence of the Principles of Orality on the Literary Structures of Paul's Epistle to the Philippians.* Journal for the Study of the New Testament: Supplement Series 172. Sheffield: Sheffield Academic, 1999.

———. "Oral Biblical Criticism: Raw Data in Philippians." Pages 96–124 in *Linguistics and the New Testament: Critical Junctures.* Edited by Stanley E. Porter and D. A. Carson. Sheffield: Sheffield Academic, 1999.

Dewey, Joanna. "Mark as Oral Narrative: Structures as Clues to Understanding." *Sewanee Theological Review* 36 (1992): 15–56.

———. "Oral Methods of Structuring Narrative in Mark." *Interpretation* 13 (1989): 32–14.

———. "Textuality in an Oral Culture: A Survey of the Pauline Traditions." *Semeia* 65 (1995): 37–65.

Downing, F. Gerald. "Word-Processing in the Ancient World: The Social Production and Performance of Q." *Journal for the Study of the New Testament* 64 (1996): 29–48.

Dudrey, R. "I John and Public Reading of Scripture." *Stone-Campbell Journal* 6 (2003): 235–55.

Fowler, Robert. *"Let the Reader Understand": Reader-Response Criticism and the Gospel of Mark.* Minneapolis: Fortress, 1991.

Gerhardsson, Birger. "The Secret of the Transmission of the Unwritten Jesus Tradition." *New Testament Studies* 51 (2005): 1–18.

Hall, Mark. "The Living Word: An Auditory Interpretation of Scripture." *Listening* 21 (1986): 25–42.

Halverson, John. "Oral and Written Gospel: A Critique of Werner Kelber." *New Testament Studies* 40 (1994): 180–95.

Harvey, John D. *Listening to the Text: Oral Patterning in Paul's Letters.* Grand Rapids: Baker Books, 1998.

———. "Orality and Its implications for Biblical Studies' Recapturing an Ancient Paradigm." *Journal for the Evangelical Theological Society* 45 (2002): 99–109.

Henaut, Bany W. *Oral Tradition and the Gospels: The Problem of Mark 4.* Journal for the Study of the New Testament: Supplement Series 82. Sheffield: JSOT Press, 1993.

Henderson, Ian H. "Didache and Orality in Synoptic Comparison." *Journal of Biblical Literature* 111.2 (1992): 283–306.

Hollander, Harm W. "The Words of Jesus: From Oral Traditions to Written Record in Paul and Q." *Novum Testamentum* 42 (2000): 340–57.

Horsley, Richard, and Jonathan Draper. *Hearing the Whole Story: The Politics of Plot in Mark's Story.* Louisville: Westminster John Knox, 2001.

———. *Whoever Hears You Hears Me: Prophets, Performance, and Tradition in Q.* Harrisburg, Pa.: Trinity Press International, 1999.

Kelber, Werner. "Biblical Hermeneutics and the Ancient Art of Communication: A Response." *Semeia* 39 (1987): 97–105.

———. "In the Beginning Were the Words: The Apotheosis and Narrative Displacement of the Logos." *Journal of the American Academy of Religion* 58.1 (1990): 69–98.

———. *The Oral and the Written Gospel: The Hermeneutics of Speaking and Writing in the Synoptic Tradition, Mark, Paul, and Q.* Philadelphia: Fortress, 1983.

Kirk, Alan, and Tom Thatcher, eds. *Memory, Tradition, and Text: Uses of the Past in Early Christianity.* Atlanta: Society of Biblical Literature, 2005.

Lohr, Charles H. "Oral Techniques in the Gospel of Matthew." *Catholic Biblical Quarterly* 23 (1961): 403–35.

Lord, Albert B. "The Gospels as Oral Traditional Literature." Pages 33–92 in *The Relationships among the Gospels: An Interdisciplinary Dialogue.* Edited by William O. Walker Jr. San Antonio: Trinity University Press, 1978.

Loubser, J. A. "How Do You Report Something That Was Said with a Smile? Can We Overcome the Loss of Meaning When Oral-Manuscript Texts of the Bible Are Represented in Modern Printed Media?" *Scriptura* 87 (2004): 296–314.

———. "Invoking the Ancestors, Some Socio-rhetorical Aspects of the Genealogies in the Gospels according to Matthew and Luke." *Neotestamentica* 39.1 (2005): 127–40.

————. "Many Shades of Orality and Literacy: Media Theory and Cultural Difference." *Alternation* 9 (2002): 26–45.

————. "Media Criticism and the Myth of Paul, the Creative Genius, and His Forgotten Co-workers." *Neotestamentica* 34 (2000): 329–47.

————. "Orality and Literacy in the Pauline Corpus, Some New Hermeneutical Implications." *Neotestamentica* 29 (1995): 61–74.

————. "Orality and Pauline 'Christology': Some Hermeneutical Implications." *Scriptura* 47 (1993): 25–51.

————. "What Is Biblical Media Criticism? A Media-Critical Reading of Luke 9:51–56." *Scriptura* 2 (2002): 206–19.

Malbon, Elizabeth Struthers. "Echoes and Foreshadowing in Mark 4–8: Reading and Rereading." *Journal of Biblical Literature* 112 (1993): 211–30.

————. *Hearing Mark: A Listener's Guide.* Harrisburg, Pa.: Trinity International, 2002.

Malina, Bruce. "Reading Theory Perspective." Pages 3–23 in *The Social World of Luke-Acts: Models for Interpretation.* Edited by Jerome Neyrey. Peabody, Mass.: Hendrickson, 1991.

Miller, J. H. "Parable and Performative in the Gospels and Modern Literature." Pages 128–41 in *The Postmodern Bible Reader.* Edited by D. Jobling. Oxford: Blackwell, 2001.

Parker, David C. *The Living Text of the Gospels.* Cambridge: Cambridge University Press, 1997.

Parunak, H. Van Dyke. "Oral Typesetting: Some Uses of Biblical Structure." *Biblica* 62 (1981): 153–68.

Riesner, Rainer. "Jesus as Preacher and Teacher." Pages 185–210 in *Jesus and the Oral Gospel.* Edited by Henry Wansbrough. Sheffield: Sheffield Academic, 1991.

Shiner, Whitney. "Creating Plot in Episodic Narratives: The Life of Aesop and the Gospel of Mark." Pages 155–76 in *Ancient Fiction and Early Christian Narrative.* Edited by Ronald Hock, Bradley Chance, and Judith Perkins. Atlanta: Scholars Press, 1998.

————. *Proclaiming the Gospel: First-Century Performance of Mark.* Harrisburg, Pa.: Trinity International, 2003.

Silberman, Lou, ed. "Orality, Aurality, and Biblical Narrative." *Semeia* 39 (1987).

Stein, R. H. "Is Our Reading the Bible the Same as the Original Audience's Hearing of It? A Case Study in the Gospel of Mark." *Journal for the Evangelical Theological Society* 46 (2003): 63–78.

Wansbrough, Henry. *Jesus and the Oral Gospel.* Journal for the Study of the New Testament: Supplement Series 64. Sheffield: JSOT Press, 1991.

Ward, Richard. "Pauline Voice and Presence as Strategic Communication." *Semeia* 65 (1994): 95–107.

Wire, Antoinette. "Performance, Politics, and Power: A Response." *Semeia* 65 (1994): 129–35.

Index of Modern Authors

Index of Subjects

Index of Scripture References